When Towns Had Teams

Jim Baumer

RiverVision Press

Cover design by Jonathan Braden. Cover photo © RiverVision Press.

Printed in the United States by J.S. McCarthy Printers.

Paperback ISBN: 0-9772052-3-1

Inquiries regarding requests to reprint all or part of *When Towns Had Teams* should be directed to RiverVision Press at the address below.

To order directly from the publishers, please add $3.50 shipping to the price of the first copy, and $1.00 for each additional copy (plus five percent sales tax for Maine residents). Send check or money order to:

RiverVision Press
P.O. Box 283
Freeport, Maine 04032

RiverVision Press is a Maine-based small press, specializing in books about Maine and its unique culture and heritage. Recognizing the need for talented writers to have a home for their works about life in Maine, our goal is to provide publishing support to a new generation of Maine writers.

Our focus is on history, memoir and other styles that capture the spirit of Maine. RiverVision Press strives to be a press that captures a side of Maine that has been lost, forgotten, or never known.

RiverVision Press   www.rivervisionpress.com

To Ted Clark, who epitomized town team baseball.
July 30, 1929 –June 25, 2005

Acknowledgements

My fascination with town team baseball began back in 1969, when as a seven-year-old I began going to my uncle's Roberts 88'ers games in my hometown of Lisbon Falls. Growing up in a town that still had a sense of closeness and community has stayed with me all of my life. I still tend to filter my perception of people and places based on the formative experiences of my youth.

When I began to develop the initial idea for *When Towns Had Teams*, it was Lisbon Falls and the experiences of those early years that informed my early research and my initial contacts for interviews. I'm still amazed that my book is the first one to attempt a treatment of local baseball of this scope. I feel fortunate to have had those early years for the bedrock upon which to build my project.

Like baseball, writing a book of this type requires a team effort. The hours spent doing research in libraries proved invaluable. I especially want to thank the staff at the Auburn Public Library, most notably Director Rosemary Waltos, for inviting me to be a part of their spring program, *Baseball on the Home Field,* featuring writers and baseball. Reference librarians Steve Bouchard and Sally Holt provided resources and helpful suggestions, as well as allowing me access to their microfilm of the *Lewiston Sun* and *Lewiston Journal*, particularly in the early stages of my research.

Historical societies play a role in the research for a book of this type. The Lisbon Historical Society in Lisbon Falls, and in particular, Dot and Al Smith, were always willing to assist me in requests for information and allowed me to give a very well-attended and well-received talk about my book in May, while still very much in draft form.

For the book, I conducted nearly 40 first-person interviews of former players, coaches and umpires. Each one of them played key roles in their towns and on the various teams they were a part of. It was these men that made town team and semi-pro baseball the central focus of most towns across the state. Without their contribution, *When Towns Had Teams* would be a mere shell of a book. Their stories, some humorous, most of them magical, are what this brand of baseball was all about.

While it's always risky to acknowledge some folks without mentioning others, I wanted to cite a few individuals who provided me with information and assistance that was truly invaluable. Roger Spear of Farmington allowed me to borrow some photos of the Farmington Flyers that he had acquired. These photos from nearly 60 years ago are priceless and give the book an authenticity that I'm pleased with. Spear also has a vast knowledge of the history of baseball in Farmington and provided me with a perspective that I couldn't have done without.

All of the interviews that I conducted yielded valuable information, anecdotes and great stories. I especially am grateful to Loren Ritchie for his help in putting his days playing for the Guilford Advertisers into the proper perspective. Not only was he willing to answer any of my questions over the phone, he sent me two large envelopes of clippings that saved me hours of library time. The interview that he arranged with the late Ted Clark during January was priceless. I'm eternally grateful for that opportunity to have met Clark and to see these two old teammates recounting their glory years playing the game they truly loved.

A writer is only as good as his editor and I was fortunate to have an excellent one in Shelley Tebbutt. She gave my manuscript the professional copyediting that it needed and I'm confident that I have a finished product I can be proud of.

Thanks to photographers Forrest Hartley for his photos of former Pine Tree League ballparks and Lesley MacVane for her great shot of my son during a 2003 Twilight League game, as well as the photo of me on the back cover. Her photo of Mark, taking his practice swings before stepping to the plate, captures baseball for me, looking down the corridor of time.

For many years, local writer, Bob McPhee chronicled the Pine Tree League on the pages of the *Lewiston Sun*. Able to provide anything that you'd ever want to know about the league from 1975 forward, he was a big help checking details of the baseball goings-on in and around Rumford. I appreciated McPhee's notes from Bitsy Ionta's induction into the Maine Baseball Hall of Fame.

I'm fortunate to have a great designer in Jonathan Braden. I'd recommend him to anyone for the quality of his work, his diligence and his uncanny ability to visually capture exactly what this book is about.

While *When Towns Had Teams* is certainly about the glory days of town team and semi-pro baseball, it's also about local baseball, as it moves forward into the future. My involvement with the Twilight League as a coach, and now serving as its president, allows me a firsthand understanding of the men who blazed the trail before me. I want to especially thank Al Livingston for keeping the league going and providing a current peg upon which to place the book. Livingston's willingness to share with me his files, clippings and stories were essential in helping me to piece together the history of the league.

Lastly, I wouldn't have been able to complete this project without my two biggest fans. My wife Mary, who patiently put up with my agitation, my doubts and provided me with a supportive environment in which to craft the story of baseball in its purest form. Not only has she been supportive, she also has acted as a proofreader, envelope stuffer and marketing coordinator. My son Mark, while providing me with someone that I'm immensely proud of, for his own accomplishments as a third generation Baumer playing baseball, as well as being a fine young man, also gave me some helpful advice and needed critique in the early stages of the manuscript.

I'm particularly grateful to my loving Sheltie, Bernie, who watched over me during countless hours at the keyboard, and always knew just the right time to suggest a needed walk, or a buzz through the woods on my cross-country skis.

Jim Baumer
July 30, 2005

Table of Contents

Introduction

It has been said that baseball is America's pastime. Whether that is still true is a matter of debate. Yet half a century go, there was nary a case to be made to the contrary. While the professional game has always had its fans, in Maine, even amateur baseball was followed with an interest and passion that many today would find hard to believe.

As communities recovered their vitality with the return of their young men after the Second World War, baseball was there to provide Mainers with entertainment on warm summer nights and quiet Sunday afternoons after church. Ask anyone who might have lived in a small Maine town or even one of the few cities in the state and they'll tell you that during the 1950's and 1960's, the local baseball team was afforded a prominent place in their parochial pecking order.

When writers like Robert Putnam wrote about the demise of social capital in our communities in his seminal book, *Bowling Alone*, he could have easily used the demise of town team baseball as the illustration of his premise. Sadly, as television and automobiles became ubiquitous staples of American culture, the aspects of community life that held them together—things like the general store, grange hall and the town baseball team—disappeared from daily life as the culture shifted. People moved away, farms were sold, local businesses closed and the town baseball team was but a memory and a yellowed clipping in a scrapbook.

From post-World War II, until the middle of the 1970's, local baseball flourished in Maine. In the 1950's, semi-professional baseball often drew crowds in excess of 3,000 or 4,000 fans to ball fields in Auburn, Augusta and even Farmington, to watch the best baseball north of Boston. Even during the 1960's, as smaller towns were dropping out of local leagues, post-season and Labor Day tournaments held across the state drew crowds numbering more than 2,000 on occasion.

While local baseball has always been an essential part of Maine's historical and cultural landscape, very little information has been preserved from this era about its players and teams. In 1960, local sports writer and broadcaster, Don McWilliams, wrote a book called *Yours In Sports; A History of Baseball, Basketball and Boxing and Bowling in Maine*. McWilliams wrote about these four sports in Maine from 1920 until 1960. While his book contained some valuable information about local teams and players, it lacked a unified focus about baseball and never received wide distribution.

During the spring of 2004, while busily preparing for the start of another summer of coaching a team in Portland's Twilight League, I began to think about the vitality of local baseball that I remembered growing up in Lisbon Falls. While the Twilight League had managed to survive for over a century, most other leagues in the state hadn't fared so well. With the six teams in our league and another seven teams in a new league in Bangor called the Bay League, these thirteen teams were all that was left of the rich traditions of semi-pro and town team baseball from the past.

From a time when there were literally hundreds of teams scattered across the state, in just about every small town, to the present day, when town team ball is found hanging by a thread, something had dramatically changed. From my firsthand experience, I knew that many men my age no longer wanted to make the commitment to multiple games per week as in former days. With the growth of the more recreational Men's Senior Baseball League (better known as over-30 baseball), older players no longer played in leagues like the Twilight League. Yet, even armed with this information, I knew there had to be more to the demise of local baseball, played by adults, than just the lack of competitive fire in those who were 30 years old, or older.

Certainly, there had to be more of a historical record from the past than Don McWilliams's account. Thus began my initial foray into Maine's baseball past. Finding little or nothing on the internet, I began foraging through the state's larger libraries—Portland Public Library, the Maine State Library in Augusta, as well as the libraries in Lewiston and Auburn. Each one of these libraries had abundant amounts of microfilm of Maine's newspapers. Unfortunately, my initial calls to historical societies around the state, even the Maine Historical Society in Portland, revealed almost nothing from baseball's abundant past.

With the realization that I had a major undertaking on my hands, I began the painstaking journey to piece together the past. Utilizing some amazing accounts from some of Maine's more comprehensive sports sections of various newspapers, in particular, the *Portland Press Herald* and the *Evening Express,* the *Lewiston Morning Sun* (as well as the *Evening Journal)* and the *Bangor Daily News*, I began to recreate a record of a bygone era, page-by-page and year-by-year.

Throughout the latter part of the summer and into the fall, I interviewed former players, umpires and managers who had been legends of the diamond 20, 30 and 40 years ago, or more. Many of these men, now in their late 60s, or early 70s, recalled their days of vigor with a clarity that amazed me. Most of the men I spoke with told me that these days of long ago "seemed like yesterday." Rarely did I explain to a former player on the phone what I was attempting to do, without them eagerly answering my questions, supplying me with additional information (and stories), as well as other names of people to contact. Frequently, they agreed to sit down with me for several hours and patiently answered my questions and tirelessly helped me with names, dates and amazing stories that I wouldn't have been able to access any other way.

While I have attempted to be as comprehensive as possible, I quickly came to the realization that this project could become endless. The hardest task became how to represent the vitality of town team and semi-pro baseball's heyday from just after the war until its decline beginning in the mid-to-late 1970's. With so much history and without any real funding in the form of grants or other means of sustenance usually allotted for a project such as this, my biggest challenge became maintaining some sense of scope, while also not ending up with a book that was 500 pages and not spending the next decade of my life trying to get it right. My goal was historical integrity, while also rendering a book that was readable and filled with the vitality that was baseball from this period of time. I also became aware of the importance of getting a book out while many of the men who played the game could appreciate it.

I don't think any writer is ever perfectly satisfied with his finished product. There is always the tension between vision and the practicality of bringing out a book to its intended audience. I have struggled with that tension over much of the past year. Overall, I'm happy that I was able to place baseball into a historical context, while maintaining a flow of events and representing the wonderful stories that I had the privilege of listening to from the variety of men I interviewed. I think *When Towns Had Teams* is a book that is long overdue and I hope most of its readers come away with a sense of the importance of the time represented. I also hope that they get a sense of my attempts to honor these former players and the towns and teams they represented on diamonds across our state.

The initial response to *When Towns Had Teams* has been very encouraging. From the talks I've done about local baseball to libraries and historical societies and the enthusiasm they've generated, I sense that there is a real hunger for some of this information. Many former players have inquired about the release of the book and the desire to purchase multiple copies. Rarely do I speak with anyone about my book without an enthusiastic response to the subject matter. All of these things, plus my instincts and personal experience, tell me that the book and the attempts I have made to represent this important subject and time period is long overdue.

With much of town team and semi-pro baseball's rich contribution to our culture and heritage fading into the hazy mist of memory, my wish is that *When Towns Had Teams* will help readers to relive and remember that special time and be able to participate in a fresh perspective on this important epoch from our past. A time when towns were alive with the crack of the ball hitting the bat, the smack of leather and the sounds of ball fields resonating with the intricate beauty of baseball played by a special group of men.

Chapter 1

War is over: Let the Games Begin

The decade that came to be synonymous with the beginning of prosperity and the advent of the middle class way of life began with high hopes and aspirations for most of the country. America's emergence as a world leader following the austerity and uncertainty of the previous two decades provided Americans with a newfound optimism going into the post-war period. With the dawning of the 1950's, an era of hope and unbounded dreams for the future characterized this new age in American life.

The end of conflict overseas ushered in the possibility of a new beginning. Mainers, like most other Americans, desired to put the darkness of war behind them and reestablish normalcy in the communities where they resided.

With business being given the opportunity to refocus its energy on peacetime pursuits, a new line of consumer products began being offered to their customers. Americans eagerly embraced the emerging technologies—electric ranges and washing machines for the home were just two of these that offered relief from domestic duties—adding quality to their lives, as well as freeing up time for leisure activities. Additionally, the return of GI's led to record increases in marriages and a growth in family life.

As these changes made their way into the towns and hamlets of the Pine Tree State, a renewed sense of normalcy returned to daily life. With this settling in period came an increased desire for new forms of entertainment. Professional baseball was experiencing new heights of popularity, as America's pastime returned to the former place of prominence that it held prior to the war. The 1950's also brought with it an unprecedented interest in higher education opportunities. High school graduates all over the country were now deciding on college as an option to jump start their careers.

All of this created a perfect climate for the formation of a fast-paced semi-professional baseball league in the state. Semi-pro baseball offered fans and communities a brand of baseball that was very close in caliber to the minor league baseball being played in states with a more urban population base. With teams comprised of premiere players, often in the midst of their college careers and recruited by coaches and general managers to play for the local team, this brand of baseball was sure to be popular with the enthusiastic fans in the state. With multitudes of young men competing for the burgeoning numbers of college baseball programs in New England and across the country, a ready-made talent pool existed to fill semi-pro rosters in Maine and elsewhere. Because these players required a top caliber brand of summer baseball to further their development, semi-pro baseball became a perfect fit for many wishing to take their games to the next skill level. Additionally, most teams included some of the better local players who had either competed in college, or may have had some brief professional experience before returning to their hometowns to settle down and begin families.

In 1949, a group of Lewiston/Auburn baseball aficionados and leaders in the business community formed the Auburn Sports Association. Led by Auburn City Manager Bernal Allen, Association President Benjamin Jones and Frank Prescott, this group was determined to raise the level of competition above and beyond what was currently provided by the local Twin City League.

While the war dampened interest in local baseball and the league ceased operations for several years, post-war Lewiston and Auburn saw the Twin City League emerge again with a renewed fervor. With an abundance of baseball talent, Lewiston/Auburn rewarded its baseball fans with entertaining baseball most nights of the week during the summer. Consisting of 10 to 12 teams, with six to eight of them capable of rivaling any league in the state, the Twin City League provided their fans with top notch amateur baseball for several years at the turn of the decade. Many local employers, as well as civic and social organizations, sponsored teams in the league. The Bates Manufacturing Company, known world wide for their fine textiles, was one of the companies in Lewiston/Auburn sponsoring a team. In addition, Cushman Manufacturing Company, Stearns Packing and organizations such as the New Auburn Social Club and the Pastime Club sponsored ball clubs.

The association knew local interest was high for baseball. With the area's abundance of talent a key to building their team, the association came up with a name for their team—they planned to call the team, the Asas—a play on the acronym for the Auburn Athletic Association. With the primary motivation being to assemble the best semi-pro team in the state, the group set its sights on choosing a field manager and assembling a roster of both local and imported talent from wherever they could find it.

For several years, Raymond "Ducky" Pond had been leading his Bates College teams into battle against the best college talent in New England. Known as a manager with a strong sense of the game, as well as being a keen judge of talent, the association felt they had the perfect field general to lead their team. In May of 1949, the association approached Pond and offered him the position as the manager of Lewiston/Auburn's newest baseball team.

At the end of May, the Asas began holding open tryouts. With word spreading like wildfire in the area about the high-powered team being assembled, the association had no difficulty getting an enthusiastic turnout for their tryouts. Any player within a 50-mile radius was more than happy to showcase their talents for a spot on the Auburn's Asas.

The semi-pro Asas were slated to play their home games at the newly built Pettengill Park. Backed by Allen as catalyst, Pettengill became the jewel of local ball yards. Its ample bleachers down both foul lines allowed the new park to seat 4,500 fans, as well as having the capability of accommodating several hundred more spectators willing to stand for nine innings.

When the newly minted Asas took the field on June 11, 1949 for their home opener, almost 5,000 fans jammed the brand new park to see their adopted sons of summer. For those in attendance, it was evident that a new era in local baseball was beginning. From the four school bands and their various routines, to the bunting and excitement crackling through the air, the association had provided an opening ceremony fit for royalty.

The opening opponents for the Asas were the Boston Colored Wolverines, a touring team of considerable reputation, brought in to challenge the locals. They proved no match however, as the Asas thrilled the spectators, trouncing their guests, 9-3.

Leadoff hitter Richie Raia pumped excitement into an already jubilant crowd by belting a leadoff home run over the wall in left. Raia also was the lucky recipient of a promised locket to be presented to the first Asas player to homer.

The unheralded Raia, a late addition to the Asas squad, was slated to attend Bates in the fall. The Wilbraham, Massachusetts native showed Pond a premonition of things to come at Bates in subsequent springs.

The Asas continued to draw large crowds and routinely beat a string of strong opponents that first summer. With Pond handling a powerful contingent of players, which included former minor leaguers Chick Leahey and Yankee's farmhand Chip Pontbriand, it was obvious that the Asas has assembled the best team the area had ever seen. Pond was able to call upon a strong pitching staff to complement his formidable line up. The mound corps that first summer consisted of Roland Chalifoux, the diminutive Canadian southpaw, former Twin City League ace Reg Masse and Bowdoin College hurler Dick Blanchard, as well as Pontbriand.

While the 1949 season was a successful one from several standpoints—attendance, field performance and administration—the lack of a league affiliation was an ongoing source of concern for the association members. Sentiment ran high that a league affiliation was essential to the maintenance of the heightened interest created in the team. The concern was that fans would eventually lose interest in the team, no matter how much talent was gathered to fill the Asas roster without the competition and rivalries provided by a league.

****

The Augusta Millionaires brought semi-pro baseball in the capitol region of the state to a new level, with their founding in 1948. While the Augusta Athletic Association had assembled high-powered teams for the first two seasons of existence, the lack of a strong league in the state made the continuity of semi-pro baseball seem doubtful. With the type of commitment and capital required to field a team of this caliber, there arose a growing urgency for the type of stability offered only by a league, preferably one with at least five or six other towns or cities in the state.

Like the Auburn Athletic Association, Augusta's baseball brain trust was seeking to create a high-powered team that would provide the kind of entertainment that would keep fans coming back to Capitol Park. Lewis Sheaffer, president of the Augusta Athletic Association, estimated that in order to make the needed improvements to Capitol Park, bringing the field up to the standards required for semi-pro baseball, it would total in excess of $30,000. Work began in the fall of 1948, as improvements were made to the new field in Augusta. In order to accommodate the crowds of 1,500 to 2,000 fans that regularly jammed Capitol Park during that first summer of baseball in 1948, additional seating was added. Additionally, several new auxiliary buildings were constructed and field grading and seeding took place to improve the park's somewhat rough playing surface. In order to permit more consistency in obtaining paid admissions, new fencing was erected to completely enclose the park.

According to an article in the *Kennebec Journal* from May 1949, Sheaffer and other members of the Augusta Athletic Association wanted to provide the Augusta area with a top-notch ball club and first-class facilities.

"The aims of the Association are to provide our fans with amusement, recreation and a pleasant facility for the people of this area," said Sheaffer, quoted from the article, as he discussed plans for the 1949 season.

In addition to the capital improvements to the ballpark, lights for night games cost $16,000, baseballs cost $1,800 over the course of a summer and insurance was $1,200. Also, in order to attract teams to Augusta, the team guaranteed visiting teams a large percentage of the nightly take, which required a healthy gate.

While the 1949 season was an enjoyable one for baseball fans in the Augusta area, the lack of league affiliation affected the team. The team reported a net loss of $4,918 for the season. This was similar to the 1948 financial statement and now had the team running deficits of nearly $10,000 for their first two seasons.

****

With the arrival of 1950, the impetus for a strong semi-pro circuit was being fueled by communities south of Augusta. Considerable interest was expressed in late April from Portland, Auburn and even Farmington for a league of five or six teams for the upcoming season.

By the middle of May, plans had been finalized for a six team circuit that would include the Millionaires, the Asas in Auburn, the Portland Pilots, Sanford's Goodalls and teams in Kennebunkport and Rochester, New Hampshire. The level of play of the newly formed Down East League was thought to be equal to a B- or C-level professional minor league, which bode well for fans seeking high-energy baseball. With several competitive independent teams filling open dates, including the Farmington Flyers, the Brewer Bluebirds, the Eastport Lobsters and the Presque Isle Indians, interest was running high for the upcoming season.

Portland's inclusion in the league was a boon, as it gave it the participation of Maine's largest city. Portland had been a successful baseball town, with a track record of support shown for its recent minor league team, also called the Pilots. The Pilots, members of the Class B Northeast League from 1946 to 1949, would have continued, but were forced to cease operations when the league lost several Massachusetts teams at the end of the 1949 season, making the Northeast League's continuance impossible.

With a number of supremely skilled players that included local pitching phenom Ed Hadlock, who would one day have the local stadium named for him, the Pilots were a solid addition to the roster of clubs planned for the 1950 season.

Maine baseball fans had a reputation for supporting well-run ventures that were properly promoted. With its solid nucleus of ownership and local business support, the Down East League was well positioned to garner the interest and support of Maine's baseball loyalists for its initial season.

The 1950 season proved to be everything that its founders had hoped for. With three very powerful teams in Auburn, Augusta and Portland coupled with other competitive teams in Kennebunkport, Sanford and Rochester, New Hampshire, the league provided fans with top-notch baseball for an entire summer.

After the Northeast League vacated the state, baseball fans were eager for a replacement and semi-professional baseball ably filled the void left by professional ball's local demise.

Augusta, led by manager Ben Houser, had assembled possibly the most powerful roster in the league. It included future Boston Red Sox players Harry Agganis and Ted Lepcio. Agganis, nicknamed "the golden Greek," was a college star at Boston University, garnering All-American honors in both baseball and football. Lepcio, a smooth-fielding shortstop and powerful hitter, would go on to play 10 years for five different major league teams. Additionally, Damariscotta's Don Bowman had been a starting outfielder for the Pilots in 1947 and 1948 and offered the Millionaires a potent bat, as well as the veteran leadership of a seasoned ex-minor leaguer. Pond's Asas squad were just as evenly matched and would battle Portland's Pilots and the Millionaires all summer long for the top spot in the league standings. By the end of the 1950 campaign, Portland had won the league title, with only a game and a half separating the top three teams.

Kennebunkport's entry, the Collegians, was run by a man who would later see his grandson, George Bush, become the first Bush in the White House. At the time, Herbert "Herbie" Walker was a well-connected figure in the world of politics, but also enjoyed dabbling in the national pastime. Using his Ivy League connections, Walker assembled a top-notch squad whose roster included several players from esteemed institutions such as Harvard, Yale and Princeton.

Late in the fall of 1950, the members of Auburn's Athletic Association organized a contest with one of the major league's barnstorming contingents. As was common practice, major league players often played ball throughout their off-season in order to supplement their meager salaries of the time. Unlike professional sports in later years, only a handful of baseball players like Ted Williams and Joe Dimaggio commanded large salaries. Most players required off-season jobs during the fall and winter to supplement their major league salaries.

On October 11, 1950, Johnny Mize brought his team of major leaguers to Pettengill Park to play the Asas players as well as other gathered local talent. With a roster that included another future hall-of-famer, Warren Spahn, Yankee star Gene Woodling and other players such as Luke Appling, the Mickey Harris All-Stars thumped the Asas by a 21-4 count before nearly 4,000 fans under the Pettengill lights. While never close in score, seeing so many major leaguers gathered to play in a local exhibition game against local talent was proof that baseball was once again at the top of the local sports pecking order.

****

Cassius "Cash" Clark loved baseball. While not a particularly skilled player in his younger days, this never prevented him from being affiliated with his passion in some capacity. As the sharp and successful owner of the local Coca-Cola bottling plant in Farmington, Clark had found various ways to support baseball in the greater Farmington area over the years. It was because of his reputation as a supporter of baseball that Clark was approached in the spring of 1948 about stepping up his involvement in local baseball matters.

According to Farmington baseball historian Roger Spear, in the spring of 1948, some high school and college-age players sought out Clark's level of interest in sponsoring a second team in the community. The current scenario had the local town team, known as the Townies, comprised mostly of older players. The arrangement often prevented recent high school graduates and local college players from Farmington State Teachers College from having a local place to compete and hone their skills on the diamond each summer. As a result, many of them ended up playing in neighboring communities and competing against their fellow townsmen.

Much to the delight of the younger players in town, Clark was found to be very enthusiastic about the idea, and the Farmington Flyers were born in May of 1948. With the Townies set to move over to the Timber League that summer, the North Franklin League had an opening and the Flyers quickly filled it.

One of the perks of sponsorship for Clark was being allowed to have a hands-on role with the Flyers as the team's general manager. This would become a Clark trademark—finding and assembling the best talent available and fielding a team able to compete with the best in whatever league, or situation the Flyers found themselves in. During this first summer, Clark cast his gaze primarily within Farmington proper to fill his roster. In subsequent seasons he would gradually widen the circle of his recruitment territory to include the local teacher's college in 1949, and then move on to bringing in the best talent he could recruit from away.

His immediate focus in 1948 was acquiring baseball bragging rights in Farmington. With the completion of the regular season campaigns of the Timber and North Franklin County leagues, Clark organized a local grudge match, pitting the older and more experienced Townies, against his young bucks, the Flyers. Not wanting to risk his reputation on the uncertainty of a single game, it was agreed that these two Farmington rivals would engage in a best-of-three series to determine the town's superior baseball club.

This hard-fought series would capture the imaginations of local fans and become one of those epic battles that locals still talk fondly about, over a half century later. According to Spear, this match was a "battle of and for the ages."

"The Townies/Flyers series had all the drama that one could witness in any rivalry—it was the Red Sox/Yankees series of Farmington," said Spear.

The Flyers quickly gained the upper hand by eking out a 12 to 10 victory to take a one game series advantage. With their backs against the wall, the valiant Townies gave the younger and more talented Flyers all they could handle, but fell 10 to 9, with the

Townies' star player, Stoogie Whittier, being tagged out at the plate in an ill-fated attempt to steal home. Clark's team was crowned champions of Farmington. Unknown at the time, the Flyers had also become the only team in town, as 1949 would find the Townies disbanding.

With the advent of the 1949 season, Clark began enlisting players from Farmington State Teachers College. While the original purpose of the Flyers had been to provide local players a place to play, his desire to win superceded his altruism in providing a home for Farmington's young stars of the diamond. Clark immediately signed the entire Farmington Teacher's College infield—Ted Clark (no relation to Cash) from Rumford, Bill Judkins and Buddy Rand of Augusta, as well as Fred Rogers. Additionally, Clark brought in the talented Pete Doiron from Livermore to play the outfield.

Norm Ferrari, who was the Flyers' first scorekeeper, remembers Clark's recruitment of this high-powered college infield.

"That first season [1948], the Flyers were just a bunch of local players—mostly high school age and guys just out of school. In '49, Cash ended up recruiting the entire infield from Farmington State Teachers College to play for the Flyers," said Ferrari. "What I remember most is that these guys—Bill Judkins, Buddy Rand, Fred Rogers and Ted Clark—they were all playing out of position for the college. Cash, along with Flyer's manager Fred Cobb, recognized that these guys were talented, but were all out of position. They switched them around—he moved Clark from short, where he was too lanky to play and converted him to first. He ended up with Judkins at third, Rand at second and Freddy [Rogers] at short. This move was a success and this group was later billed as Clark's 'million dollar infield' by the local paper."

Clark's pull-hitting prowess enabled him to clout 20 homers during the 1949 campaign. While Hippach Field was notorious for its short porch in right, many of Clark's homers were mammoth shots over the pine trees in right. Gaylen Sayward, who hailed from Farmington and would later be "the local backup" for the Flyers, as he calls it, remembers some of Clark's majestic home runs.

"Teddy had one of those picture book swings that you stopped to watch. When he hit the ball, it just took off," said Sayward. "That summer, he had one of those magical seasons that people still talk about."

Both Clark and Doiron provided a solid one-two punch in the middle of the Flyers line up and the retooled Flyers easily won the league crown in the North Franklin County League. Additionally, Farmington also ended up beating a number of strong teams from outside the state such as the New York Colored Giants, the Boston Hobos, the powerful House of David barnstorming team and even an all-star club from Puerto Rico. At the end of the 1949 campaign, the team's overall record stood at a stellar 49-14. Now that Clark had seen his team claim superiority in the town of Farmington and show their abilities in the North Franklin County League, he set his sights on assembling an even better club for the 1950 season. This quest to be the best would be the impetus for Clark's practice of importing the best out-of-state talent he could find to supplement the regional talent pool. Playing an independent schedule for the season, the 1950 Flyers began drawing substantial crowds to Hippach Field to watch the talented team play.

Clark's embrace of importing players from away didn't always sit well with local players or some of the townspeople. Both Ted Clark and Pete Doiron assumed that their prior season's exploits assured them a place on the 1950 squad. The Flyers' general manager had other opinions and told both Clark and Doiron at the season's first workout that they wouldn't be needed for the summer.

"Pete [Doiron] wasn't real pleased," recalls Ted Clark. "Cash told us both that he was bringing in some college boys and we wouldn't be needed. Pete grabbed Clark and put him up against the dugout," said Clark. "Cash was an old man and Pete was ready to kill him. Luckily, the other players grabbed Pete and the two of us packed up our stuff and left," said Clark.

Both Clark and Doiron had been key offensive performers for the '49 Flyers and the opinion of locals is that both would have been able performers for 1950. This incident is an indication of the importance that the Flyers' owner placed on winning.

According to Ferrari, it wasn't a malicious thing with Clark in not continuing to use local players with the Flyers.

"I liked Cash a lot. I was a high school kid when he came and asked me to be scorekeeper. Most people in town thought the world of him—it's just that he was a competitive guy who wanted to have the best team around," he said. "I think having both Auburn and Augusta nearby got him fired up and made him want to be able to beat those guys. It wasn't a mean thing with him or anything."

In 1949, Clark's "import" had been pitcher Cliff Hall of Gorham State Teachers College. It was rumored that he had received "gas money" for driving up to Farmington from Portland when it was his turn in the rotation to pitch. The odds were now higher for Clark and the Flyers as 1950 would see them playing an independent schedule which would bring them head-to-head with the teams in the Down East League. As a result, he brought in his first out-of-state talent, this time from Rutgers University in New Jersey. It would also be the start of Clark's paying players on the Flyers' roster. The four players were lodged by local members of the community. In addition to being paid $40 per week in the form of a minimal job, the players received their meals at Ma Voter's restaurant, with Cash picking up the tab.

The 1950 Flyers were fast out of the gate and were winning 75 percent of the contests they played during June and early July. On a scorcher of a July 12th, the Flyers played before their biggest crowd of the season. Fifteen hundred fans witnessed the Flyers pound a barnstorming team from Indiana, the Kokomo Klowns, by a score of 17-1. At that time, Hippach didn't have lights (permanent lights would be installed at the end of the summer), so playing lucrative night dates and the accompanying bigger crowds they garnered required the rental of portable lighting. Unfortunately for Clark, the lighting truck toting his lights for the evening broke down in New Hampshire. Unable to procure lights and facing the possibility of postponement and a loss of revenue, the resourceful Clark decided to move the game up to six o'clock. Clark, in an attempt to reach as many fans as possible with the time change, began phoning stores and other establishments across Franklin County to spread the word. In addition, he hired a local college student and sent him around in a sound truck to the outlying towns in Oxford, Androscoggin and Somerset Counties, blasting the news via loudspeaker!

Later in the summer, the Flyers would play several night games under portable lighting, as the team rolled past league and outside opponents. Attendance continued to grow as a result of Clark's incessant promotion and marketing and by the end of the 1950 season, attendance was averaging around 2,000 fans per outing.

In just two seasons, Clark had taken a local team that had been an afterthought and assembled one of the best semi-pro units in the state. Part of it was a result of Clark's shrewdness and inclination towards recruitment. His business background also taught him the importance of networking, long before it became a corporate buzzword. One relationship that would pay enormous dividends was a friendship Clark had developed with a local summer resident. Clark had befriended David Bender, who spent his summers on the lake in nearby Mount Vernon. A Rutgers University grad, as well as an avid supporter of their athletic teams, Bender allowed Clark access to a steady stream of talented Scarlet Knights ballplayers. He would use this pipeline numerous times over the next few seasons to further his baseball goals.

Clark wintered in South Carolina; this would prove useful to him, from the contacts he made, to making him a bit less gruff, as his Yankee upbringing had socialized him to be. Never far from his roots however, the New Englander in him aided him during those times when he needed to be a tough negotiator.

Sayward, who had the opportunity to observe Clark up close while being a part-time player and Flyer gofer, had an interesting analysis of Clark and his success in building his teams of the 1950's.

"Cash had two sides that he utilized very well in baseball. He could be the charming southern gentleman when he needed to be—this made him persuasive in building relationships with others, particularly out-of-state college coaches—he was also part frugal Yankee, from his New England roots. Cash knew how to get the best in any deal, which he learned as a practical business man," said Sayward.

"He was an interesting man. He had a black lab that he used to decide which players he would keep on the team. When the players first came to town, he'd bring them over to the field and say they had someone to meet—his dog. If the dog liked you and you could play—you were all set. If he didn't like you, then you probably wouldn't be playing baseball for the Flyers," laughed Sayward.

The Flyers had been regular opponents of various Down East League teams during 1950, so it was logical that they would join the league for the 1951 season. Even though Clark had gone out and assembled what many consider his best team ever, the Flyers struggled out of the gate. By midseason however, the Flyers were battling Augusta for second place. A late-season surge saw them finish a solid second to the Asas of Auburn. Clark was upset that his team couldn't overtake his rivals down the road. The Flyers got some measure of revenge however; as Clark arranged a best-of-five season finale between the two teams. The Flyers beat the league champs three games to one to conclude another exciting baseball campaign in Franklin County.

****

The first two seasons of the Down East League had provided baseball fans with top caliber baseball from Sanford to Augusta and even over into Rochester, New Hampshire, a hotbed for baseball in the Granite State. With college players flooding north into Maine and New Hampshire that summer to fill the rosters of each of the teams, the Down East League had become the premiere college talent showcase in the Northeast, if not the eastern part of the country.

Despite the level of skill being flashed on the diamond, the 1951 season saw the league down to only four teams for that summer's campaign. Sanford, Rochester and Kennebunk had dropped out. Added to the loss of these three teams was the decision by the Pilots in Portland to go the independent route for the season. Fortunately, the Dow Air Force Jets, from Bangor and the addition of Farmington brought the league to the minimum number of clubs necessary to make another campaign worth undertaking. However, there were obvious dark clouds on the horizon concerning semi-pro baseball's future in the state. It appeared that despite the superior talent on the field and the occasional overflow crowd, particularly in Auburn and Farmington, Maine just didn't appear to have the needed capital and population base necessary to guarantee crowds in excess of 2,500 to 3,000 for each game to justify the current expenses of most clubs.

Gaylen Sayward's affiliation with the Flyers and the Down East League, as both a part-time player and regular attendee at Hippach Field gave him a unique perspective on the strength of the league.

"The league was as good a league as Maine has ever had. We had players coming in from Rutgers, Seton Hall, Michigan; these guys could play ball," said Sayward. "I'd have to say that the Down East League was comparable to today's Cape Cod League," he said.

With the cost of running teams in the neighborhood of $10,000 or more, prospective general managers of clubs seeking entry to the league felt this was a prohibitive amount of money. In hopes of attracting additional interest from Waterville and Fairfield and luring Sanford back into the fold, some general managers were proposing capping each team's salary at $3,500.

Farmington's Clark, who had spent a considerable amount of his own money to put together a very strong independent team in 1950, along with the Auburn ownership, were opposed to capping each team's payroll in expenses in 1951. The concern was that the limit might prevent some clubs (namely Auburn and Farmington) from fielding the college-laden teams of past seasons that their fans had grown accustomed to seeing. They were voted down, four votes to two and the Down East League entered its third season in 1952 with Auburn, Farmington and Augusta, as well as the Waterville Wrens, Fairfield Comets and Dow Air Force Jets from Bangor.

As always, Clark was not to be outdone in anything he was involved in, particularly in running a baseball team. For the first time, Farmington began selling season tickets for the 1952 season. Clark, hearing increased complaining from locals about the lack of local talent being represented by past Flyer rosters, began a tradition of early June tryouts for local players. While this was mostly a goodwill gesture and a token to the local community, the addition of local star Billy Linscott quieted some of the grumbling. Additionally, Sayward continued in his occasional, fill-in role, as did Alden Small, who served as bullpen catcher, so Farmington was represented with a presence on the Flyers' roster.

With the league now back up to the healthier number of six teams, the summer of '52 saw the Flyers battling Waterville for most of the season for the third spot in the standings. Playing consistent ball during the campaign, the Flyers would nudge out the Wrens for third place behind Auburn and Augusta. Ten Farmington hitters batted over .300 for the campaign. While Clark had assembled another powerful combine, local interest appeared to be waning in Farmington, as well as other locales around the state. Crowds began dipping below 1,000 in Farmington, Auburn and Augusta—former leaders in attendance—throwing up red flags regarding the long-term health of semi-pro baseball in the state. With these clubs being the only three in the league with lighted parks, the pressure for them to draw large crowds was intense. By the end of 1952, word was going around that Augusta would fold and that Farmington might not have a club in 1953.

Early in 1953, *The Franklin Journal* reported that the team's fate rested on the response of volunteers who had been solicited to help with the burden of running the team. There was even talk of the Hippach lights being sold if the team didn't operate for the upcoming campaign. With only Clark and four other individuals shouldering the financial burden of fielding a semi-pro team, sentiment ran high that the community needed to become more involved if the Flyers were to continue. With the cost of fielding a league franchise reduced to about $3,500 to accommodate more participation and to offset poor attendance, it was hoped that the league could get off the ground for the '53 campaign.

In April, the new Franklin County Flyers Association was founded to remove the burden from Clark's bank account and to ensure the continuance of the Flyers' franchise. After five years of being the primary financial vehicle for the Flyers, Farmington's baseball benefactor had expressed a desire to begin lessening his role with the team, to a more supplemental, rather than primary role with the franchise. With memberships being offered for $2 each, the goal was for several hundred members to join during its inaugural offering in 1953.

By meeting time on April 13, 1953, the goal of $2,500 was still a few hundred dollars short. Membership reported that $2,000 had been gathered. With such a large group in attendance, the Association went forward and adopted new by-laws and former University of Maine star Ed Woodbury was named manager, as the Flyers were going to be one of six teams again in the Down East League.

With Woodbury supplying the team with special bats from his home-based wood-turning factory and a roster consisting of top-notch talent such as All-American Jim Reardon from Seton Hall, University of Maine player Al Hackett and the return of Michigan State's Jackie Corbett for another summer, the Flyers were once more poised to challenge the top teams in the still-competitive league.

In early August, the Flyers were sitting on top of the pack, with a 16-8 record, having won six of their previous seven outings.

On August 15th, the Flyers knocked off second place Auburn before a capacity crowd at Hippach.

As August wound down, the Flyers were clinging to first place for the final week of the Down East campaign. While they ended up losing their final two games, the Flyers clinched their first league crown, ending up with a half game lead over Augusta, with a league mark of 25-13 for the summer.

****

When Bill Thurston was growing up in Norway, Maine, he never envisioned that he'd later become a respected baseball coach at Amherst College. From the humble beginnings on a dairy farm in a rural Maine community, the former Norway High flamethrower was able to rise through the ranks of baseball to where he is now considered one of the deans of the college coaching fraternity. While he certainly didn't know it at the time, his brief stay over two seasons in the Down East League would be one of the deciding determinants of his later success in the baseball world.

It was obvious to all that saw this skinny boy perform athletically, that he had something that the other boys didn't. His powerful right arm and exceptional speed allowed him to rise through the ranks of youthful games in football and baseball, to eventually become a high school star athlete in both of those sports.

During the summer following his junior year of high school, Thurston was pitching for the local town team in Norway. Unlike many players of high school age, Thurston opted to play for the town team instead of joining the local American Legion team.

"Town team ball was a 'stepping-stone' for a young player like me," said Thurston. "When I was in high school, if you were a pretty good player, you might get asked to play for the town team," he said. "I probably should have played Legion ball, as my first summer, I got lit up pretty good. I was a hard-thrower and I thought I could just blow it by people like I did during the spring in high school ball. These old country ballplayers could hit the crap out of a guy like me who didn't know enough to change speeds."

While Thurston certainly would have dominated his own age group playing Legion baseball, that summer of 1952 gave him an education as a pitcher that would propel him to the next level, that being semi-pro baseball.

Word had gotten around the area that Norway had a young 16-year-old pitcher that could really throw the ball. Talk reached Cash Clark in Farmington about the pitching prodigy, so he took a ride down to watch Thurston toil on the mound for the Townies.

"Cash had obviously heard about me and being that he was always trying to get an advantage over the other clubs, he thought he'd see if I might be good enough to fill some holes in his pitching staff," said Thurston.

On this particular night, young Thurston was pitching against a weaker town team and had a particularly strong outing. Clark was obviously impressed enough to offer Thurston a contract to play the remainder of the summer for Clark's powerful Flyers.

"This was pretty heady stuff for a 16-year-old," said Thurston. "While I didn't know it at the time, high school players were not supposed to be eligible for the Down East League," he said. "But Cash being Cash, that didn't matter. He needed a pitcher and he went out and got one.

Despite his relative inexperience, Thurston had considerable success over the last month of the Flyers campaign. Being utilized mostly as a spot starter and long-reliever, Thurston pitched a couple of shutouts against Skowhegan and Waterville and impressed Clark enough to be offered a contract for the 1953 season following his senior year at Norway High School.

As so often happens, one's life direction can often be altered by a decidedly innocuous event or series of events. For Thurston, playing for Farmington provided him with that event which later propelled him up baseball's Darwinian ladder.

Thurston had filled out to where he was now a wiry 6'1" and weighed 175 pounds. With his exceptional foot speed and above-average arm, he was filling the role of a part-time outfielder, but wasn't getting many innings on the mound for the Flyers.

"I was staying at the Clark's that summer," said Thurston. "I was playing some outfield and pitching very little and somewhat erratically," said Thurston.

Thurston recalls Clark calling him in for a meeting one afternoon. "He brought me in and told me, 'Bill, you're not pitching very well for us. I've got to go out and get another frontline pitcher. Since you're from Norway, you can go home and still catch on with the town team for the summer'," said Thurston.

The young player from Norway was devastated. While he knew his performance wasn't what he would have liked on the mound, he thought that for a 17-year-old player, he was holding his own against some of the top college talent in the nation. He knew that many family members and friends were driving down to Auburn to see that night's game against the rival Asas, and all young Thurston could envision was telling his family he'd just been released. He was mortified with the thought of the embarrassment.

"As fate would have it, that night, we're playing the Asas in Auburn. All my friends and family are at the game. I haven't told anyone I've been released and that this is my last game with the Flyers," he said.

"I'm out in the bullpen watching the Asas light up our pitcher, Sid Griffin, from South Portland," said Thurston.

"The Asas have eight runs and our manager, signals for me to warm up. Meanwhile, Griffin gets out of the inning, but in the second, he gives up a couple more hits and a run and the call comes down for me to come in to pitch. I come in, walk the first guy to load the bases, but wiggle out of the inning with no more additional runs and I end up retiring the next 21 guys I face, " he said.

"In the seventh inning, Clark comes down and says to me, 'Hey kid! Forget what I told you earlier—you can live with me the rest of the summer and you're still on the team,'" laughed Thurston.

Thurston went on to have a pretty good summer. "That one event made a big difference for me," said Thurston. "As a result of playing for the Flyers, I ended up going to the University of Michigan on a scholarship, instead of the University of Maine where I was originally headed."

During August of 1953, Jack Onslow, a scout for the Boston Red Sox wanted to sign Thurston and send him to the lowest rung on the minor league ladder at the time—Class D ball. Being set to go to school at Maine, to play both football and baseball, with an athletic scholarship in tow, Thurston didn't want to end up going to some town that was even smaller than Norway, where he'd play baseball that was a step below the Down East League.

"I told Onslow of my situation of going to Maine and that I wasn't really interested in leaving the deal I had at Maine—which I was looking forward to—to join a team in the middle of nowhere, at the lowest rung of the minor leagues and bypass the sure deal at Maine wasn't what I thought was in my best interest," he said.

Onslow then asked Thurston if he'd be interested in attending a bigger school—a national power like Michigan—coached at the time by the legendary Ray Fisher.

Thurston was supremely interested. He knew that Michigan was just coming off a national championship season. One of his Flyer teammates—Jackie Corbett—played at the perennial baseball power.

"It was like a dream to me," said Thurston. "Here I was, just a farm boy from Norway and the next thing I know, I'm being offered the chance to go to the University of Michigan, a place where my dorm had more people than my hometown," he marveled.

Thurston ended up taking the train to New Jersey from Maine, where he met his teammate Corbett and his girlfriend. He then rode westward to the next stop on his journey—playing baseball for the University of Michigan.

"When I got to Michigan, it took me three weeks just to relocate Jackie," laughed Thurston. "The campus at that time was approaching 75,000 students and my dorm alone had over 1,200 residents," he said.

The 1953 season would be Thurston's last summer playing ball in Farmington. While in college, Thurston showed his stuff on diamonds much further north. He pitched in the Maine/New Brunswick League for Edmundston, just across the border from Madawaska, in New Brunswick, Canada. At the time, the league had Maine representation with teams in Houlton, Grand Falls, Presque Isle and Limestone Air Force Base. In 1956, he compiled a 9-1 record as he and his teammate, Ron Perranoski, led the Edmundston team to a league championship. Perranoski would later go on to have a distinguished major league career and eventually serve as the Los Angeles Dodgers' pitching coach under long-time manager, Tommy Lasorda.

Recalling Cash Clark, Thurston had this to say about the man who made the Flyers possible in Farmington.

"Cash could be a gruff New England SOB—he didn't always have a lot of patience when it came to winning or losing," said Thurston. "But he cared deeply about baseball and keeping the game alive in his community. He also took care of his players. I remember getting a letter from Cash one time when I was at Michigan, and in it was a $100 bill," he said.

****

For all intents and purposes, the heyday of the league was over. Both Augusta and Waterville were done—Augusta folding by mid-season in 1953. While the Down East League cobbled together four teams in 1954, the trend was towards clubs like the new Dixfield team. The Dixies would join the league and draw upon the town's strong baseball heritage and amazing support from its small but determined community. The *Lewiston Sun* announced that Dixfield was playing "for the love of baseball and not money."

A rainy summer plagued the league's attendance and revenues were down all over. With each team losing money once again, Auburn had to resort to moving many of its games from the usual weeknight tilts under the lights, to Saturday twi-nighters to avoid going head-to-head with televised Red Sox games, which now siphoned away attendees from Pettengill Park.

On May 18th, 1954, the Boston Red Sox/Baltimore Orioles night game was broadcast for the first time on a Maine television station. WCSH, channel six out of Portland, brought major league baseball into the comforts of homes around the state. While trumpeted as the beginning of something major and important, the convenience of watching professional baseball with a beer and a snack in your hand, made leaving the confines of home to watch local baseball not quite as appealing. In just three more seasons, semi-pro baseball would be all but dead and the Down East League would be but a memory.

In 1956, the ill-fated Western Maine League formed, with hopes of reviving the ghost of the former Down East circuit. While trumpeting itself as the offspring of the former semi-pro pioneering loop, the level of talent in the league was seriously diluted from the days when the top Division One college players flocked to Maine.

The Western Maine League became just another league in the state, not much better than some of the stronger town team leagues. While Auburn's Asas were still recruiting players, most of them were in-state college boys, a far cry from when their roster was filled with the best college and ex-pro talent around. Town team ball had recovered from the absence of players due to the war and were providing many small town baseball fans a viable alternative to traveling into Auburn, Farmington, or elsewhere to see a game.

By the end of the 1957 campaign, semi-pro baseball died in southern and central Maine. While there continued to be semi-pro baseball in Aroostook County near the Canadian border for another decade, the 10-year run of this high-powered brand of baseball had reached the end of the road. While isolated towns would make attempts to revive it over the next decade, the heyday of the post-war semi-pro era of baseball had ended.

But with any ending comes the hope for rebirth and renewal. As the 1950's gave way to the dawning of the 1960's, town team baseball was starting to make noise again. While both the Down East and Western Maine leagues had folded, the Androscoggin

River Valley would again resound with the crack of the bat and the slap of glove leather, this time pitting town against town, into the next decade and then some.

Chapter 2

Mill Towns and River Valleys: Town Team Baseball Experiences a Revival

With the escalation of the war, young men from across the state left their communities to fight for Uncle Sam. With a dwindling stock of baseball talent to draw from, many town teams and affiliated leagues ceased operations during the war. Some leagues, like the Pine Tree League, continued, but most experienced several years of inactivity between 1941 and the end of the war.

As young soldiers returned from global conflict, bursting with competitive natures in their primes, leagues began to reorganize and resume play. This process was gradual, as it took time for town team ball to return to the prominence that it once held prior to the war. Semi-pro baseball was wildly popular in the early 1950's and represented a thorn in the side of town team ball by siphoning away its best players. In smaller communities, the loss of one or two key players to a semi-pro club could be the difference in being able to field a team or not. With the dawning of the 1950's, town team baseball began its gradual comeback. As the popularity and feasibility of semi-pro baseball waned during the latter years of the decade, town teams were poised to fill the baseball void and attract the top players once again.

****

Representing communities nestled along the banks of the Androscoggin River and others dwelling in the shadows of the western mountains, as well as the smokestacks of the mill towns dotting the region, the Pine Tree League had provided local inhabitants of these varied communities with competitive baseball dating all the way back to the 1920's. The league, along with Portland's Twilight League, was considered one of the oldest in northern New England. Unlike the Twilight League, which imported many of its players, the Pine Tree teams consisted of players that were based predominantly in the community where each team was domiciled.

During the 1950's the league struggled to remain viable, with fierce competition for players coming from the rival Timber League. Several towns that had traditionally affiliated with the Pine Tree League had been coaxed over to this competitor. The Timber League had been particularly vibrant around the turn of the decade. With both Dixfield and the powerful Wilton Loggers providing a solid cornerstone, the league attracted talent that had previously worn the uniforms of Pine Tree teams. The Loggers, in addition to being the top team in the Timber League, regularly waged battles against the better semi-pro clubs in the area such as the Auburn Asas and the Farmington Flyers. During the time of the Timber League's prominence, the Pine Tree League limped on, fielding five or six teams and grappling to maintain the level of competition that fans were accustomed to.

As the 1960 season arrived, the Pine Tree League was back up to seven teams, with Dixfield's Dixies rejoining the fold from the Timber League. Dixfield had consistently been one of the strongest towns playing baseball along the Androscoggin River and its inclusion in the league in 1960 served notice that the Pine Tree was once more a league to be reckoned with.

****

The small town of Dixfield hasn't changed dramatically over the past 50 years. Tucked into the western Maine foothills, a visit to the town these days reveals a bit more traffic, as well as a new mural on the side of the IGA located at the junction of Routes 2 and 143. Other than that, the town remains remarkably the same as it did during the days when the Dixies' games at Harlow Field were each summer's main attraction.

Standing in the parking lot of the IGA, hearing the sound of pulp trucks downshifting to a stop at the traffic light, it's not hard to envision what it might have been like to be a visiting player driving into town during the 1950's and 1960's to play the Dixies.

Dixfield's recent baseball history includes the town team Dixies, which were perennial Timber League and Yankee Amateur Baseball Congress (YABC) champs in the late 1940's and early 1950's. The Dixies regularly made trips to Auburn's Pettengill Park to steal the coveted state baseball crown from larger and more prominent communities. From 1949 through 1952, Dixfield won four consecutive YABC championships, the longest stretch of post-season dominance in YABC history. With the likes of the Horne brothers—Stan pitching and Harold catching—the Gordon brothers—Linc in center, Robert and Sheldon forming the double play combo at short and second—as well as Dick Morang providing power at first base, the die was cast for a local dynasty that became the basis by which all other Dixfield teams would be measured.

In 1953, the Dixfield club decided to sample the competition at the next level and entered the semi-pro ranks with its more rigorous competition. This led to the demise of town team ball in Dixfield for several seasons. The semi-pro Dixies lasted for three seasons in the Down East League and then joined the new Western Maine League for 1956. The Dixies were always competitive, but lacking the budget of larger towns like Auburn and Farmington, they often relied on locals and a couple of college transplants to compete with the deeper pockets that stocked rival rosters with high-powered and highly touted college talent from away.

With the demise of semi-pro ball after the 1956 season, the town team Dixies rejoined the Pine Tree League and became a fixture over the next decade, save for two years in 1960 and 1961, when they rejoined the Timber League during its brief revival.

****

One player who symbolizes many, if not all, of the qualities that made town team baseball and its players so special is one Theodore "Bitsy" Ionta. Ionta, along with the Swan brothers, Artie Taylor, Newt Stowell and Big Bill Elliot were mainstays on the Dixfield teams of the late 1950's and early 1960's. All of these players brought passion and a burning desire to compete each time they sprinted out to their positions.

Ionta, a slender right-handed hurler and middle infielder, brought with him a similar competitiveness, as well as carrying himself with a quiet dignity that has served him well over his six decades of participating as an active player in one variety or another of local baseball.

Baseball has always occupied a central place in Ionta's life. While he played baseball at Mexico High School, Ionta characteristically admits that he wasn't a star player.

"I was average at best," said Ionta.

Interestingly, while it was as a pitcher that he received most of his notoriety during his days for the Dixies, and later the Rumford Townies and Pirates, during high school he never pitched as much as one inning.

"I never pitched in high school," he said. "After graduating in 1952, I went into the Air Force for four years, getting out in 1957. While I was in the service, I had a friend who was a catcher. Clair Fletcher and I would play catch every night between the barracks. I would pitch and he would catch and we'd play these simulated games—my Red Sox against his Dodgers. Whenever we'd get a chance, we'd go over to the nearby ball field on base and I'd throw off the mound or shag flies. The combination of all that throwing, as well as decent mechanics, which I had apparently picked up from somewhere, gave me the confidence to believe that I could be a pitcher."

After receiving his discharge from the service in July 1957, he approached manager Claude Belyea of the Rumford Rams about playing. Belyea asked Ionta what position he played.

"I didn't hesitate," said Ionta. "I told him I was a pitcher."

Because the Rams were in need of pitching, Belyea issued Ionta a uniform and he suited up for a weekend doubleheader against the powerful Auburn Asas. During his very first game with the Rams, Ionta received his baptism by fire. The Rams starter was in trouble most of the first few innings and with the bases loaded and no outs, the Rams manager summoned Ionta from the bullpen to make his debut.

"I came in with the bases loaded and no outs," he recalled. "After I struck out the first two hitters on curve balls, up comes the dangerous Norm Davis. I was feeling pretty confident—I had two outs and I was ahead of him in the count by getting a couple of sweeping curves over. I think the count was one ball, two strikes. I thought I'd be cute and try to blow the fastball by him— he hit it and I think the ball is still going," laughed Ionta. "The funny thing was I wasn't nervous at all. With all the pitching I'd done between the barracks and off the mound while in the service, I was confident that I could be an effective pitcher."

And effective Ionta was to become. When he was inducted into the Maine Baseball Hall of Fame in 2001, writer and historian Bob McPhee of Rumford calculated that during Ionta's career— spanning over 40 years—he won an amazing 223 games, while losing only 41. Most of these wins came between 1960 and 1980, when Ionta regularly pitched nine-inning complete games.

Like most players who continue to play baseball for any length of time, the game was their hobby—like hunting, skiing, or even restoring cars for others. During the 1950's and throughout the 1960's, being a member of a local baseball team involved a substantial commitment of time.

"Town team ball usually involved playing two times during the week and doubleheaders on Sunday," said Ionta. "Dixfield, as well as many of the other teams, practiced one or two nights a week, so baseball was a five-or six-day-a-week commitment for us."

Reflecting back over his career, Ionta recognized that there had been a progression for him, as a player with inauspicious beginnings.

"When I was at Mexico High, I was an average, average player," he said. "I guess I just got better as I matured. When I came out of the service, I played for Farmington State Teachers

College (now the University of Maine at Farmington) for four years, and then I played all those years of town team ball."

When asked about his pitching style and its apparent effectiveness, Ionta mentioned that his delivery and sound mechanics lessened the usual stress put on an arm as it performs the unnatural task of throwing a baseball at maximum velocity.

"I threw with a three-quarters delivery, which didn't put much stress on my arm," said Ionta. "I always could throw strikes. I probably threw in the low 80's (his velocity), but I could always hit my spots."

In 1960, Ionta was a member of the Norway-Paris Twins team that won the YABC Tournament at Auburn's Pettengill Park and made the long journey to Battle Creek, Michigan, for the National Amateur Baseball World Series.

"Dixfield didn't qualify for the post season tournament," recalled Ionta. "Each team that qualified for the tournament was allowed to pick up three players from other teams in their league, according to YABC rules," he said. "I was one of Norway's pick ups along with Artie Taylor [his catcher from Dixfield]."

The national tournament brought teams from all over the country and was divided up during the preliminary rounds by whether or not a team was east or west of the Mississippi River. During past appearances by Maine teams, it was a rare feat for them to win a single game in the tournament. As so often happened with teams from Maine, they would make the two-day sojourn only to lose their first two games. They would then turn around and make the long trek back to Maine and their non-baseball lives.

Norway-Paris lost their first game and appeared destined for another two and out appearance by a Maine team. According to Ionta, "We had our bags packed and on the bus. The rules of the tournament stipulated that dorm rooms and other perks for players only applied while you were still alive in the tournament. If we had to go back to our rooms on day two after losing, we'd have to pay for our rooms for that day. By being packed up and checked out, if we lost, we would have our things and not have to pay that final day's charges."

So much for our positive thinking, huh," he laughed.

The strategy apparently worked—the Twins reeled off three consecutive wins—prolonging their stay in Battle Creek. Finally, playing the previous year's defending national champions, a strong Dearborn, Michigan team, the underdogs from Maine went down to defeat, 9-6. The upstart Norway club actually out hit Dearborn 14-8, but four costly errors behind Ionta sealed their eventual fate.

We really won over the fans at the tournament," said Ionta. "The fans were pulling for us hicks from Maine, in our mismatched uniforms and odd assortment of street clothes," he said. "When Phil Martin [the team's player/manager] came to the mound to take me out, the entire crowd of several thousand gave me a standing ovation. It was quite a thrill," said the humble Ionta. "I think we impressed them and won their respect—a team from a little state like Maine, competing against city players with populations larger than our entire state's," marveled Ionta.

Playing in five decades as a player, Ionta has seen many changes take place in local baseball. During the 1980's, Ionta took on the additional task of becoming Pine Tree League co-commissioner with player/coach Mark Thurlow of West Paris. Despite his new administrative duties of running the league, he continued to play for the Rumford Pirates, mostly as a part-time player. Ionta shared his thoughts on how the local game has changed over the years and why he thinks local baseball is dead and won't be revived.

"When I first started playing, the emphasis was on offense and pitching," said Ionta. "We didn't play on terrific fields, plus the gloves weren't the high tech products that the kids have today. The modern player also works harder on his defense than most of our players," he said. "We didn't spend much time taking ground balls or working on defensive drills like I see teams doing today."

As far as the hitting is concerned, he's not convinced that modern hitters are any better.

"We had some big raw-boned guys who could hit," said Ionta. "That Norway-Paris team that I went to Battle Creek with in 1960—we didn't win any games with our gloves. We were out hitting some pretty tough competition," he recalled. "Today, when I go to games, I see kids taking pitches down the middle. Most of the players today rarely choke up on the bat with two strikes—I rarely struck out as a hitter."

Reflecting on his own career and his successes, Ionta offered the following.

"I never took myself too seriously. I went game to game—looking forward to the next time I could play—just hanging out with the guys. We played hard and always tried to win. If we didn't, it wasn't the end of the world. We always thought about doing our best and having a good time."

When considering the demise of town team ball, Ionta offered a couple of thoughts that he had as to why a once-vital part of small town Maine has disappeared.

"Job availability for kids has a lot to do with it," said Ionta. Kids all have cars and money. It's more fun to go to the beach on Sunday than play a doubleheader," he said. "Also, when the older guys got done, you needed some younger guys to step in and take over. The younger players didn't have the same respect for the game that we did. If they weren't going to show up, they wouldn't call. You have players today who want to play when they feel like it. For town team ball to flourish, you have to have 12-15 guys committed to one another and the team."

Ionta laments the loss of community that led to the demise of town team ball.

"Our towns have lost some type of connection that they used to have," said Ionta. "I'm not sure what it is, but people just don't do things together, as a community the way they used to. As for sports, so much of the modern day variety is all about the individual. Guys standing at the plate, watching the ball when they hit a home run. That just didn't happen when I played," declared Ionta. "If someone did that to a Red Dean [Farmington, Strong-Phillips pitcher renowned for his competitiveness] when he was pitching, well the next at bat, he'd have had the ball planted in his ribs."

Ionta shared his thoughts about some of the players that he played with or against that stand out in his memory over his long and illustrious career.

"Stan Timberlake of Turner was a great athlete. He was big, but he could run and throw hard and would do a lot of little things to beat you. My teammates in Dixfield, Cary Swan and Newtie Stowell, as well as Artie [Taylor] who later went with me to Rumford; they were real good ball players," he said.

Ionta paused for a minute, reflecting back over the many years and teams that he played with or against.

"Let me see, Bobby Downs who I played with in Rumford was a good ball player. I also thought Clyde Pingree and Red Dean of Strong-Phillips were top-notch. Like I mentioned, Dean was a tremendous competitor. Rangeley had some good teams during the early 70's, but most of their players were imports—they worked there during the summer."

****

When the Auburn Asas semi-pro team ceased operations following the 1957 season, baseball in Lewiston and Auburn suffered. Gone were the crowds that had numbered in the thousands during the early 1950's. The Twin City League, which often fielded a roster of 10 to 12 teams during much of the early 1950's, was nearly dead. Only a handful of teams remained and many of them were based outside of Lewiston and Auburn—this was almost unheard of during the league's heyday.

Reynolds Tree Experts stepped forward with a sponsorship and this club provided a strong Lewiston/Auburn nucleus in 1956 and 1957. The growing popularity of softball was putting a serious strain on baseball in Central Maine's most populous area, however, as more and more former baseball players found the quicker games and diminished travel an easier commitment to make.

The Andy County League formed in 1960, to pick up the slack left by the demise of semi-pro baseball and the Twin City League. With a viable pool of talented ballplayers preferring the superior competition offered only by baseball, the initial season of the league found five teams competing within a 30-mile radius. With clubs from Turner, West Minot, Mechanic Falls, Chisholm-Livermore, and a combined Lewiston/Auburn entrant sponsored by the Hotel Manoir in Lewiston, the area's local baseball heritage was kept alive for at least one more year.

Turner provided the league with a capable bedrock team to spur on the other towns joining the league. The Townies had gone to Battle Creek in 1957 to compete in the National Amateur World Series. Still considered a formidable team by those who followed the local baseball scene, the Townies were dubbed the preseason team to beat for the upcoming 1960 season.

The most interesting team in the Andy County League was the West Minot Townies. Anyone who has ever driven through the town of West Minot knows that the town center is easy to miss, if you happened to blink. With only a couple of buildings that signify that you are passing through a town at all—the abandoned train station, a holdover from the days when train travel was the primary mode of transportation, as well as the general store at the forks—it's easy to miss this center of rural commerce. The major means of employment in West Minot was dairy farming, so most of the players milked cows and farmed by day, while legging out base hits and snaring line drives by night in front of family and friends.

The town of West Minot didn't number many more than 300 people. The unique character of a rural outpost like West Minot and participation in town team baseball becomes apparent when you consider that the combined populations of Lewiston and Auburn, the largest communities fielding a team in the Andy County, were more than 100 times that of West Minot's. Even Chisholm-Livermore, much smaller than Lewiston and Auburn, had more than ten times the inhabitants of West Minot.

****

Frank Gammon began playing for West Minot in 1954 while still in grammar school. In small towns similar to West Minot, fielding a team of 10 –15 players was a constant challenge. Often, players as young as 13 or 14 were recruited to provide nine players during a crisis. Like any sport, players get hurt and conflicts arise regarding work or family. The birth of a calf, haying season, as well as other work-related conflicts could wreak havoc with small town rosters. Padding the roster with a few extra players, such as a grammar school player like Gammon, afforded teams like West Minot the luxury of riding out the occasional absence of a regular player, without having to take a forfeit.

Gammon, along with his older brother Calvin, followed in the footsteps of their father, Woodrow. "Woody" Gammon had been a crack player during his days at Buckfield High School in the late 1920's. After graduating, Gammon married and began a family, while moving to the fertile pastures of West Minot and a life of farming. Like many of his peers, Gammon still found time to maintain his town team baseball career, tacking on evening and Sunday contests to a full work and family schedule. Gammon continued his career throughout the 1930's and 1940's, even playing some games in the 1950's with his teenage sons, if player shortages required it.

The Gammons, along with the Trundy and the Clough families, formed the nucleus of the West Minot team. Looking at a box score from this period usually reveals two or three Gammons, several Trundys and a Clough or two, with one or two other names sprinkled in for variety.

The West Minot students attended Edward Little High School in nearby Auburn, as West Minot was too small for their own high school. The Red Eddies were always one of the premiere high school baseball teams in the state. Their roster usually was dotted with a couple of the West Minot players, such as the Gammon brothers. According to Gammon, playing ball for Edward Little helped West Minot to have such competitive town teams.

"We would usually have nine or ten players from our town, but we'd have to get a couple of pitchers from 'the city,'" said Gammon.

The city was Auburn, or even Mechanic Falls, West Minot's larger neighbor to the northwest. Over the years, West Minot imported solid pitching with the likes of Dick Osgood, Dick Small and Ralph Pederson from Auburn. Additionally, Don Verrill, who hailed from West Minot and perfected his craft for Edward Little, provided additional depth to the Townies' pitching staff.

****

Jeff Trundy recalls that town team baseball was part and parcel of what it meant to grow up in a small Maine town like West Minot.

"Growing up in a small town of about 300, you learned very early in life that you were supposed to play baseball," said Trundy. "If you were good enough, then you would one day get to wear the uniform of the town team and represent your town against rival communities," he said. "All of us kids, who played sandlot ball growing up, aspired to one day put on the uniform and take our places out there with our fathers, uncles, or neighbors on the local team. We knew that if we were good enough, then we would one day get to wear the West Minot uniform and represent our town against surrounding communities like Mechanic Falls, Turner, and even Lewiston and Auburn."

Town team baseball is remembered by Trundy as being both fun and also very competitive.

"I recollect that it was extremely competitive, but also extremely fun," he said. "You had guys that were playing for the sheer joy of the game. None of them were going to make any money, or get signed to play professionally. They were just going out to represent their town and keep their pride intact," said Trundy. Occasionally, the competition got out of hand.

"I think I was around 15 or 16, when one night, the Lisbon team was playing West Minot at the old Sanatorium Field, which was up on a hill overlooking the White Mountains. My cousin Warren, who was quite a competitor, was on first and Lisbon had a big first baseman [Bob Ransome]. For whatever reason, Warren and the first baseman got shoving one another and before I knew it, my uncle Maynard, who was a bit of a hot-head, came running down from the crowd; the next thing I knew, there were punches being thrown, spikes were flying and we had ourselves a good old-fashioned donnybrook on our hands. I was watching this all from the perimeter, not really taking it all in," laughed Trundy. "Then, as quickly as it started, order was restored by the umpires and probably a few calmer members of the crowd, and the game resumed as if nothing had ever happened."

Recalling the heyday of the West Minot teams just prior to his own playing days, Trundy cites the years of 1962 and 1963 as being the high points for baseball in the town. Like teammate Frank Gammon, Trundy also got his town team start at an early age.

According to Trundy, it was at the end of his freshman year in high school at Edward Little in 1964. Trundy remembers joining the West Minot lineup for good that summer, although he seems to think he logged a few games the previous summer at the age of 14.

"I can remember coming down to Pettengill Park in Auburn for the end of the season tournaments [YABC]. The winners got to go to Battle Creek. For me and my family, it was better than going to Fenway Park for today's kids. I used to love to come down and watch guys like Artie Taylor, who played for Dixfield and later Rumford," he said. "What was an even bigger thrill was finally getting to play in these tournaments, which often drew crowds of 1,500 to 2,000 people."

West Minot continued to play in the Andy County League through most of the early 1960's, although in 1964, they joined the less competitive Spruce Tree League with Poland, Casco, Danville, Naples, Norway-Paris and Gray. For several years during the mid-1960's, many area teams including West Minot bounced around, playing one year in one league and the next in another area loop. For the most part, the level of talent and team depth dictated where teams would affiliate, with travel convenience also factoring in.

By 1965, interest in baseball was beginning to wane in West Minot as the team was aging without replacements available from the town. As farming communities like West Minot began to see the agrarian way of life diminish, many long-time families began to move away. For West Minot, 1965 became a struggle to field enough players to be competitive, although with talented, multi-dimensional players like Jeff and Warren Trundy, Frank and Calvin Gammon, as well as some solid pitching, the Townies still finished near .500 for the season. Sadly, 1966 would be West Minot's swan song as a town team participant. The death of local baseball in communities such as West Minot began another winnowing of towns from the roster of local baseball. Continuing a trend that began ten years earlier with semi-pro baseball's demise, baseball was merely mirroring society at large. As baseball died in small towns like West Minot, it signified a loss of rural values that had promoted civic participation and interest in things like town team baseball. The increased mobility offered by automobiles also provided more options for entertainment. The greater influence of television proved too strong for small towns like West Minot to resist. As a result, the town dropped out of participation for good. In 1967, Jeff and Warren Trundy, along with the Gammon brothers, took their talents to the northeast and went to play for their former rivals, the Turner Townies.

While many of the stories he remembers are nearly 40 years old, Trundy vividly recalls the incidents and exploits as if they were yesterday. Like many former players interviewed, Trundy's memories connect him to a bygone era that remains a fond testament to a special period in our local culture and town histories.

"The field in Turner was at the old Leavitt Institute," remembers Trundy. "There was a building out in right field and it was two different colors. If it hit the bottom half of the building, then it was a double, if it hit the other color higher up, it was a home run," he recalled. "You can imagine what kind of problems this presented from an umpiring standpoint," laughed Trundy. "I remember Drig Fournier, a wiry left-handed hitter from Livermore, hitting balls over the building. For a kid, that seemed like he hit the ball 500 feet. Or big Steve Lancaster of Chi-Livermore hitting two balls over the oak tree in center at the Sanatorium Field in West Minot; the tree was some 450 feet away, so you can imagine how far he hit the ball."

Trundy's days beyond town team ball have been kind to him. After high school, he starred at the University of New Hampshire, where he was an all-conference selection and also won a batting title. When he left college, he entered the coaching ranks where he has achieved considerable success coaching the game that he learned to love as a child, growing up in an idyllic, rural corner of Maine. For nearly 20 years, he coached at Cony High School in Augusta, where his Cony Rams teams were consistently near the top of the pack in Eastern Maine high school baseball. Currently, he is the head baseball coach at the Gunnery School, a prep school in Connecticut. Trundy fills his summers by managing the Falmouth Commodores, members of the prestigious Cape Cod League. The Cape Cod League is the summer home of many future major league stars, as the rosters of Cape teams are amply stocked with the top college talent from around the nation. In 2004, Trundy was voted Cape Cod League manager of the year.

When asked if the experience of growing up in tiny West Minot and his involvement with town team baseball factors into his present-day successes in the game of baseball, Trundy offered the following.

"I'm just a country bumpkin from West Minot who's gone quite far from those magical days of playing in front of family and friends in my little village. I know my upbringing around the game has had a lot to do with my love for the game and whatever successes I've been able to achieve, particularly as a coach."

****

For Adrien "Drig" Fournier, the mill and athletics would be converging elements in his life. Born the youngest of seven boys and five girls, he learned early about the expectations that chase a boy growing up in working-class towns like Jay. According to Fournier, all his brothers played baseball.

"It was a given that I'd play also," said Fournier.

After graduating from Jay High School in 1951, Fournier, along with many of his classmates, went to work at International Paper's Otis Mill. He would spend many of his waking hours in the shadows of the mill's massive smokestacks.

Like many of his town team contemporaries, Fournier answered the call to local competition while not yet of high school age. Since Jay didn't have a team, the 14-year-old Fournier joined his older brother Lawrence, playing for the neighboring team in Chisholm-Livermore. The Chi-Liv Townies became Fournier's team, as he continued to play for them during each subsequent summer of high school. While baseball was Fournier's forte at Jay High School, he also starred in other athletic pursuits as well. The multi-talented Fournier lettered in three sports. In addition to his accomplishments on the diamond, he was an excellent quarterback on the gridiron and a capable scorer on the basketball hardwood during Maine's long winters.

The summer following his graduation, Fournier again played town team ball before shipping off for Uncle Sam, where he would serve an overseas stint in the military. With America once again facing international conflict, this time with the nation of Korea, Fournier brought his characteristic focus to the duties assigned to him by his superiors over the next two years.

In 1956, he returned to his job at the mill, bringing with him the added maturity that comes from being a young man in a foreign land, away from familiar surroundings. Because Fournier's talents were well-known in the area, his return didn't go unnoticed by local baseball "sharpies." Fournier was recruited to play for the Wilton Loggers team, who had just left the potent Timber League to join the newly formed Western Maine League. The Western Maine League was primarily the reformed Down East League, a semi-pro circuit that continued to attract premiere college players to the state for the summer. The Western Maine League wasn't as strong as the Down East League was during its peak in the early 1950's, but it was still a pitching-rich league and a good test for Fournier's prowess as a hitter.

The 1956 Loggers boasted a duo of strong hitters in the middle of their line up to compliment Fournier. Joining Fournier was former Jay High School alumni, Will Laverdiere, who had starred at Colby College. Laverdiere was a veteran of several summers of semi-pro ball and added slick fielding as a shortstop to his offensive production. Additionally, slugger Bill Linscott from Farmington was joining the Jay duo, which formed the core of the Logger's batting order. Linscott had originally played for his hometown Flyers for two seasons before coming over to Wilton when the Flyers folded following the 1955 season. Every team needs strong pitching to compliment hitting and the Loggers had a quality arm in veteran lefty, Alvin Davis.

While the 1956 Loggers were certainly competitive, they lacked the depth of a team such as Auburn or even Rumford and finished a disappointing third in the four team league, just ahead of cellar-dwelling Dixfield. Despite the team's struggles in the league, Fournier didn't miss a beat against the better pitching, as he finished as one of the Western Maine League's top hitters, finishing the 1956 campaign with a batting average just under .400.

The arrival of the 1957 season saw Fournier playing for Turner in the Andy County League, as the mill's shift work schedule made the semi-pro commitment impossible for him. In his first season with the Townies, Fournier helped lead them to a league title, as well as providing the spark necessary to allow them to claim the YABC championship at Auburn. This qualified Turner for a trip to the nationals in Battle Creek, Michigan.

Fournier's first stay in Turner would be brief, as the budding of May's warm days in 1958 saw interest rekindled in reviving the Townies in Chisolm-Livermore. Chi-Liv [as they were referred to by most local fans] became a powerful team for the next five years, winning the Andy County League championship in 1958 and claiming another league crown in 1961, as the revived Timber League was the venue for that summer's successes.

What began as an inauspicious beginning in 1961—the Chi-Liv team was late joining the revamped league and forfeited their initial outing—ended on a high note, as the Townies beat out Timber rivals such as Jay-Wilton, Phillips-Strong, Rumford and Dixfield, qualifying again for the YABC tourney. Battling tough competition from around the state, the Townies swept through the local tourney to qualify for a trip to Battle Creek.

For the veteran Fournier, this would be his second cross-country jaunt to play against the best amateur talent in the nation. In addition to his on-field responsibilities, Fournier was now the team's business manager and responsible for gathering the $1,500 necessary to cover the team's trip to Battle Creek. A local fundraising dance and Fournier's veritable charm led many businesses in Jay and neighboring Livermore to pitch in, which allowed the Townies to venture westward.

The team left Livermore in five cars in order to make the two day Midwestern excursion with hopes running high for a repeat of last year's strong showing by Norway-Paris. Unfortunately, the team took an opening pounding from the host team, 11-1. They bowed out on their second day of the tournament, falling 10-3 to Savannah, Georgia. Though he didn't know it at the time, this would be Fournier's last appearance in Battle Creek.

"I was a little disappointed we didn't do better," said Fournier. "We had added some real good players like Bitsy [Ionta], Newtie Stowell and Milt Gardner from the Adams [Massachusetts] team, so I thought we'd do well. The western teams were always tough, he said. "A lot of these teams had players who would eventually play professional baseball, while we were just a bunch of country ballplayers."

The Timber League ceased operations for good following the 1961 season, so Fournier, along with fellow Chi-Liv stalwarts Frank Franchetti and Steve Lancaster were off to Turner to rejoin the already strong combine. Fournier would become a key component for the Townies over the next five seasons, providing them with a consistent line drive hitter from the left side of the plate.

In 1967, Fournier fittingly returned to play his farewell season with the Chi-Liv Townies. Fournier and long-time teammate Steve Lancaster revived the Townies for that summer's Pine Tree League battles. After 20 seasons of local skirmishes, Fournier finally hung up his spikes for good and ended his prolific career in the place where it all began, back in 1947.

****

As a player, Fournier was never content to merely go through the motions while playing the game he loved. Over his career, Fournier became a student of all aspects of baseball. As a left-handed hitter, he could hit the ball wherever it was pitched, spraying drives all over the ballpark. When called upon, he was capable of providing power also, as those who played with him and against him will attest to. If the game situation dictated a stolen base, Fournier was always up to the task.

After his playing days, Fournier stayed connected with baseball by pursuing umpiring with the same passion and professionalism that he brought to the game as a player. For 28 years, Fournier arbitrated games and was considered by many coaches and fans alike as one of the finest umpires in Western Maine. During the late 1960's and early 1970's, high school coaches selected their own umpires and Fournier's schedule was always quickly filled by the area coaching fraternity, desirous of his firm, but fair skills he brought to the profession.

Over Fournier's career, he stole home a remarkable 25 times. Fournier attributes this to being a student of the game and an observer of every aspect of a pitcher's routine as reasons for his success in accomplishing one of baseball's rarest of feats.

"I wasn't blessed with blazing speed," confessed Fournier. "The key for me was knowing the pitcher's tempo and I watched everything he did out there on the mound," he said.

Fournier credits high school coach Bob St. Pierre, for teaching him much of what he knew about running the bases.

"He was a great at coaching the art of base running," said Fournier. "With a runner on first and less than two outs, he'd steal the runner at first and have me lay down a bunt. St. Pierre told me to make the third baseman handle it. More times than not, he'd throw it over third and we'd have a run, and I'd be on second or third," he remarked.

Like most players recalling the heyday of their youth, Fournier has several stories that stand out in a cavalcade of memories culled from nearly two decades of playing local baseball. Like any good hitter, Fournier has a couple of hitting yarns to share from back in the day.

For years, the Thomaston Penitentiary team had some great prison baseball teams. They were happy to have outside teams come inside the imposing walls of the ancient facility, to provide opposition for a team that played all of its games at home. On several occasions, Fournier's Chi-Liv team made the trip to Thomaston and waged battle against the prison team.

"Our Chi-Liv team went up to Thomaston to play the prison team," said Fournier. "The base of the wall in center was about 420 feet from the plate. I hit a ball half way up the building located behind the wall. Roger Doiron, one of my teammates said it was one of the longest home runs he had seen."

On another occasion, Dick Small was pitching for the Auburn Asas. Small was a crafty lefty with a big sweeping curve. Fournier told how he loved to sit back on the "hanger" and drive it into the gaps. On this occasion, Fournier heard Small's second baseman make the comment, "This guy can't hit you."

"That was a big mistake," said Fournier.

Fournier recalls hearing Small tell his teammate to "shut up," knowing the comment was sure to get Fournier's dander up. Sure enough, on the very next pitch, Fournier lined a shot to the left of the second baseman that took his glove "completely off from his hand," chuckled Fournier.

Fournier had respect for the many opponents that he competed against over the years. A few stood out in his memory for various reasons.

"Bob Baumer from Lisbon Falls—he and I had some battles when I played for Turner," said Fournier. "He was a tough lefty, but I had success against Bobby because he was always around the plate. I was fortunate because he could be a bear on lefties."

Fournier also mentioned the strong Rumford teams that he played against over the years and players like Artie Taylor, Larry McKenna and Mike Puiia.

"Those guys always played hard, but they were great guys," he said. "You'd slide hard into second or run into Artie Taylor at the plate, but after the game, they'd invite you over to their car for a beer."

One player Fournier especially wanted to recognize was Warren "Red" Dean, the competitive right-handed pitcher, whom Fournier batted against for nearly 20-some years.

"Red was the ultimate competitor; a guy who hated to lose," said Fournier. "He'd do whatever he had to do to beat you."

One of the best players he saw over his 20 years of baseball was his long-time teammate Steve Lancaster. The two of them played most of their careers together, bouncing back and forth between Chi-Liv and Turner.

"Steve had all the tools—he could run, hit, throw, and hit with power," said Fournier. "I've never understood why he didn't go further as a player, because he certainly could have."

Fournier still follows local sports. He loves to go to high school football games at his alma mater of Jay High School. The school continues to dominate high school football in the area, nearly 50 years after Fournier starred as a Tiger quarterback.

Looking back over his career and whatever successes he attained, Fournier attributes it to the lessons he learned about work.

"I knew the value of work," he said. "When I was in high school, I'd get up at 3:30 in the morning each school day to deliver milk for the local dairy. On Saturdays before football games, I would usually work four or five hours before grabbing lunch and heading over to the high school to suit up for that afternoon's game. Growing up in a mill town, all us kids learned what work was, because our fathers and uncles all worked six days a week, plus overtime," said Fournier.

Upon his retirement, he had logged over 41 years behind a papermaking machine. During that time, he had become proficient at this specialized craft, as well as being proud of his union involvement, which included being "locked out" during the infamous and very contentious International Paper strike of 1987. Because of the hardball tactics taken by the parent company, Fournier and other coworkers were forced out of their hometown employment. In order to make a living, they had to take their skills and talents elsewhere. Many of them moved downriver to the Pejepscot Paper mill in Pejepscot, Maine. This is where Fournier retired from the papermaking trade in 1993.

Fournier, like many former players, had a deep love and respect for the game of baseball. Playing town team ball for nearly 30 years required a deep passion for the game, as well as a commitment to his teammates, and ultimately, his community.

"We lived to play the game," said Fournier. "Working shift work in the mill, there were many times I ended up playing on Sundays with little or no sleep. Looking back, I don't regret it at all," he said. "It's hard to believe it's been almost 40 years since I played. Sometimes it seems like yesterday."

****

During the mid-1960's, the Andy County League was on solid footing. With a stable roster of affiliates, the league had both Lewiston and Auburn fielding teams, which gave it an urban focal point that most leagues in Maine didn't have. Additionally, Auburn's inclusion provided an additional benefit to the league; while the Asas were no longer the powerful team they once were, they played their home games at Pettengill Park, the best ball field in Central Maine. Having lights allowed night games and the league was able to schedule twi-night doubleheaders between four league teams on Sunday nights. These semi-regular Sunday night bills produced healthy crowds and a decent gate. With crowds ranging from 750 to 1,000 paying fans, the proceeds allowed the Andy County League to be on much firmer financial footing than many other leagues during this period.

****

The 1964, 1965 and 1966 seasons were considered by many long-time local baseball observers as the heyday of town team baseball in the Central Maine region, particularly the twin cities of Lewiston and Auburn, as well as the surrounding towns.

Jimmy Bouchles offers a perspective on local baseball rivaled by few in the Lewiston and Auburn area and beyond. Beginning with his involvement in the twin cities, first as manager of the stellar Bates Manufacturing teams of the Twin City League, a year managing the semi-pro Auburn Asas, several years as commissioner of the YABC, as well as thirty years as the primary force behind legion baseball in Auburn, Bouchles' grasp of the area's baseball culture is keen.

"The period in the middle 1960's brought a resurgence of local baseball in Lewiston and Auburn," said Bouchles. "It wasn't quite up to the level of competition and fan interest of the prime of the Asas and the Down East League, but the town team ball played by the Townies in Turner, Rumford, Lisbon Falls, and some other towns was very strong," he said. "The success of the YABC tournaments and the crowds really sparked a lot of interest during that time. We were drawing crowds close to 1,500 to 2,000 during 1964 and 1965," he said. After that, they started to drop off, except for a handful of times after that."

With the Andy County League and its six to eight teams, the Spruce Tree League and its six teams, as well as the Pine Tree League with an additional four or five teams, the area now had three solid leagues within a fifty-mile radius. This greatly contributed to the kind of excitement that was necessary to hold the interest of fans, who now had many more choices than those of a decade before.

One feature that also sparked additional interest and contributed to the resurgence of baseball during this period was the mid-summer all-star tilt organized between the Andy County and rival leagues such as the Spruce Tree League. While the Spruce Tree teams didn't have the depth of talent of their rivals due to the smaller towns of that league, each Spruce Tree team had players that were every bit as skilled as their Andy County counterparts.

The first all-star game was a success, with around 600 fans coming out to Pettengill Park to experience the crack of the bat against the ball under the lights and the humid late-August night air. The Andy County stars beat up on their Spruce Tree counterparts by a 14-5 score. Dave Begos led the way with a home run and a double and snagged the MVP trophy for his exploits. Several pitchers split the mound duties with Bob Baumer, Dick Small and Chris Houlares being most effective.

The Spruce Tree contingent made some noise of their own, with Gary Mingo's home run in the fourth cutting the Andy League lead to 4-3, but that's as close as they would come. Subsequent matches between rival leagues continued over the next few seasons and would continue to stir up local fan attention, as well as additional media coverage.

As with any league, competition between strong teams will create a buzz and hold the focus of players and fans alike. Beginning in 1964 and continuing over the next three seasons, local leagues such as the Andy County League would have some of the fiercest kinds of rivalries around.

With the revival of baseball in Lisbon Falls and the success of the Roberts 88'ers in 1964, plus strong opponents in Turner, Lewiston, and Norway-Paris among others, local baseball was once more a conversation piece. By garnering outstanding regular coverage in local dailies such as the *Lewiston Morning Sun* and the *Evening Journal*, area sports fans were once again turning out to support town team baseball.

On July 20th, locked in a tight battle for the league crown, Turner rolled into Lisbon Falls determined to avenge three straight previous losses. A Turner win would cut the 88'ers lead to half a game in the standings with only four games to go.

The anticipated match up between pitching aces Gerry Henry for the Townies and lefty stopper Bob Baumer for Lisbon's 88'ers, offered the promise of one of the classic matches of the summer.

With local baseball once again on sound footing and holding the interest of area players and fans alike, town team baseball appeared to be back with a vengeance for several years to come.

Chapter 3

The Roberts 88'ers: A Coming Together of Town and Team

Passion for baseball runs deep in the veins of many in Lisbon and Lisbon Falls, the villages, which along with Lisbon Center, make up the town of Lisbon. Historical records indicate that town team baseball has been played in this mill community as far back as 1894. The first clash of opponents in the town is recorded as being played on the old fairgrounds in Lisbon Falls, located on the site of the present-day Getty gas station on Lisbon Street.

Lisbon, like similar mill communities across the state, attracted a substantial influx of European immigrants in the early part of the 20th century. Lured by the promises and opportunities offered to all who came to America seeking a better life, these settlers were quick to acquire the customs and culture of their new homeland. Sports provided the chance for many immigrant children to assimilate into their adopted surroundings. What was any more American than for a young immigrant boy playing on the local baseball team?

These newcomers, many of whom were Slovakian, Polish, German or French, settled in Lisbon to work in the Worumbo Mill. The mill sits at the base of Main Street in downtown Lisbon Falls. Bordered on one side by Route 196, the busy thoroughfare passing through the town, and the Androscoggin River, the mill was renowned for its textiles, particularly the wool cloth it produced. For many of these immigrants, a job in the mill allowed them to establish an economic foothold that had often been denied to them in their former countries.

Textiles weren't the only thing the Worumbo Mill was known for. During the 1930's and 1940's, the mill fielded a formidable baseball club, providing residents of the town with ample and spirited entertainment of the finest variety.

The Worumbo Indians were a semi-professional team that was sponsored by the mill. Begun by Oliver Moses III, or "young Moses," as his workers called him, Moses "the younger" was the third generation of his family to run the storied manufacturing facility. An avid baseball fan, Moses recruited top baseball talent from all over the state and beyond, to work at the mill and play baseball for the team.

Playing 45-50 games each summer, the Indians attracted large crowds to their home games at beautiful Worumbo Park. With the park's location along the river and home runs to right field landing in the water, the park had its own contingent of boaters in search of baseballs, long before the days of San Francisco's McCovey Cove and scrambles for Barry Bonds' home run balls.

Fans gladly paid their admission fee to watch their hometown heroes play sharp competition from Winthrop, Lewiston, Portland and Brunswick, as well as strong New Hampshire semi-pro outfits from Manchester, Lancaster and Berlin. In 1937 and 1938, the Indians qualified for the National Amateur Baseball Tournament in

Wichita, Kansas. After their first trip in 1937, the team returned from their Midwestern battles to a welcome worthy of a conquering army. The players were greeted by a parade, and Moses closed the mill for the day, with each employee receiving paid leave from work to attend the parade in honor of the Indians. The Worumbo's beloved stars of the diamond rode up Main Street in cars to the greetings of music, confetti and banners, informing them of the town's adulation. The celebration was important enough so that even Governor Louis O. Barrows traveled down from Augusta to participate in the festivities.

While the Indians' roster was populated by the best talent available in Maine, players were also brought in from places far and wide. The best known of these outside players was Eddie Waitkus, who after his stint with the Indians, went on to play professionally for several years in the National League with the Chicago Cubs and Philadelphia Phillies.

With the coming of the Second World War and the loss of able bodied baseball players, the Indians passed out of existence. After the war, town team ball became popular again, with Lisbon having several different teams in town, playing in several different leagues. Most of these teams were knows as the Townies and even the Merchants, as local town businesses kicked in contributions to pay for baseballs, bats, umpires and uniforms.

During the summers of 1960 and 1961, the town of Lisbon failed to field a team. This was not the norm for a town that prided itself on its heritage of strong, competitive teams. During these years, some of the town's better ballplayers like Dick Pohle, Dave Begos and Bob Baumer played for teams outside of town. Pohle and Begos logged time with Hotel Manoir in Lewiston, while Baumer, after a year in the Army during 1960, pitched outside the state in 1961 and for the Auburn Asas in 1962.

In 1963, Lisbon town manager Amel Kisonek decided that the time was right to revive baseball in Lisbon Falls. An avid enthusiast of the national pastime, as well as a long-time supporter of the game in the community, Kisonek began talking to local players early in the year in preparation for the team's entry into the fast-paced Andy County League.

Kisonek recruited a solid contingent for the upcoming season, acquiring commitments from such stalwarts as Baumer, Stan Doughty, Marty Roop, Begos, Bob Ransome and Steve Karkos, to build his team around.

The initial season was a success, with the Merchants finishing second during this season of baseball revived. The team that the Merchants finished runner-up to was the Turner Townies, who also won the 1963 Yankee Amateur Baseball Congress (YABC) tournament at Pettengill Park in Auburn and qualified to play in Battle Creek, Michigan, at the nationals. While finishing second to Turner, the Lisbon upstarts made their presence felt. The Merchants defeated Turner three times during the regular season providing ample indication of their strength. This ability for Lisbon Falls to beat Turner regularly would become a source of irritation in subsequent seasons for Turner, as well as staking out a rivalry that was every bit as ferocious as that of a Red Sox/Yankees series.

****

For Bob Baumer, the talented southpaw hurler, it was an opportunity to once again play for his home town, after a sojourn as a baseball mercenary. Since baseball rhetoric says that pitching is 90 percent of the game, then it follows that quality pitching is a coveted possession. In particular, a left-handed pitcher with Baumer's ability, as well as baseball guile and experience, made him a valuable commodity.

After graduating from Lisbon High School in 1954, Baumer was offered a scholarship to pitch for powerful Rollins College, which was located in Florida. Not wanting to attend school so far from home, nor spend a year at a prep school such as Bridgton Academy, Baumer opted to stay in town and began working for Morse Brothers Oil, a local heating fuels distributor.

Pitching for the Lisbon Falls Merchants from 1954 –1959, he helped them wage battle in the competitive Lakes Region League against the likes of Winthrop, Richmond and Randolph AC, the strongest clubs in that loop. In 1956, Baumer was added to the Randolph roster as a post-season play-off pick up. He was instrumental in Randolph's post-season success, as the team claimed the YABC crown and journeyed to Battle Creek, Michigan, to take part in the National Amateur Baseball World Series.

Like most young men of this era, Baumer fulfilled his military requirement with a year spent abroad in 1960, stationed in Europe. While in the service, Baumer was a member of one of the stronger service teams that consisted of college players, professionals, and talented amateur players.

Baumer returned home to Lisbon Falls in 1961 to find that there was no town team available. Friend and fellow Lisbonite Dick Hlister, along with Dick Pohle, had been invited to play in the powerful Cape Cod League for the Orleans Cardinals that summer. Hlister apparently was able to convince the Cardinals of his friend's abilities as a pitcher, because Baumer was asked to spend the summer on the Cape twirling for the Cards.

In 1962, Baumer once more found himself lacking a hometown team, so this time he ventured up the road to pitch for the Auburn Asas, before baseball made its triumphant return to the town for the 1963 season. With the revival of the team in Lisbon,

Baumer once again found himself able to represent his hometown in baseball battles against surrounding communities.

The Lisbon Falls Merchants received some important financial backing at the start of 1964. Noyes Lawrence, along with his wife Rae, were co-owners of Roberts Pharmacy on Main Street in Lisbon Falls. Lawrence believed in giving back to his community by supporting local endeavors. Seeing that The Merchants' uniforms were over 10 years old and getting a bit threadbare, Lawrence approached Baumer with the offer of outfitting the team in updated apparel for the coming season.

The pharmacy had been founded by Lawrence's grandfather, George Roberts in 1888. Lawrence suggested naming the team, the Roberts 88'ers. The idea was met with enthusiastic support from both Baumer and Kisonek, so Lisbon Falls' 1964 entrant in the Andy County League would now be known as the Roberts 88'ers, a name that would resonate with recognition in Lisbon proper for decades to come.

Going into the 1964 season, sentiment in Lisbon Falls was running high that this year's team was going to give the rest of the Andy County League a run for their money. With Baumer and Kisonek doing their off-season legwork, the 88'ers added some additional cogs to the team that gave them confidence entering 1964 that the 88'ers were a better ball club.

The 88'ers opened the 1964 campaign with an efficient 5-0 whitewashing of Mechanic Falls, behind Baumer's two-hit pitching. New players making immediate contributions were the talented Pohle at short, providing stellar glove work as well as two hits. Pohle, a true baseball nomad, had played briefly in the Kansas City A's system. A decade later, Pohle would be featured in a *Sports Illustrated* article, as a player who at the age of 38, attended a San Diego Padres tryout in disguise. With an elaborate ruse and makeup, Pohle managed to shave 20 years off his visage and eventually was signed to a minor league contract. Playing under the alias Rocky Perone, Pohle was able to play in one game before a manager that had played with him years before, outed him from his charade.

Pohle's double play partner was Jim Cornelio, the former Jay High School player. Cornelio, with considerable experience in both the Pine Tree and Timber Leagues, had moved to the area to fill a teaching assignment in Brunswick. The two of them gave the 88'ers one of the slickest middle infield combos in the region, if not the entire state.

****

When the Lisbon Merchants folded after the 1959 season, Stan Doughty thought he was hanging up his spikes for good as a player, save for an occasional Sunday afternoon pickup game or old-timers outing. The veteran Doughty had been playing amateur baseball since the age of 15, when he teamed up with the adults in his hometown of West Paris, competing against the neighboring towns of the Pine Tree League.

With his considerable experience as a college and semi-pro player, as well as recent summers providing veteran leadership and all-around solid play for the various Lisbon town teams, Doughty was a valuable commodity for a team looking to challenge the league leaders. However, with a young family, the responsibilities of teaching at the high school level, as well as holding the head baseball coaching position at Lisbon High, the farthest thing from Doughty's mind was a return to town team baseball.

After three years away from active duty as a player, Doughty missed the competition. Several of his former players such as Pohle, Begos, Stevie Karkos and Joey Harakal were set to play for the newly formed Lisbon Merchants in 1963. When Kisonek ran into Doughty one day on Main Street and jokingly suggested that the Merchants could use a third basemen, Doughty thought about how much he missed the game as a player—the camaraderie, the sound the bat makes when you hit a baseball squarely and the feeling that resonates through your hands as you complete your swing—but he quickly put the thoughts out of his mind.

When Baumer saw Doughty a week later, he asked him if he had any desire to play for the Merchants.

"We've got a good looking team," said Baumer. "We could use another left-handed bat to go with Begos' in the line up, though."

Unbeknownst to Baumer, Doughty had been turning the idea of playing over in his mind since running into Kisonek.

"I had convinced myself I'd give it another shot," said Doughty. "Sylvia [his wife] was all for it. She told me that if I was going to play again, I might as well do it now because I wasn't getting any younger," he said. "When Bobby talked to me, I had made up my mind to play."

With Doughty's bat added to the Merchants line up, they had a solid order, particularly one through six. While it might take Doughty a few games to get his stroke back, everyone that had seen him play during his prime knew he would be rattling line drives around the park behind the high school in no time.

In late June, Doughty was just starting to feel like his old self when the bane of older, amateur players—the hamstring pull—knocked him from the Merchants line up and made him question the sanity of playing again, at the age of 32. For Doughty, the pull never got much better and he wasn't able to play regularly for the remainder of the 1963 season.

"We were playing the Lewiston Merchants and I was on second base," Doughty recalled. "Stevie Karkos hit a ball to the gap and I figured I'd score. I thought there was a throw at the plate so I gave it that little extra burst of what speed I still had and I felt it [the hamstring] pop," he said.

Going into 1964, Doughty's decision to give it another try with the 88'ers also brought an additional bonus to his hitting and defense. Herbie Whitman, a powerful right-handed slugger, had moved to the Falls in his job with Hood's Dairy, after playing the previous two season's for Mechanic Falls. Whitman also happened to be the brother of Doughty's wife, Sylvia, so the 88'ers of 1964 were becoming a family affair.

With Baumer and Marty Roop, a righty from Bowdoin College, the 88'ers had a solid one-two combination on the mound. Mix in strong defense and hitting from the likes of Begos, Doughty, Whitman and big Bob Ransome, as well as Pohle and Cornelio, and it was easy to see why there was so much excitement about the 1964 Roberts 88'ers.

Not wasting any time, the 88'ers reeled off nine straight wins to open the '64 campaign. It wasn't until the end of June that the 88'ers lost their first game, a 1-0 nail biter to the Norway-Paris Twins. In one of the classic tilts of the summer, Baumer and the Twins' Leon "Stubby" Truman hooked up in a duel, witnessed by nearly 1,000 fans at the old Fairgrounds in South Paris.

With darkness descending on a field without lights, the scoreless battle was settled in the bottom half of the seventh when former minor leaguer Neil Jesseman's 350-foot single off Baumer provided the Twins with a hard-fought walk off victory at dusk, over the surging Lisbon Falls club.

Not to be deterred, the 88'ers next reeled off eight more wins in a row before being edged by Norm's Café of Lewiston on the

20th of July, 6-4. After suffering only the team's second loss of the summer, the 88'ers record stood at 17 wins and two losses. During the club's first 19 games, the defense had played 13 of them without a miscue. Pitching, defense and hitting made the 1964 88'ers, a team to be reckoned with.

On Sunday August 4th, 800 fans jammed the field behind Lisbon High School, as the 88'ers, behind Baumer's pitching and Dave Begos' tape measure home run, beat their rivals from Turner, 3-1. The victory was their fourth straight triumph over the Townies. This was to become commonplace over the next three seasons, as the 88'ers would eventually reel off 15 consecutive victories over their archrivals up the road. Of the 15 victories in a row, Baumer would collect 11 of the mound decisions. When asked why the 88'ers had such great success against a team that ordinarily won over 70 percent of its games, Baumer shrugged and offered the following explanation.

"They were a team with a lot of good hitters. Good hitters tend to like to hit fastballs. I didn't ever throw two balls the same speed—I just changed speeds and hit my spots against them," he said. "After awhile, I think it became a mental thing."

Baumer's dominance over the Townies was beginning to get under the skin of a few of the Turner fans, however. Not only was he the team's ace pitcher, but Baumer also filled the role of the team's player/coach. According to baseball etiquette, the home team supplies all the baseballs for a given contest. Over the course of a game, it's not unusual to lose balls, particularly at fields like Lisbon's, which had a thick grove of pines along first base and a swamp behind the stands at third. In addition, some of the balls become scuffed or cut and are no longer adequate for use in the game.

Baumer usually kept extra baseballs in the trunk of his car, which he parked about 75 yards beyond the small spring and grove of trees behind the backstop. During the seventh inning of another apparent victory over Turner, Baumer ambled out to his car while the 88'ers batted, to grab a fresh box of balls.

"Old man Trundy of Turner saw me go out to my car and he started shouting from behind the Turner bench—'there he goes! He's going out to get those baseballs,'" laughed Baumer. While there was no logic inherent in that charge, it does illustrate how the 88'ers had gotten inside the heads of their opponents from Turner. From that point on, whenever Lisbon was playing Turner at home, Baumer would practice this ritual designed to irritate and psyche out their chief rivals.

"For years, whenever I'd run into Trundy, he'd insist that I used doctored baseballs," chuckled Baumer.

In the win over Turner, Dave Begos hit what many in town consider one of the longest home runs ever witnessed at the high school. Estimates are that it traveled some 450 to 475 feet to right center.

In a case of the rich getting richer, the 88'ers added a talented late season pickup to its existing murderer's row of hitting talent. Recent Lisbon High graduate George Ferguson had just completed his legion campaign, leading the New Auburn team to a runner's up finish in the state American Legion tournament. Upon joining the 88'ers, Ferguson proceeded to hit safely in seven of his first 10 at bats for the 88'ers, proving that he wasn't intimidated by the markedly better pitching.

****

When boys grow up with fathers that are renowned for their athletic prowess, there is an expectation that they will follow in their footsteps. Whether or not those hopes are spoken, small towns can be tough places to hide from the shadow of a parent's reputation.

For young George Ferguson, growing up in Lisbon Falls carried with it the baseball bloodline of his father George, as well as his uncle Art. The senior Ferguson had been a good enough baseball player to be offered a contract by the Boston Braves. After a couple of seasons in the minor leagues, the elder Ferguson found himself playing at manicured Braves Field in Boston after the war, a far cry from the days of playing on the ball fields and pastures of Lisbon Falls. Only bad knees prevented him from having a long professional career. Additionally, uncle Art Ferguson was also an outstanding player, a member of the powerful semi-pro Auburn Asas teams of the early 1950's. During his latter years, he played locally in the Twin City League in Lewiston.

Many old-timers in Lisbon Falls still talk about when the elder Ferguson returned to Lisbon Falls after his release by the Braves. He was playing some variation of town team ball at old Worumbo Park. Despite his damaged knees that would have disabled men with less heart, Ferguson was still the best player on the field, competing against younger players cavorting about with two good legs.

Young George was like many of the boys who came of age in mill towns and rural communities across the state. Days were filled with friends, games, riding bikes and of course, playing sandlot sports, including baseball. As a young boy, Ferguson probably showed a precociousness on the diamond—he probably hit the ball with greater force and more distance, as well as throwing harder than most of the boys his age and older—all which would later get him noticed by professional scouts when he matured and got stronger. As a pre-teenager however, he was just another kid, able to play baseball and other sports with friends, for the sheer thrill and enjoyment of the game. During the late 1950's and early 1960's, kids could still be kids, without the pressure put on children in later years by organized leagues and overzealous adults.

"We played baseball from morning, until it was too dark to see the ball," said Ferguson. "You had to get to the field early at [Joey] Harakal's or Worumbo Park, or you didn't get picked for a team," he said.

During high school, Ferguson became a hitter that baseball people took notice of. All those years of playing pickup baseball against players three or four years older had allowed him to become a good enough player to one day be offered a contract to play professionally upon graduating from Lisbon High.

Ceding to the expectations of his father however, young Ferguson opted for college. Instead of the long bus rides and minimal pay of rookie league baseball at the professional level, he was headed off to textbooks and lectures at the University of Maine in Orono. The decision showed its wisdom when Ferguson continued his diamond excellence under the tutelage of legendary Black Bear coach, Jack Butterfield. After a stellar career at Maine, Ferguson ended up being drafted and signed by the New York Yankees in 1968.

Like many youngsters growing up during this period, Ferguson was part of a progression of elevated expectations. With the 1950's newfound affluence beginning to push back some of the older ways, there came an increased recognition and respect given to education by many second-generation immigrants. Ferguson and many of his peers would become the first members of their families to attend college, unlike most young men a decade before who didn't have the push or see the need for higher education.

Ferguson played a couple of seasons with the 88'ers, including the 1965 season, when he was their regular shortstop, replacing Pohle, who was off to his next stop on his baseball odyssey. Teaming with Cornelio, Ferguson gave up some of Pohle's range and defensive skills, but ably replaced them with power and more offensive production.

Buoyed by the completion of his freshman year at the University of Maine, Ferguson rejoined the 88'ers for the start of their 1965 summer campaign. Although just 19, Ferguson was being counted on to be a key offensive component for the team, as the 88'ers sought to build upon 1964's successes.

"The 88'ers were as good a town team as any in the area," said Ferguson. "We felt we could beat anyone. We consistently beat the bigger city teams like Auburn and Lewiston. It was a big thrill for us—being from a hick town—to beat these city teams," he said.

"Our 1965 team was real strong. We had good pitching with Bob [Baumer] and Laddie Deemer [who played baseball and basketball at the University of Maine]. Stan [Doughty] was on his way out at third, but could still hit. We just had a great bunch of guys who enjoyed playing together," he said.

The summer of 1965 would be Ferguson's last season playing baseball in his hometown for the next seven years. He wouldn't return until the 1972 season, after his spring training release by the Yankees. He came back to begin his first teaching job in the rural, former farming community of Durham, across the river from where he grew up. He eventually landed a position in his home town, where he would continue to teach at the elementary level for the next 30 years.

Ferguson fondly recalls how much fun he had playing for the 88'ers during the 1965 season. As a 19 year old, being able to play ball with many experienced players in their late 20's and some, like

Doughty and Roop, in their 30's and married, taught him to respect the game, but also to enjoy playing it.

"I just loved playing for them [the 88'ers]. We took it serious, but we had fun while playing," said Ferguson. "Guys like Herbie [Whitman] were something else; we were constantly joking and riding each other, but players respected one another," he said.

Ferguson brings a valuable perspective to town team baseball, because he played amateur baseball at many levels—town team ball in Lisbon Falls, semi-pro baseball in the Maine/New Brunswick League, as well as a summer on Cape Cod, which is considered the pinnacle of amateur baseball, and two seasons in the Twilight League in the early 1970's when that league was at its strongest—in addition to his college and professional experience. In his opinion, town team ball in the Andy County League was an excellent caliber of baseball.

"For the brand of baseball that town team ball offered, the 88'ers were as good as it gets in this area," said Ferguson.

When asked for players he remembered that stood out, Ferguson listed Dave Begos and Doughty as hitters who he played with that were a cut above the rest. Opposition players that garnered Ferguson's respect were big Bud White from Auburn, a tough lefty who pitched for Holy Cross, and Larry Gowell who pitched in the majors for the Yankees.

"Larry Gowell had the best slider I've ever seen. You could hear his fingers snap when he broke it off," said Ferguson. Gowell played with Ferguson on several Yankee farm clubs.

"I used to think 'thank God he's on my team and I don't have to face him,'" said Ferguson. "He and Mike Garman [who would later pitch for nine years in the big leagues, including several years with the Red Sox] were the best I saw in my time in pro ball."

****

By the end of the 1964 Andy County campaign, the 88'ers had finished with a 24 and four record, besting the second place Turner team by some two and a half games. Leading the way had been Baumer's amazing 13 wins, as well as Begos and Doughty who had hit over .400. Whitman had batted .350 and added five home runs.

Over the next three years, the 88'ers would rule Andy County League foes to the tune of a combined 66-9 record during the regular season. In addition to their two post-season trips to the American Amateur Baseball Conference (AABC) regional tournament in Waterbury, Connecticut, in 1964 and 1965, the 88'ers also dominated the local league play-offs in the Andy County League. Beginning in 1964, the 88'ers won six consecutive league play-offs and claimed the Seltzer & Rhydholm trophy awarded to the league champs. Finally, at the end of the 1970 season, the Auburn Asas finally wrested the Andy County League crown from the 88'ers, after an amazing run of local post-season superiority.

Not only did the 88'ers play top-notch baseball against league rivals, but Kisonek and Baumer scheduled an additional 15 to 20 non-league tilts against other town and semi-pro teams. While most teams were content to play their 20 –25 league games and call it even, the 88'ers often hooked up with opponents from the Spruce Tree, Pine Tree, Lakes Region, Knox-Lincoln and Twilight leagues to wage battle with their leading teams during the 1960's and early 1970's.

****

The AABC was the governing body of amateur baseball in the United States. Beginning in 1964, the AABC instituted a regional tier to their national championship that was held annually in Battle

Creek, Michigan. Maine teams would no longer be allowed direct access to Battle Creek after winning their state tournament.

Like most local teams that were part of the AABC, the 88'ers began each season with a goal of qualifying for the YABC tournament at Pettengill. The 1964 YABC winner would be required to travel to Connecticut and play in a regional tournament, in order to qualify for a trip to Battle Creek and the National Amateur Baseball World Series.

Bringing their stellar 24-4 regular season league record with them, the 88'ers were considered the pre-tourney favorites. With three of the four Maine leagues that were members of the AABC being represented in Auburn, each league was entitled to send two representatives to the state tournament, most often the first and second place teams from each circuit. The leagues represented in 1964's YABC tournament with their respective teams were as follows: The Andy County League and the first place Roberts 88'ers and second place finisher, the Turner Townies. The Spruce Tree League was making their first appearance in the tournament in 1964 and would be bringing their top two teams, The Gray Merchants and the Poland Townies. The Pine Tree League was sending league champ Dixfield, along with their runner-up, the Norway-Paris Twins. The fourth YABC member and usual participant, The Lakes Region League, decided not to send representatives in 1964.

Each participating team had the luxury of picking up three additional players from other league teams not qualifying for the post-season tournament. As a result, the play-off rosters were well stocked with an assortment of arms and potent bats coming off the bench. This combination yielded late-inning heroics and excitement on more than one occasion.

The Dixfield Dixies opened the 1964 tournament on Friday night with an 11-2 trouncing of the overmatched Gray Merchants. The offensive firepower provided by the likes of Artie Taylor, Newt Stowell, as well as former Farmington Flyer Ted Clark, one of Dixfield's pickups from Rumford, were too much for the upstart Merchants.

On Saturday afternoon, the 88'ers served notice to the rest of the combatants that they were the team to beat, by blanking Turner 5-0. Behind Baumer's five-hit, nine-strikeout performance and Whitman's two-run single, the Lisbon Falls juggernaut once again rolled over their chief rivals from Turner and veteran hurler Stan Timberlake.

On Sunday, the 88'ers, behind tournament pickup Rudy Leavitt of Mechanic Falls, handed Dixfield their first loss of the tournament, 6-2. While Dixfield managed 14 hits off Leavitt and threatened the entire game, four double plays got him out of several jams. Meanwhile his 88'er teammates got to Dixie ace Ted "Bitsy" Ionta, led by Whitman, Jim Cornelio and Bob Ransome, each with two hits apiece. Ransome belted a two-run homer to left and finished the day with three runs scored. It was a rare play-off defeat for the wily Dixfield veteran.

Dixfield staved off elimination on Monday by winning the evening's opening tilt, sending the Turner Townies home for the season, with their 4-3 nailbiter. The Dixies' Newt Stowell out dueled Tink Wagner of Turner and Bobby Downs contributed a two-run double for the Dixies. Art Cotton homered in the seventh to cut the margin to one run, but Stowell buckled down over the final two for the victory.

This set up an exciting nightcap, with the two strongest clubs vying for all the marbles. Lisbon got on the board first in front of the 1,000-plus fans gathered for the excitement. Dave Begos' long sacrifice fly to center field plated Whitman to put the 88'ers on top in the bottom of the fourth.

With starting pitcher Marty Roop utilizing an effective sinker, the 88'ers took a 1-0 lead into their half of the fifth inning. With two outs, Tom Fortin rifled a sharp single to left off Dixie starter George Barker. Dave Moulton followed with a double to the gap in left-center and Fortin held at third to bring up Roop with the opportunity to help his own cause. The former Bowdoin College star rapped a one-hopper up the middle, which plated both Fortin and Moulton and put the 88'ers on top, 3-0.

That would be all that the lanky right-hander would need. Roop finished strong, ending with a six-hit, six-strikeout performance, propelling the 88'ers to the YABC crown and the opportunity to represent Maine the following weekend in Waterbury, Connecticut.

****

On Friday, August 22nd, 1964, an optimistic Roberts 88'ers squad boarded their Hudson Bus Lines charter coach at 8 in the morning for the six-hour trip to Waterbury, Connecticut. The 88'ers believed that this year's team had the horses to compete against the top amateur talent in all of New England and the New York region.

With the addition of infielder Bobby Gammon and pitchers Leon "Stubby" Truman and Charley Huff of the Norway-Paris Twins, the 88'ers thought they had the additional depth and pitching necessary to compete effectively against the more populated regions of southern New England, New York and New Jersey.

Whether being forced to play two hours after their long bus ride had an effect, or that the local Gleem Painters team of

Waterbury was that much better, is fodder for speculation. Regardless of the reasons, the 88'ers and their optimism was dealt a serious blow, as they were trounced 11-3, in a game that was concluded after seven innings due to the tournament's eight-run mercy rule.

In a rare sub-par performance, left-handed ace Baumer was rocked for nine hits and eight runs, as the Gleemers proved too strong a foe for Maine's representative. Scoring in every inning, the Waterbury nine jumped out 8-0, before the visitors managed to rally for three runs in their top of the seventh, led by a Gammon two-run triple and Whitman's RBI single.

Facing elimination on Saturday, the 88'ers bowed their necks and played some spirited ball, refusing to go quietly. Opening with a 3-1 afternoon victory over Corkey's Café of Waterbury, the 88'ers lived to play another game in the early evening. Roop continued his late-season clutch pitching and Begos crushed a two-run fourth inning homer to power the Maine boys to victory.

Charley Huff, the late roster addition from Norway-Paris got the mound nod for Lisbon Falls. Facing highly touted college pitcher Jack Marucz of Seton Hall, Huff was masterful. The wily right-hander kept the powerful New Jersey club off balance with an assortment of off-speed junk and the 88'ers managed to push across two runs off Marucz, for a hard-fought 2-1 victory. This back-to-the-wall gut check propelled the Lisbon Falls squad into Sunday's championship game, a rematch against Gleem.

In a move that some second-guessed, the 88'ers manager Amel Kisonek decided to start Leavitt on Sunday against Gleem, instead of the crafty lefty Leon Truman of Norway-Paris. With Truman available and well rested, Kisonek opted for Leavitt and he was hit hard by the lefty-laden line up of the Painters. Leavitt left the game in the sixth, trailing 6-1, and the 88'ers couldn't overcome the deficit against a superior opponent. While the loss was disappointing to the warriors from Maine, it was a memorable performance and won the upstarts from the Pine Tree state the respect of the assembled field of teams, as well as the fans in attendance.

The 88'ers would again win the YABC tourney in 1965 and travel to Waterbury. On this trip south, they finished a respectable third in the field of teams, eliminated by that year's regional winner, a strong Puerto Rican contingent from New Jersey. This appearance was tempered somewhat by the loss of Kisonek. The driving force behind baseball's resurgence in Lisbon, Kisonek passed away unexpectedly of a heart attack during the off season.

Maine continued to send representatives to the AABC Regional tournaments through the 1969 season. Auburn of the Auburn Rec League (formerly the Andy County League) would represent the YABC in 1966, with Rumford of the Pine Tree League in 1967 and 1969 and Guilford of the Penquis League in 1968 being the Maine representatives involved in regional play. However, the 1964 and 1965 performances by the 88'ers would remain as highwater marks for Maine teams competing against the more populated towns and cities to the south.

With Rumford's appearance in the AABC regionals in 1969, another chapter in Maine's town team baseball history was about to close. Beginning in 1970, and continuing for several seasons through 1974, the state held their own tournament and crowned a Maine amateur champion. These contests were raucous affairs and fiercely played, but never quite matched the luster of going to the regionals or the trips to Battle Creek a decade earlier.

Chapter 4
A League of Its Own

Baseball in Portland goes back well over one hundred years. As far back as 1828, *The Daily Argus,* Portland's newspaper at the time, reported that the Portland town fathers were complaining because "...boys are playing bat-and-ball at noon-day in the most frequented streets, with windows all about and horses continually passing."

The first recorded contest of a Maine team playing baseball was in September of 1858, when the Portland Baseball Club played a Boston ball team at the Boston Commons, reported on September 11, 1858, in the *Portland Daily Advertiser.*

Baseball in Portland has been around for as long as the game, or some variation of it, has been played in Maine. The Portland Twilight League is the oldest league of its kind in Maine and arguably, one of the oldest amateur or semi-professional leagues in the country, dating back to 1903. Only Boston's Park League claims to have been in existence longer, and there is some debate whether Boston's league is in fact older than the Twilight League. Regardless, the Twilight League has been a fixture in Portland nearly every summer, for the past century.

The origins of Portland's Twilight League go back to the early years of the 20th century, when Portland was experiencing the pangs of growth and the burgeoning culture reminiscent of many northeastern cities at the time. Industry, commerce and the invention of the automobile would begin to change Portland from a sleepy seaport town, to Maine's first urban environment.

The Twilight League has traditionally been considered a semi-pro loop, as select players have been known to receive compensation for playing baseball in the league, from time to time over its varied past. While not a true town team league in the sense that the majority of its players reside in the geographic locale of Portland, the league's longevity, history, and competitiveness make it one of the most significant aspects of local baseball in Maine. Because Portland is Maine's largest city, this commercial center on Casco Bay forms the basis of much of Maine's culture—from commerce, to entertainment, to politics—and baseball is no exception to that rule.

Because Portland's population was large enough to provide an ample pool of baseball talent—enough to fill several team rosters—the league in its earliest years was comprised entirely of teams from within the city limits.

While town team baseball was played primarily in Maine's smaller towns scattered across the mostly rural reaches of the state, in the more urban areas of the state, cities such as Portland, Lewiston and Bangor were able to field multiple teams. Only Portland and Lewiston, however, were able to support entire leagues comprised of teams situated in one geographic locale— Lewiston and its Twin City League and Portland's Twilight League. Unlike the Twin City League however, which eventually folded by the late 1950's, the Twilight League has maintained a near-continuous presence in the city since its inception.

****

The initial formation of Portland's Twilight League in the early 1900's originated from the custom of the era, with various neighborhood teams squaring off against one another, usually on a Sunday afternoon.

The old Cunningham Grounds, which were situated in the heart of what is considered today to be the Bayside section of the city, was the site of these battles for city superiority. As the competition ratcheted up weekly in these contests, team officials and players began talking about the feasibility of forming a league in the city.

Beginning with a group from the Munjoy Hill section of Portland that went by the name of Buffaloes, a league was formed to play for the Forest City championship. Other early teams were the Mohawks, the Maine Centrals (sponsored by the railroad), the Knights of Columbus, as well as the Knight of Pythias.

During the formative years of the league, the Cunningham site saw crowds numbering as many as 5,000 spectators for crucial matches, particularly the end of season city championship. For the next 35 to 40 years, the league evolved and eventually adopted the name Twilight League as its moniker, primarily due to the time of day that weeknight games would be played.

With war on the doorstep and a pressing need for the fortification of the country's naval fleet, Portland's coveted harbor was an ideal location to utilize for the shipbuilding needs of this era. Additionally, the Navy began staffing the forts that dotted Portland's Casco Bay, on the mainland, as well as the nearby islands. With this influx of young men, most being of the prime ages for the display of baseball prowess, Portland's availability of baseball talent grew incrementally. The first few years saw the formation of a shipyard team from the East Deering area, contingents of players from the various military units forming squads, as well as a shipyard team from across the bridge in South Portland, all squaring off against one another in spirited contests that provided baseball fans of Portland with more than their fill of local baseball.

Other leagues outside of the city such as the Sunset League south of Portland and a competitor league in the city, the Mercantile League, which consisted of teams from the gas company and other utilities, provided outside opponents for Twilight League teams to supplement their league schedule with. At the end of the summer, a city-wide championship was held and the predominant winner was the Twilight League.

The number of leagues and teams afforded the better players with ample opportunities to play baseball, often being paid for each game they played. According to a column written by the late Blaine Davis, former sports editor for the *Portland Press Herald,* Davis recounts a day when he had been able to play third base in both the Twilight and Mercantile circuits, plus other teams that would call him to play for pay.

"You could be playing every night of the week and twice on Sunday. The better players in the area got paid $5 per game, which wasn't bad money for the time," wrote Davis.

With the arrival of the Second World War, the city's rolls swelled to their largest numbers in its history. Thousands of shipyard workers flocked to Portland to fill available jobs supplying the U.S. Navy with ships. The Twilight League expanded and became the Western Maine League during those years. Old-timers will recall the names of Cliff Blake, who would later lead the professional Northeast League in hitting in 1947, with the Portland

Pilots, as well as future Red Sox farmhands Ralph Lapointe and Dick Jude, gracing diamonds across the city.

With increases in the number of players and teams playing, the need for new ball fields became a pressing concern. During this time of heightened participation, several new diamonds sprung up across the city. A new field was built behind the Expo, on the site of the current Hadlock Field. Additionally, there was the nearby Richardson Field, Cunningham Grounds, as well as fields at Deering High School and the Grand Trunk ball yard near the Presumpscott Street rail facility.

During the years of the war, crowds routinely numbered between 4,000 and 5,000 fans, lined several deep along both the first and third base lines. Without television and other forms of entertainment, the nightly or Sunday Twilight League tilt was, literally, the only game in town.

Probably no field in Portland has any more history than the field located at spacious Deering Oaks Park, located in the heart of the city. Known to players and baseball fans of the city simply as "the Oaks," this field was first constructed in 1948, with federal money. In later years, lights were added and with the coming of the interstate in the late 1960's, the addition of permanent fencing enclosing the diamond. With the building of the Forest Avenue off ramp from the Interstate bisecting the city, came the necessity of moving the railroad tracks to the east side of I-295. As a result, the Oaks inherited its current odd dimensions of left field being the deepest part of the park, at 347 feet. The 10-foot-high chain link fence angles in from left to right with both center and right field being 313 feet from home plate. This provides an inviting target for left-handed hitters to go for the long ball.

Deering Oaks Park was designed by a noted urban planning firm, which was founded by well-known architect and designer,

Frederich Law Olmstead. Olmstead, who also designed parks for many major municipalities in the U.S., including New York City's Central Park and Boston's noted Commons, had provided Portland with a jewel of an outdoor gathering place, located in the heart of the city.

The field at the Oaks was built in a location between two banks, providing the field with a natural amphitheater for the game at hand. With fans occupying the banks on both the first and third base sides of the diamond, under the cover of the mammoth oak trees, which just happen to factor into the unique ground rules of the field, there isn't a better place to watch a baseball game in the city. As for the ground rules, they often drive players and coaches to frustration, particularly pitchers. Any batted ball that comes in contact with a tree on either side, or behind home plate, with its overhang of branches, is ruled out of play, whether a player catches it or not. On more than one occasion, this has allowed a batter an additional swing, which often resulted in the opportunity to redeem himself with a key hit, or even a home run.

With the arrival of highways and other urban additions, the Oaks in Portland offers an oasis from the hustle and bustle just outside its perimeter, particularly on those lazy summer evenings when the lights go on and the players are illuminated like actors on a stage.

As the United States grew more involved in the conflict in Europe, many local men were called away to serve Uncle Sam on foreign shores. The summer of 1942 was the first year since the league began that a formal season wasn't played. With diminished numbers affecting most local leagues like the Twilight League, the ability to fill rosters with able-bodied young men became increasingly difficult, if not impossible.

With the cessation of conflict and the end of the war, other rival leagues in the city folded, leaving the Twilight League as the city's only semi-pro league. As the need for baseball fields diminished, many of the former diamonds were turned into houselots, paved over, or grew up with weeds. The Oaks took on a new significance and became, along with the Stadium behind the Expo, Portland's primary venues for the Twilight battles in the city. In later years, the Stadium would become Hadlock Field, which would give way to new modifications to the former ball yard—in the 1990's, it would become the new stadium for Portland's professional team, the Sea Dogs—leaving the Oaks as the last holdover from a bygone era. Other fields were built across the city, such as Haverty Field, constructed by Haverty Buick's John Haverty, who built a ballpark behind his home in the Auburn Street area of Portland during the 1960's for use by the team he sponsored at the time. Regardless of what other fields came and went, the Oaks maintained its place as the Twilight's primary battleground.

By 1946, the Twilight League was once again back to its normal number of teams and skilled players, filling the various team rosters. For the first time however, the league faced competition from a new professional team located in Portland. As was happening all over the country, minor league baseball was expanding and many northeastern cities, with populations of 50,000 or more, such as Portland, were prime areas for the expansion.

The Portland Pilots became members of the Class B Northeast League in 1946, and began siphoning fans and interest away from the Twilight League for next four years. The Twilight League began to encounter its first rocky stretch, as the league experienced financial difficulties, struggling to find sponsors for the first time. Many local businesses preferred to have their money pay for ads adorning the walls of the Portland Stadium and the exposure this provided, rather than sponsor a Twilight League team, or have their company name merely displayed on the back of a player's jersey.

The Northeast League folded after the 1949 season, with several Massachusetts teams withdrawing. Unable to field enough teams to warrant another season in 1950, Portland was left without a league for the Pilots.

With semi-pro baseball expanding around the state in towns such as Auburn, Farmington, Augusta and Sanford, Portland decided to form its own semi-pro team and join the fledgling Down East League. A group of Portland businessmen, led by Sam Aceto and Herb Curry, two prominent members of the community, formed the Portland Baseball Trust and began recruiting top college players and former professionals to play for the new, semi-pro version of the Portland Pilots.

For much of the 1950's, the Twilight League found itself in a position of having to scratch and claw for survival. With interest in amateur baseball lagging and some of the league's better players being signed by the Pilots, the league struggled to field its usual allotment of teams. Fortunately, Portland's large population provided enough players to field a minimum of four teams, and in some years, as many as six. In addition, teams were able to draw some of the better players into the city from some of the surrounding communities of Westbrook, Scarborough, Buxton and other towns nearby.

With the arrival of the 1950 season and the league down to five teams, rumors began flying that the league was going to fold for good at the end of the season. However, in 1951, the league meeting in the spring found interest enough for the possibility of at least the minimum number of four teams and possibly a fifth. The group elected James Speirs as league president for the upcoming season and the league once again began its summer campaign.

According to long-time Twilight supporter and league commissioner, Francis "Babe" Anderson, the Twilight League struggled to keep going during most of the decade and into the 1960's.

"Just after the war, the league was fairly strong. During much of the 1950's, the league struggled to stay afloat. Partly, this was because of the popularity of semi-pro baseball in other areas of the state," said Anderson. "Also, businesses in Portland were no longer as willing to sponsor teams, as they were in the past. Softball was becoming popular and for some reason, the papers were not as willing to give the league the coverage it had received in the past," he said.

****

With the arrival of the summer of 1951, the Portland Pilots had dropped out of the Down East League and were going the independent route. While the Pilots had won that league's title in 1950, the cost of being in the league, with its requirements for visiting teams getting part of the gate, and the tremendous expense of operating as part of that league made Herb Curry, Sam Aceto and other board members decide that the independent route was best for the team. An additional factor was that in a city the size of Portland, there were other things competing for fans attention and the Pilots didn't draw as well as hoped for in 1950. There were nights when their amateur counterparts up the street at Deering Oaks outdrew the paid, semi-professional Pilots at the Stadium. This created some rancor between the Pilots and the upstart Twilight Leaguers. Professional baseball had made the baseball fans of Portland increasingly fickle and less enamored of the semi-professional Pilots, or even less likely to support the Twilight League as in years past.

There were also those in Portland, mainly member of the local press, who felt that some of the Twilight League's better players, such as the sweet-swinging Merv Kilgore and the powerful Johnny Mancini, as well as others, could easily play for the Pilots—better yet, some sportswriters intimated in the pages of the local papers that these players would be better choices for the Pilots than some of the more expensive talent imported from away. That theme made its way to the pages of the *Press Herald* and *Evening Express* more than once in 1950. This of course stoked the competitive fires of resentment that some Twilight players felt towards their "pampered" semi-pro counterparts down the street, not forced to toil all day before playing ball each evening, as most Twilighters were.

During the summer of 1950, there had been some rumblings about a play-off at the end of the 1950 campaign, between the Twilight champion and the Pilots of the Down East League, to crown a city champion. Scheduling issues and other logistical matters prevented it from happening.

As the 1951 campaign got under way, Speirs recognized an opportunity to get the Twilight League some needed publicity and to show local baseball fans how strong his league was. While the Twilight League rosters were not filled with former professional players, or bright-eyed college phenoms, Speirs knew his league was strong, and worthy of greater respect.

The energetic and often outspoken Speirs, decided to issue a challenge to Herb Curry, the Pilot's president of operations.

"Speirs was a talker and he had started in on Curry one day, telling him that his league could beat the Pilots and that his Pilots weren't good enough to make any of the teams in the Twilight League. You know how these things get started," mused Anderson. "Obviously, Curry was none too pleased by Speirs' talk and I think he began to consider his challenge," he said.

Certainly, Curry and the Pilots had more to lose than the Twilight League in this possible *Clash of the Titans* plot. If the Twilight League lost, they could offer up the easily accepted excuse that the Pilots had paid players—college stars and ex-professionals—while their players were amateurs in the truest sense.

For Curry, the easiest way out of the noose, without failing to answer the challenge, was to turn it into an act of charity and goodwill on the part of his organization. It was a clever ruse on his part, as he turned the challenge back onto the head of Speirs and the Deering Oaks' diamond men.

In the June 3rd edition of the *Portland Sunday Telegram,* the feud between Curry and Speirs became the public's privy, however. Speirs, used the oldest tactic in the book, by throwing down the gauntlet, for all to read in Maine's largest paper. Spears is quoted as saying, "We'd like to help out the treasury of the Twilight circuit and we think our best can beat your world wonders with ex-professional careers behind them. Have the Pilots got enough nerve to play us?"

At this point, Curry obviously lost the art of decorum and grace, as he exploded with, "Nerve enough?" he is quoted as screaming. "We'll play the Twi Leaguers, the best they can find, and give 'em ten men. How about June 12, if you want some action?"

With that exchange, there was no going back. June 12 became the date that baseball fans marked on their calendars as the must-see game of the summer season. The site was chosen to be the Portland Stadium and a large crowd was expected.

The *Press Herald/Evening Express* got into the act by starting a campaign for readers to send in postcards and vote for the Twilight players that should be chosen to make up their roster against the powerful Pilots squad. The paper, in an effort to insure objective status, chose Bill Riley, of the city's recreation department, to receive and tabulate the votes.

The anticipation was palpable throughout the city, as talk was all about the coming match between the competing two groups— the upstart amateurs and the heavily favored semi-professionals.

When game night arrived, a crowd estimated by some to be around 2,000 to 2,500 fans, filed into the stadium behind the Expo, to witness the David versus Goliath match. With the votes tallied, the Twilight All-Stars, managed by long-time Portland baseball man Pete Pompeo ended up with a formidable group of challengers—veteran Merv Kilgore (the leading vote getter), ex-Cheverus High star, Sonny Conley, Bob Adair, who played college ball at Bates, and big Ed Madigan, who already had two no-hitters under his belt for the season, on the hill for the upstarts.

The Pilots roster was filled with the likes of Elbie Fletcher, Skippy Roberge, Barney Olson and George Yankowski, all who had spent time on a major league roster. In addition, shortstop Lenny Merullo had also played for the Chicago Cubs. Tapped to start on the mound was ace Ed Hadlock, the top pitcher in the Down East League in 1950. Hadlock, who hailed from Kezar Falls, formerly starring for Gorham State Teachers College and now manning the Portland High post as baseball coach, was one of the toughest mound men the area had seen.

The fans weren't surprised when the Pilots jumped out quickly in the bottom half of the first, 4-0, against Mardigan, the former Deering and New Hampshire prep star. Mardigan's early problems began with a two-out walk and then Elbie Fletcher unloaded a bullet over the right field wall for two runs. Two more scored with two more walks and a miscue by Johnny Mancini in right.

A lesser team would have folded from intimidation at that point, but many of the Twi Leaguers like Mancini, Kilgore and others, had played enough baseball to know that baseball is a nine inning game for a reason. The all-stars just bowed their necks and went about chipping away at the weakness of Goliath.

Johnny Redmond was issued a one-out walk by starter Jack Campbell (surprisingly starting ahead of Hadlock). Bill Ladd followed with the first of his two doubles and Sonny Conley's single plated Ladd and Redmond.

The all-stars weren't done as Campbell was relieved by Hadlock to start the fourth. Ladd blasted a double to the left-center gap and when Merullo booted Conley's routine grounder, the all-stars were looking at second and third and one out. Johnny Gleason's flare over second plated Ladd and after a Hadlock wild pitch, Yank Silverman's rocket to center allowed Conley and Gleason to trot home and the crowd was chirping, as the Twilighters were now in front, 5-4.

A Merullo inside-the-park homer that rattled around the right field wall area, tied it. Remarkably, the Pilots were done scoring for the night, as skinny lefty Dave Redmond, just graduated from Portland High the previous Thursday, went the final six innings, hurling shutout ball, in which he fanned nine Pilot hitters.

Ladd, who would finish the night with four hits, drove home Merv Kilgore from second in the top of the fifth with a sharp single and the all-stars had a lead they would not relinquish.

Adding an insurance run in the top of the eighth to make it 7-5, Redmond, pitching like a veteran, shut the door on the Pilots and the upstarts from Deering Oaks had slain the semi-pro giants, with a stunning victory that would be talked about for years to come.

****

By the end of the 1950's, the Twilight League was once more on life support and wheezing to catch its breath. While Speirs certainly added color and energy to the league, the administrative details were often not attended to. Often, the best commissioner or president of an amateur baseball league is the quiet sort, who labors behind the scenes, collecting money, enticing sponsors, paying umpires, and generally doing a little of everything that's required to keep a league running smoothly, or functioning at all.

By 1958, the Twilight League had folded. Years of neglect in collecting fees and lack of aggressive recruitment of new blood into the various administrative roles had left the league rudderless and its coffers empty.

In 1959, Gene McClure of Westbrook organized a new semi-pro circuit called the Cumberland-York League. McClure was able to stimulate enough interest outside of Portland to begin the season with five clubs. One of the teams, the Harris Oil combine from Cape Elizabeth, was a former Twilight League participant and had a number of former Twilight players on their roster. In addition to the Oilers, Yarmouth's Townies, led by Charlie Turner, the Buxton Bullets, Scarborough A.C. and the Westbrook Merchants rounded out the five team circuit.

With the dawn of spring in 1960, a number of former Twilight League players began encouraging Anderson to revive the Twilight League for the coming summer season. Anderson was determined to put the league on solid financial footing, although the task was a major one from the start. With the league at a crossroads and struggling to continue into the future, Anderson realized he had to be diligent in attracting sponsors, as well as making sure that league fees were collected up front, in order to get the league to a place of self sufficiency. Anderson became the driving force behind the league's revival, beginning the 1960 campaign with commitments from eight teams for the summer.

Not everyone appreciated Anderson's diligence. With teams accustomed to a more laidback approach regarding administrative details, some team officials expressed resentment towards Anderson's new policy stipulating that no team would be allowed to play without half of their league fees paid before the first game.

"In the past, teams were lackadaisical about getting their money collected and turned in," said Anderson. "Umpires wouldn't get paid and the league had developed a reputation that wasn't a good one. I wanted to establish the league on a more stable footing and bring it back to what it had been in the past," he said.

Anderson's tenacity and attention to detail, along with his frugality, became key components in ushering in one of the league's most stable periods with the start of the 1960's. Often getting baseballs and bats donated and scouring the city for opportunities to do things as inexpensively as possible, Anderson ran the league on a tight budget during his three years at the helm.

"I didn't have the financial backing that came later, with Bernal Allen [from South Portland] and the other sponsorships," said Anderson. "I was running the league on a shoestring—if there's something less than a shoestring, then that's how we got by those first few years I was president."

While his efforts probably didn't receive the attention and appreciation they deserved, it's obvious to see that without someone like Anderson involved during this key juncture in the league's history, the league might have folded for good. Not wanting any special recognition for his efforts, Anderson was quick to point out that his motivation for doing the necessary things to keep the league afloat stemmed from his love of the game. Anderson's recognition of the pressing need to achieve better organization and paying strict diligence to the administrative details and acceptance of the headaches that came with keeping the league afloat probably prevented the Twilight League from folding for good.

"I loved baseball too much to see the city without the presence of the league," said Anderson. "I saw an opportunity to keep the game alive in Portland and I did what needed to be done."

The addition of two new clubs in 1960 did more to change the dynamic of the league than anything. With both the Yarmouth Townies and South Portland Merchants coming to the Twilight League during the summer of 1960, the rivalry created between these two teams would become the fodder for stories and spirited showdowns for the next decade or more. Both teams were headed by an enterprising and competitive general manager; Charlie Turner in Yarmouth and Bernal Allen in South Portland. Both Allen and Turner hated to lose, and both men were skilled in evaluating talent and recruiting players to their squads.

By tightening up the administrative process and bringing on board several new teams to compliment old league standbys such as Harris Oil of Cape Elizabeth, Anderson allowed the league to embark on its most dynamic decade since before the war.

The league in 1960 boasted strong teams, parity and on most evenings or Sunday afternoons, fans were treated to well-played and competitive baseball over the three-month season.

Lastly, for any league to maintain strength and provide for longevity, there is a periodic need to retool, or bring in new blood. The 1960 campaign provided that, as many former schoolboy stars such as Dick Dolloff of Westbrook and the University of Maine and Dick Loubier of South Portland High School, joined veterans such as former semi-pro star Ed Hadlock and former Milwaukee Braves' farmhand Dick Carmichael, providing the league a healthy mix of youth and veteran leadership.

****

The Yarmouth Townies joined the Twilight League at the start of the summer, in 1960. The previous year, Charlie Turner, the driving force behind the Townies, had brought his upstarts from Yarmouth from the Casco Bay League, where they had been a fixture for many years, over to Gene McClure's Cumberland-York Semi-Pro League. Facing much stronger competition than the usual Casco Bay League fare, the Townies had finished a respectable third behind the strong Harris Oil nine and Scarborough A.C.

Turner, a long-time Yarmouth resident, had been organizing and supporting baseball for as long as anyone in Yarmouth could remember. If there was a senior league team needing uniforms, a little league group needing a coach, Turner could be found, nurturing baseball in any way he could in this town 10 minutes north of Portland.

Yarmouth was a farming community that in later years would become an upper-middle-class suburb of Portland, when land speculation drove values through the roof and farmers sold off their acreage to make way for subdivisions. During the late 1950's and 1960's however, it was a quiet community, with farms just outside of town and a friendly Main Street with a drugstore, hardware store, a couple of banks, a lumber yard and several other businesses comprising the town's tree-lined business district. Yarmouth was symbolic of small town southern Maine during this era.

Like many who lived in the smaller towns throughout the state, Turner was an entrepreneur, long before the word achieved its later credibility and panache. In a time when milk was delivered to your door and other grocery items were brought to the customer, rather than the customer being required to shop in a faceless box store, Turner sold eggs and vegetables to the residents of Yarmouth and neighboring towns, door-to-door.

Pat Feury, who played for Turner beginning in 1962 and would stay with Turner for most of the next 14 summers, remembers Turner and the door-to-door vendor that he was.

"Charlie sold eggs," said Feury. "I remember he always had a car full of tootsie pops also, which he gave out to the kids on his delivery route."

Taking the Townies southward in league play was the logical next step for Turner, a competitive organizer, who always sought to have a strong team, regardless of the league he was competing in.

The Casco Bay League, while typical of many town team leagues in the area, was not a particularly strong league. With teams in Freeport, Gray, Falmouth, Cumberland, New Gloucester and various surrounding communities, the league provided a competitive outlet for men wanting the play ball, giving them a more intense experience than the Sunday afternoon pickup games that others engaged in, but it lacked the intensity of competition of the Twilight League.

During the 1950's, Turner's teams won the majority of league titles, which were based on seasonal records, with no post-season play-offs. For several years, Turner had thought about taking the

Townies to a more competitive league. There was talk of Yarmouth joining the Andy County League, but geographically, it didn't make as much sense as going into greater Portland to compete.

With the Twilight League's up-and-down character of the late 1950's however, Turner was reluctant to leave the stability of the Casco Bay League. When the Twilight folded in 1958 and McClure sought to revive baseball in greater-Portland, he sought out Turner, knowing of his wishes to upgrade the competition for his Townies.

When Anderson sought to revive the Twilight League in 1960, he put out a call for players and teams wanting to join the league. Turner decided that if his Townies were ever going to make the move, then this would be the year. With fellow Casco Bay League opponent Gray moving over to the Twilight loop, Turner made the decision to bring his boys from Yarmouth into the more competitive circuit for 1960.

The Townies tended to have a few local Yarmouth players, but Turner always was actively recruiting, using his delivery route to locate and flush out talented ballplayers from neighboring communities. Long-time Townie pitching ace Johnny Thoits was from Falmouth and Turner had located him during one of his egg deliveries to Falmouth.

The Townies didn't take the Twilight League by storm. Their fourth place finish made Turner recognize that his team was now playing in a more competitive league, which required him to upgrade his talent in order to move up in the standings. In 1960, Harris Oil of Cape Elizabeth won the regular season crown and awaited the winner of the South Portland Merchants/Scarborough AC best-of-three play-off preliminary.

In late August of 1960, Westbrook, behind the pitching of Jimmy Burrill and Dolloff, swept the South Portland Merchants, 8-

2 and 2-1, to advance to the finals against regular season champion, Harris Oil.

In what would become league protocol over the next decade, the regular season champion was awarded the league's championship title. Each year, however, a play-off series was waged between four to six league teams, with the finals being determined by a best-of-three championship series.

The Oilmen from Cape Elizabeth, after losing to Dolloff, 2-1, came back to take the next two games, 5-3 and the series final, 3-1, as Dick Densmore, the big right-hander from Duke University, out dueled John Gillette, giving the Oilers the playoff title to go along with the regular season championship. In what seemed improbable at the time, this league title by Harris Oil would be the last time for the next decade that anyone other than Charlie Turner's Yarmouth Townies or Bernal Allen's South Portland contingent wore the league's regular season crown as champs of the Twilight League.

In 1961, Turner began putting together the makings of a team that would establish the Twilight League's longest reign of supremacy by winning their first of six consecutive league titles. In 1967, when the South Portland team, now sponsored by the Ametek Corporation, won the title in a single game play-off, enough controversy and accusations swirled around South Portland's title win to forever taint South Portland's dethronement of Yarmouth and continue to be hotly debated for the next 35 years.

During the infamous 1967 campaign, Yarmouth won the first half and ended up being tied with South Portland for the second half of the season. South Portland player/coach Bob Philbrick arranged a one game playoff, that wasn't an official championship game.

"Neither Bob or Charlie could get together on a time for a playoff series; we had guys leaving for school and others who wouldn't be there," said Feury. "Bob said, 'why don't we play a game Sunday,' and of course, Charlie was willing to play any time, so he agreed, with the stipulation it wouldn't be for the championship. We didn't have Dave Seabury, who was our top pitcher that had beaten South Portland during the season," he said. "We also didn't have Eric Hayward and some of our other top players. Bob ended up going to the paper and saying they won the championship. Charlie was mad as hell when he found out about it."

"That's always bugged me to this day, that South Portland claimed the title, when we actually won it again that year," said Feury.

Not only did the Townies become a dominant team in the Twilight League, but Turner arranged for the team to play an additional 25 games or so against other teams from all over the state. Many a player/coach or other administrator from various town teams located up and down the state, has a story of receiving a late-night phone call on Friday night from Charlie Turner, seeking an opponent for a weekend doubleheader, because the Townies had an open date.

Yarmouth was also one of the Twilight teams that made annual Labor Day weekend trips to Lamoine for the statewide semi-pro tournaments hosted by the strong Lamoine ball club. The Townies claimed the state title in 1963, in the first annual Carlton Willey Invitational Tournament, by defeating the host team, Lamoine A.C., by a resounding 9-4 count on Labor Day of that year.

The tournament, named in honor of Cherryfield's Carlton Willey, who was pitching for the New York Mets at the time, had been organized by local baseball maven, Gifford Cochran.

Cochran, a painter and artist who originally hailed from New York City and had been a big Brooklyn Dodgers fan, had moved with his wife, Fletcher, a best-selling author, to the solitude of Lamoine to paint and enjoy the Maine coast. While there, both Fletchers took an interest in the local ball team. Their interest and enthusiasm resulted in their building one of the better ball fields in the area, where the annual season-ending tournaments were hosted.

Cochran also owned the Hancock House in Ellsworth, one of the area's finer lodging establishments, and would provide rooms for the out-of-town teams, such as Yarmouth, and feed them at his expense.

With Johnny Thoits providing two victories—an opening 14 strikeout performance over Winthrop and the title game's 6-hit limitation of a strong Lamoine line up, the Townies came away with their first statewide semi-pro title to go along with their Twilight crown for the summer.

By 1964, the Twilight League was back to being one of the top leagues in the state, with a regular roster of teams. Strong rivalries developed between Yarmouth, South Portland, John Haverty's Haverty Buick team and Harris Oil, all competing for the top spot each summer.

****

Bernal Allen made a career out of getting things done. As a city manager in both Auburn and later, South Portland, he was known as a person who possessed vision, insight, as well as the skill to negotiate the landmines prevalent in local politics. Most of all, Allen loved baseball. Regardless of the city he was running at the time, he always managed to immerse himself in local baseball in some form.

While serving as city manager in Auburn, Allen was the prime mover and principal architect for designing and then implementing a plan that gave the city one of Maine's finest baseball venues, Pettengill Park. Allen also was directly involved with the Auburn Athletic Association in forming the semi-pro Asas in 1949, as well as serving in various league capacities during the height of the Down East League's popularity.

When Allen moved to South Portland, he began looking for an opportunity to involve himself with a baseball club. While he certainly was an able administrator and was instrumental in bringing many beneficial changes to the city, including developing the city council procedure still used today, as well as overseeing the planning and construction of South Portland's public library, to name but a few, his first love and passion was the game of baseball. He brought the same focus and vision to assembling his team, as he brought to the machinations of city government.

Allen got the team off the ground in 1960, but it was his affiliation in 1961 with another name that became synonymous with South Portland baseball for over a decade, that really legitimized Allen's baseball operation in that city.

In 1961, Bob Philbrick had moved back to the area from New Brunswick where he had been playing semi-pro baseball in the Maine/New Brunswick League and was looking for a place to play.

Philbrick, a native of Bath, where he played on a couple of state legion championship teams, had played ball for Boston University, during which time he summered in the Twilight League during the late 1950's, before his stint in the semi-pro Maine/New Brunswick league. A knowledgeable and colorful baseball man, Philbrick's competitiveness and Allen's desire to put the best team on the field would lead to the establishment of one of the league's best rivalries of all time, with Yarmouth. These two teams matched some of the best town team rivalries, such as the Lisbon/Turner rivalry in the Andy County League and the fierce rivalry that existed between the Auburn Asas and Farmington Flyers back in the days of the Down East League.

The acquisition of Philbrick by Allen gave him a field general to run his team that Allen lacked in 1960. Philbrick became his player/coach and would stay involved with the Twilight League for the entire decade of the 1960's and early 1970's as a player and then serve in various capacities from president to commissioner until the late 1980's.

Another fixture for South Portland with ties to town team baseball was Phil Martin, who had moved from the Norway area to take a teaching and baseball coaching position at Scarborough High School. Martin had played on the 1960 Norway-Paris Pine Tree League team that played in Battle Creek Michigan.

In 1961, Allen had talked Martin into joining the Merchants. Martin gave the South Portland squad a veteran pitcher with experience in pitching against strong opponents. Martin was known for his elusive knuckle-drop that he was eager to teach to any pitcher that was willing to learn.

With Allen and Philbrick assembling a strong club across the bridge in South Portland, this would lead to annual dogfights between Allen and Philbrick's South Portland's summer contingent and Turner's Yarmouth Townies for the next 10 years or more.

During the mid-1960's, Allen was able to convince the Ametek Corporation of South Portland to become a sponsor for the South Portland team. The manufacturing firm, which made washer parts for Maytag, sponsored the South Portland team through 1970. It was the Ametek team (known as the "Redskins") that legitimately dethroned Yarmouth during the regular season in 1968. Ametek would go on to win the league title for the next two seasons, also, in 1969 and 1970.

The South Portland/Ametek team, along with Yarmouth and Harris Oil were regular participants in the Lamoine semi-pro tournaments over the Labor Day weekend, through the 1967 season, which was the last year for one of the state's most competitive and highly sought statewide tournaments.

The Twilight League always made a strong showing in the annual Labor Day tournaments downeast. This tournament was a yardstick that measured how your team and/or league stacked up against the best competition from other areas of the state. In addition to Yarmouth's victory in 1963, South Portland won the tournament in 1962, beating Mattawamkeag, and would win it during the final season of the tournament, as the Ametek Redskins team at the time, in 1967. The 1964 Harris Oil team would add another Twilight team to the list of semi-pro champs, with their 4-0 end-of-season win, behind one of the greatest pitching performances ever seen in the Pine Tree State. Dick Joyce, local high school phenom at Chevrus, college star at Holy Cross and future major leaguer, beat a strong Mattawamkeag team, striking out 18 hitters in the process.

****

If there is one constant that insures the survival of local baseball leagues, it's the changing of the guard that must occur each decade or so, bringing in new administrators, players and sometimes, new methods of organization. Al Livingston, who spent time with both Allen and Turner, offers an interesting perspective on the league, from his many years of involvement, to having the opportunity of knowing both men, who epitomized Twilight League baseball for most of the 1960's and 1970's.

Livingston started playing in the Twilight League at the tail end of 1968. Having just finished his summer legion schedule, Ametek's Bob Philbrick added Livingston to the roster for a new, local Labor Day tournament that Philbrick had organized over the first two weekends in September.

"Bob [Philbrick] asked me if I was interested in playing for Ametek. I was a South Portland kid and playing for Ametek was a big thrill for me," said Livingston. "I played at the tail end of 1968 and stayed with Ametek for the next year, after my freshman year at the University of Maine."

With Livingston playing baseball at the University of Maine, Allen had acquired access to the kind of talent that he was always looking for. Livingston would become the liaison for Allen in recruiting college players for the next few seasons, while Livingston played for Ametek.

As had been the case throughout the 1960's, Allen did almost all the recruiting and Philbrick molded the players into a cohesive unit. Livingston recalls Allen calling him at school often during April and May, asking about players and whether they'd play for Ametek for that summer.

"Bernal would call me several times per week, any time of the night to keep me posted on who he was looking at and interested in picking up for the season," said Livingston. "He really took it seriously and wanted me to try to use my influence with the Maine guys and get them to play for him," he said.

Livingston remembered the league changing during the end of the 1960's; some of the older, more established players changed teams, and the league began to get younger, as the older guys finished up and many college players came in to the league at the start of the 1970's.

"Phil Martin had played with Bob [Philbrick] at Ametek through the mid-1960's. He then went over to Yudy's Tire in the middle 60's and teamed up with Ziggy Gillespie and had some strong teams over there," said Livingston. "Phil's calling card was the knuckle curve. He taught it to a lot of pitchers who became successful with it. One such guy was Leon "Stubby" Truman, when Phil was at Norway-Paris," he said.

Truman was a legendary pitcher in the Norway-Paris area, who ended up playing in four decades as a pitcher, primarily due to being able to throw the elusive pitch that Martin taught him.

Livingston would be with Ametek through 1970; in 1971, he stayed in Bangor for the summer and played for the Bangor Merchants team, managed by former University of Maine two-sport star, Dick Devarney. Devarney was a member of the 1964 Black Bear team that went to Omaha and played in the College World Series, winning two games—the first time a Maine team had won in Omaha. After graduation, Devarney was talented enough to have played football professionally in Canada. He had returned to Maine and his alma mater, where he was coaching the University of Maine freshman baseball team.

"We had a bunch of University of Maine guys playing for the Merchants that summer—Tommy Fortin and George Ferguson from Lisbon Falls; Devarney was playing short and running the team—we had Ronnie Soucie, a Bangor kid, now at Husson and Mike Jones from Maine on the mound; we had a very strong team and we actually won the tournament that summer at Pettengill," said Livingston.

In 1972, Livingston was back with Allen and Philbrick, playing for South Portland, which now was the South Portland Merchants.

"Bernal was now managing the new Maine Mall and he got sponsorship money from them and other businesses to run the team, as Ametek had closed its South Portland plant."

The Merchants won the Twilight crown again that summer, their fourth title in five years, although Yarmouth would win the semi-pro championship in Auburn, which was now called the Governor's Cup and was held at the end of the summer.

Livingston remembers the level of play in the league really ratcheting up a notch during the 1970's. Due to his connections earlier, bringing Maine players to the Portland area, more and more Division I players were spending their summers playing in the Twilight League.

"The competitiveness of the Twilight League really ramped up in the 70's; in order to compete, you had to compete with Bernal, who was always going out and recruiting the best players he could find and stocking the South Portland roster," said Livingston. "We started bringing guys up from Massachusetts. Bernal was actually finding guys jobs, providing gas money; it got real competitive," he said.

"Bernal would have me go around in the spring and watch college games for the express purpose of recruiting college players to play for South Portland that summer," said Livingston. "He had contacts and was aggressive and he wanted to win. He was like the George Steinbrenner of the league, without the arrogance," he said. "Bernal was a quiet guy—very unassuming—he didn't say boo."

In 1974, Livingston moved over to Yarmouth to play for the other pillar of the league, the one-and-only Charlie Turner and the Yarmouth Townies. Like Allen, Turner always had someone run the team and Livingston had become Turner's manager for the summer, taking over from Pat Feury.

"Charlie was just nuts about baseball—he and Bernal were similar in makeup as far as baseball was concerned; Charlie would go out and get the town to contribute money every year," said Livingston. "When Charlie died, that was the last time anyone got any money from the town or any of the businesses—they'd only give it to Charlie.

Livingston would stay involved with the league, playing throughout the 1970's, into the 1980's. After his playing days, he has remained active in the league for much of the next 20 years and has served as league commissioner for the past several.

Spanning some of the league's strongest years, he has witnessed the league become a summer playground for many University of Maine players, such as Mike Bordick, Billy Swift and Billy Reynolds, all who were drafted. Swift, who followed in the footsteps of his father Herbie, who pitched for Forest City Chevrolet in the late 1950's, pitched for South Portland, before being drafted in 1984. Swift pitched at the major league level and won 20 games for the San Francisco Giants in 1993. Bordick, of course, went on to a long and distinguished major league career and is best known for being a good enough shortstop to force the legendary Cal Ripken to third base, when Bordick was traded to the Orioles in 1997.

Livingston learned the lessons well that were taught to him by mentors like Bernal Allen, Charlie Turner, as well as players such as Bob Philbrick and Phil Martin, and has passed them on to a younger generation, many of whom are still active in baseball as coaches, players and administrators.

While local baseball has dwindled and all but disappeared in most areas of Maine, the Twilight League continues into its second century of existence, a league that was, and still is, a league of its own.

Chapter 5

Getting There (From Here)

Baseball in Maine had established a healthy foothold in the towns and cities south and west of Augusta. If you lived in the lower half of the state during the 1950's and had witnessed the post-war reemergence of town team ball in that part of the state, it was natural to overlook the more remote areas of Maine to the north and downeast.

Until the arrival of the interstate in Maine during the late 1960's, travel north was limited to roads such as U.S. Route 201 and other north/south corridors of the state. A trip downeast meant the coastal highway of U.S. Route 1, which was becoming a busy thoroughfare, especially each summer, as the automobile took on greater importance in the life of all Mainers.

Yet, despite whatever perception those in the lower regions of the state had, baseball was alive and well and amazingly vibrant, with a wealth of leagues and teams as talented, if not more so, than some of their southern and western counterparts.

Driving north and east on U.S. Route 1 from Portland will take the traveler into the Brunswick and Bath areas. Both of these towns saw local teams that competed at the higher levels of local baseball. Brunswick had several different teams during the 1960's and early 1970's that played in Portland's Twilight League. Bath's team, after an early go in the Knox-Lincoln Twilight League, joined the Andy County League and the Bath Iron Works team, sponsored by the famed shipbuilding firm, was a very solid contingent during the mid-1960's.

Carl "Stump" Merrill, who would later become a manager of the New York Yankees, was a Brunswick native who summered locally for Brunswick's representative in Portland's Twilight League, while a star for the University of Maine Black Bears. Other players of note in the area were Ed "Bobo" McFarland, who was a two-sport star at Bowdoin College in both baseball and basketball. McFarland formed a formidable battery combination with Merrill during the late 1960's with the Brunswick Stars (and later, the Bath-Brunswick Whalers). Prior to that, Jim Dumas was one of the best players in the area, playing first for Brunswick and later, the Yarmouth Townies, prior to graduation from Holy Cross. Dumas was drafted and played several seasons at the minor league level.

Traveling up or down the coast (let's just call it eastward), you pass through a number of smaller towns nestled along Route 1, such as Damariscotta, Waldoboro, and Thomaston. All of these towns had teams in the Knox-Lincoln Twilight League, which flourished during the late 1950's, until it disbanded in 1966.

****

For Don Bowman of Jefferson, a small town of several hundred just north of Damariscotta, local baseball was something he had always been aware of. Jefferson and the gathering of houses to the west, which was known as West Jefferson, or affectionately called Oakdale by the locals, also had a ball team.

A rural community of a 200 to 300 people with two ball clubs would certainly qualify as a baseball hotspot, which is how Bowman recalls the area's passion for baseball.

"Before the war, I was playing as a 12 year old with my uncles and other relatives for the Jefferson A.A.," said Bowman. "Just down the road, in West Jefferson, which was basically a fork in the road, they also had a team."

Bowman was a talented enough player to have caught the eye of Clyde Sukeforth, the legendary scout for the Brooklyn Dodgers. Sukeforth would later be the scout who signed Jackie Robinson, the first African-American major leaguer and future hall-of-famer. Sukeforth hailed from Washington, a similarly small community, located just to the east of Jefferson. He had seen Bowman play for Jefferson High School and asked him if he wanted to attend an upcoming tryout in Brewer.

"Clyde Sukeforth saw me play one day for Jefferson High School. I had a pretty good day; I had a couple of hits, a home run and I pitched," said Bowman. "I guess he liked what he saw, 'cause he asked me if I wanted to go to Brewer for a professional tryout camp."

Bowman recalls that he had a pretty good camp, but wasn't offered a contract.

"I hit a home run and pitched pretty well. I struck out a couple of guys that they signed, but I guess they weren't interested enough in me," he said.

Bowman was offered a contract to play professionally for the Portland Pilots in 1947. The Pilots, an unaffiliated Class B minor league team, were members of the Northeast League, which included the Nashua Dodgers, a farm club for the major league Brooklyn Dodgers. They had a big right-handed pitcher named Don Newcombe, who would later go on to a distinguished major league career in which he won 20 games on three different occasions and finished his ten-year career with 149 victories at the big league level. The only player to ever win Rookie of the Year, Most Valuable Player, and the Cy Young awards, Newcomb was a hard-throwing rookie when Bowman faced him in 1947.

"I was playing for Del Bissonette in Portland in 1947. We had a real good club and I was the fourth outfielder, coming off the bench late and getting occasional starts," said Bowman. "I faced Newcombe late in the season—boy could he throw. Anyways, I was a left-handed hitter and Del decided to start me against Newcombe; I ended up having two hits off him, one of them a double down the line."

Just two years later, the 6'4" 225-pound flamethrower would join fellow African-American Jackie Robinson on the Brooklyn Dodgers, where he would be named the 1949 National League Rookie of the Year.

Like many players of this era, Bowman became a baseball gypsy, moving from town to town. As leagues folded, he'd have his contract picked up by other similar leagues. There were thousands of players like Bowman, good enough to warrant a spot on a roster of the many minor league teams of that era of expanded farm systems and leagues stretching east and west of the Mississippi River and deep into remote areas of the south.

Bowman wasn't offered a contract by Portland in 1949, so he came home to Jefferson where he worked on a farm and got called by Ben Houser of the Augusta Millionaires, to see if he was interested in playing baseball for one of the best semi-pro outfits in the state.

"Houser called me and wanted to know if I wanted to pitch some and play the outfield," said Bowman. He told me they'd pay my gas and give me a few bucks per game to play. I loved baseball and still hoped to catch on with another professional club, so I thought 'heck, why not.'"

Joining a talented club with a Red Sox affiliation, the Millionaires had future major leaguers Ted Lepcio, Billy Porter and Harry Agganis on their roster. In addition, they had notable Maine players such as Augusta's Marty Dow, Jim DiFrederico from Millinocket, and now Bowman.

While Bowman was quick to downplay his abilities or importance as a player that others would seek out for his talent, he was the most experienced player on the Millionaires roster of highly talented college and future professional ballplayers. Possessing size (6'1", 200 pounds), power and a strong left arm, Bowman had pitched professionally, as well as being a good enough hitter to also warrant time in the outfield for both Portland and Providence of the New England League.

"I guess I was a pretty good hitter and I could pitch. They liked left-handed pitchers—they still do," said Bowman. "When I went to my first Millionaire tryout, Don Brennan, who ran the team for Houser [Ben Houser, Augusta General Manager], had me grab a bat and get in the cage to hit. I ended up hitting five or six out over the fence in right during my first time in the cage, so I guess he liked what he saw," laughed Bowman.

After the 1949 campaign, Bowman ended up being signed by a team in the Border League, located in upstate New York, which had clubs in Auburn, Geneva, Ogdensburg and Watertown, where Bowman played.

The league operated in 1950 and most of 1951, before folding in July. Bowman had his contract purchased by a club in Lamesa, Texas, so off he went on another baseball odyssey, a young man from Jefferson, Maine, now deep in the heart of Texas, some 2,000 miles from his little village back home.

"I guess you could call me a baseball gypsy or vagabond at the time," said Bowman. "I loved to play the game and was surprised to be good enough to get paid to play it," he said. "We didn't make much money, but I was still playing professional baseball and doing something I loved to do," he said.

Located in the high plains region of West Texas, only about 50 miles from the eastern border of New Mexico, the city of Lamesa, population 10,000, while small by Texas standards, must have seen like the bright lights of the big city to Bowman, a young man from the rural state of Maine.

"It was definitely different than Jefferson, or some of the other places I'd played in, but I was used to bigger towns, as I'd played for Portland and Providence," said Bowman. "I liked Texas and the fans really supported baseball in the town. It sure was hot to play there, though," he said.

Bowman recalled an incident that he'd never run across before in any of the other towns he had played in.

"We had played a game on a Sunday afternoon and it was a real scorcher; it was always hot in Texas when I was there," he said. "A bunch of us decided to drive out to a swimming hole nearby. We had picked up sandwiches and some cold drinks; soda and some beer and we were going to swim and cool off. Next thing I know, I'm about five feet away from the biggest snake I've ever seen. One of my teammates to my left pulls out a pistol and shoots the snake dead as a doornail, just like it was something he did every day. Now I wasn't real keen about going into the water after that, but none of the others seemed to mind and most of them were boys from Texas, so I just followed their lead and never saw another snake, not that I hoped to," laughed Bowman.

After his time in Texas, Bowman's contract wasn't renewed. At 23, it had become obvious to him and the baseball decision makers that Bowman was always going to be a Class B or C player at best, so he decided to return to Jefferson and get on with his life.

Still in baseball shape and desiring to play the game he'd come to love at such an early age, Bowman joined the Damariscotta Redlegs team, just down the road from Jefferson. Bowman would play for another decade, until the age of 35. Damariscotta was a member of the Knox-Lincoln League and played fellow towns in Friendship, Hope, St. George, Thomaston and Waldoboro.

"It was a pretty good league. We had some good local players; semi-pro baseball was much stronger, but the town team in Damariscotta gave me a chance to play at night after working and I didn't have to travel very far; all the teams were close by," said Bowman.

Obviously for a hitter as good as Bowman, the level of pitching wasn't nearly as strong or as sophisticated as he was used to. He routinely is found in old newspaper clippings as being one of the leagues leading hitters. In 1960, he was batting .458 in early July, leading the Damariscotta Redlegs to the top of the Knox-Lincoln standings.

Bowman looks back fondly on his baseball days. From the earliest of years, playing for the old Jefferson A.A. as a youngster, to his experiences of professional and semi-professional baseball, to the days at the end in the Knox-Lincoln League, Bowman had a long and varied career.

"I was fortunate to play as long as I did," said Bowman. "I had some opportunities professionally and got to travel a bit. I played with and against some really good players like Newcombe, Agganis and Lepcio and others. Sometimes it's hard to believe that some of it was 50 years ago," he said. "Where did the time go?"

****

Not only was baseball flourishing in the midcoast area of the state, it was being played locally all over the state. Leagues were being revived, renewed and begun anew in the northern territories of Maine and making their way into the downeastern hamlets, along the state's rocky coastline.

In a *Bangor Daily News* article by reporter Stuart Haskell, with a May 29, 1956 dateline, Haskell reports that "organized baseball is on the way back in Eastern Maine!" The reporter goes on to write that, "while baseball was nearly dead from 1951 to 1954 in this part of Maine, 1955 saw a resurgence of seven separate leagues stretching from the Knox-Lincoln circuit in towns like Thomaston, to the Central Valley League with towns such as Milo and Dixmont."

Taking baseball down the coastline to Ellsworth and Hancock and surrounding communities was the Waldo-Hancock League. Two new leagues had formed along both the northern and eastern sections of the Canadian border, respectively. The Maine-Quebec League and the towns of Madawaska and Van Buren and Canadian outposts in Edmundson were playing to the north and along the eastern border. Towns such as Calais on the Maine side and St. Stephen across into New Brunswick added an international flavor to the local battles on the diamonds of the area.

One league that began back in earnest around this time was the Quoddy League. With teams in the larger Washington County towns of Machias and Eastport, as well as some of the smaller villages of Cutler and Jonesboro, to a grouping of a few houses along a back road such as Dixie and their high-flying team, the Dixie Eagles, the Quoddy circuit would become a fixture of Eastern Maine local baseball for the next 40 years.

Beginning as a six-team grouping, the Quoddy League's first season back in action was in 1955. In 1956 the Cutler Cardinals became members of the Quoddy circuit, along with another nearby club, the Dennysville Townies. These two, added to the clubs from 1955 of whom were the Jonesboro Jets, Machias Bruins, Lubec Red Wings, Eastport Lobsters, Pembroke Hornets and the Dixie Eagles, brought the Quoddy League to eight teams.

The league got off on the right foot by stressing organization and administration in order to make sure that those willing to commit to a summer of baseball got what they bargained for. The downfall of the prior Quoddy incarnation had been its lack of organization. Shifting schedules made it difficult for players as well as fans to know when and where teams were going to play.

As a result of the emphasis on structure, the Quoddy League in 1956 regularly saw Sunday afternoon crowds of 200-300 fans at ballgames, often exceeding the populations of the town where the game was played.

While the league didn't have the ambitious schedules and abundance of outside games that their counterparts to the south did, the focus was on playing a schedule of one to two games per week, starting at the end of May. With its anticipated and well-attended annual midsummer all-star tilt in July and play-offs at the end of the season in September, the league had developed a structure that worked well in rural communities, many of which depended on commercial fishing for their livelihoods.

****

Howard McFadden from Lubec might be one of the best baseball players to come out of downeast Maine. Beginning his local baseball career at the age of 14, just after his freshman year of high school, McFadden joined the semi-pro Dixie Eagles in 1949.

According to McFadden, the Eagles had just started up again, after being one of the area's top-notch clubs prior to World War II. As was common in small towns across the country, communities were robbed of most, if not all, of their able-bodied men for a period of two or three years, as the war escalated in Europe, drawing in American military participants.

The loss of young men caused the team to disband in 1942 or 1943 and it didn't begin again for six or seven years.

Growing up in Lubec, the easternmost town in the continental United States, McFadden was exposed to local baseball at an early age. The town, like Don Bowman's hometown of Jefferson, while slightly larger at around 1,000 inhabitants, was still a small town by southern Maine standards. Despite its diminutive size, the town fielded two competitive local ball clubs—the Lubec Seals and up the road just west of town, the Dixie Eagles.

"Dixie was this little grouping of houses just west of Lubec," said McFadden. "There were about 20 or 30 houses out in the country on the back road [just off what is Route 191 today] between Cutler and Lubec. This is where the Eagles played," he said.

McFadden remembers games between Dixie and Eastport or Jonesboro having such large crowds in the 1950's that current day Route 191, near to where it joins Route 189, would be blocked off by parked cars, and no one could get through.

"These three teams—Dixie, Jonesboro and Eastport—were the powerhouses. When they played, they drew fans from all the neighboring towns," said McFadden. "People couldn't wait until Sundays for these games. We'd have several hundred people at a game and you know these old country roads; once one car parked on one side and another on the other side, people couldn't get through. Maybe that's why we had such big crowds," laughed

McFadden. "No one could get through so they just decided to come to the game. Seems to me that we used to practice almost every evening and we had people coming out to watch us practice. The kids would be there wanting to participate and people would sit and watch us practice," he said.

The town of Lubec was originally incorporated in 1785 as a town. For over 200 years, its isolated location has yielded a community with its own unique character and heartiness. During the years after the war, the town was the sardine capital of the world. With the large draggers gathering ample catches off the coast, Lubec's location made it an ideal place for the many canneries that dotted this eastern community's waterfront.

Like most of his classmates at Lubec High School, when McFadden graduated, he went directly to work for one of the sardine factories in town. With seven canneries running three shifts, seven days per week, McFadden had a job waiting for him at American Can in 1952. Continuing to play ball nights and weekends, McFadden was aware of the possibility of being drafted to serve in the military, as the draft was in full swing during this period in history. Knowing that being drafted meant a four-year tour of duty, versus only two years if a young man volunteered, McFadden signed up as a volunteer in 1953, but didn't get his call to service until 1957.

"I didn't exactly want to go right then, but I knew if I volunteered, I'd only have to go for two years, instead of four," said McFadden. "I volunteered for the draft and continued to work and play baseball and didn't get my notice until 1957."

Baseball was an event in rural outposts like Dixie. With a hotdog stand and soft drinks offered, people made a Sunday afternoon of it.

"Everyone would show up, even the town drunks would be there," said McFadden. "Things have changed so much since then," he said. "Today, you have so many things; the snowmobiles, four-wheelers and camps on the lake; TV—we never had a TV back then," said McFadden.

Illustrating the differences between then and now, McFadden recalled that there was one television in the community, at a garage in town.

"Back when I first went to high school, there was a garage in West Lubec. It was called Knowles Garage," he said. "They had the only TV around in the whole area. From baseball practice after school, a lot of times we had to walk home and catch rides with the folks coming home from the sardine factories. We'd often stop at the garage to watch TV, but it was like watching that wall over there; you couldn't see anything," he laughed. "A lot of the workers did the same thing on their way home and that's how we'd get our rides."

Like many young men of military age during the 1950's and 1960's, when Uncle Sam came calling, you had no choice but to forsake career, family, and of course, town team baseball.

McFadden's call finally came in 1957 and he was off to Army basic training at Fort Dix, New Jersey. While at Fort Dix, McFadden found out about a tryout for the military base's baseball team and decided to give it a shot. McFadden's talents were evident to the Army coaches and he made the team and ended up playing third base. Normally a shortstop back home, the Fort Dix team had several professional players on their roster including shortstop Jim Mahoney who later played for the Boston Red Sox, as well as three other major league teams.

"Halfway through the season at Fort Dix, I got shipped to Fort Benning, Georgia," said McFadden. "I wanted to continue playing, but the team at Fort Benning was in the middle of their season and wouldn't take any new players on.

"The next year, I got shipped to Germany in 1958 and made the Berlin Bears, which was the Army baseball team in Germany."

Returning home in 1960, McFadden went back to work at the Cutler Navy station. Part of his release involved being kept on reserve status. Many of the local Army reserves were involved in building the Navy tracking station in Cutler and McFadden was part of the work crew at the base. He resumed playing town team ball, this time for the Dennysville A.A. Later in the summer, he received a notice of standby for summer training in Fort Drum, New York.

"I didn't go right off because I had this good job and I was making good money. I wanted to wait to see if they'd call me and I never heard anything," said McFadden. "I probably should have gone, because later, when the Berlin Crisis and Cuban Missile Crisis unfolded in 1961, I got called in with all the reserves and sent to Fort Bragg, North Carolina. I think they sent me there with the artillery unit because I didn't report to Fort Drum in the summer— I had been in the infantry before," he chuckled.

Once again, there was a tryout for the base team and McFadden attended, not knowing how he'd do, as the team was stocked with many major league players from the Baltimore Orioles, such as pitcher Steve Barber and shortstop Ron Hansen, as well as pitcher Dick Drott from the Chicago Cubs. There were also a number of AAA players in camp at the time.

"We had an 8 A.M. tryout and the wind was really blowing out. I ended up getting some good fastballs to hit and got under them and they ended up going and going; the coaches were asking, 'who is this guy; where is he from?'" said McFadden.

"We played teams from all over the area on weekends. We played Duke and the University of North Carolina in exhibition games and we beat all of them. We had major league and AAA pitchers, so we were very tough," he said.

With the major leaguer Hansen playing short, McFadden got moved over to second base and ended up winning the non-professional MVP award for the team.

"There were five military teams on the base, made up with all the reservists, plus Polk Air Base, but we never played them, because we had such dominant pitching and it wasn't fair."

In 1963, McFadden was picked up to play for the Eastport Lobsters, which played teams from northern and eastern Maine, including Dow Air Force Base in Bangor, as well as traveling up to Canada to play some of the semi-pro teams across the border in Edmundson and Fredericton, New Brunswick.

The Lobsters traveled over to Calais and St. Stephen on the Canadian side and picked up games and also played the Indian team at Pleasant Point.

"We played Back Bay and St. Stephen, which had good ball clubs. We also played the Dana Point Indians which had a very good team," said McFadden.

Baseball was an important part of community life in the deepest reaches of downeastern Maine, with the small communities along the coast all having teams. For the rest of the decade of the 1960's and into the 1970's when softball began making inroads, the Quoddy League, along with the Border League and others downeast, played competitive baseball that stacked up well with any other league across the state.

It was in 1964 that McFadden decided it was time to go to college, after working for nearly a decade. He enrolled at Washington State Teachers College (now the University of Maine at Machias) where he began pursuing his teaching degree. This is when McFadden began playing for the team that he would become forever associated with, the Cutler Cardinals. McFadden's first season with the Cardinals was in 1964 and he would end up playing for the Cards for 22 seasons, retiring after the 1985 season, at the age of 45.

"I knew Cutler's Neil Corbett back from my days playing for Dixie and then Eastport. We played his team back in the 1950's," said McFadden, when asked how he came to play for Cutler.

"Neil Corbett is one of the nicest and most honest people you'd ever want to meet," he said. "When I was playing for Eastport in 1963, Neil called me a couple of times and asked where I was playing next year. He never asked if I wanted to play for him, but just that if I needed a place to play, he'd be happy to have me in Cutler."

Machias was also in pursuit of McFadden's powerful bat and steady play at shortstop. They had a strong pitcher in the University of Maine's John Sawyer and there was talk that former major league pitcher Carlton Willey, back home in Cherryfield, might play a few games.

"Steven Smith had asked me to play for Machias. I knew they had John Sawyer [who pitched for the University of Maine], but I knew Carlton [Willey] probably wouldn't play for them. Neil had also called me, so I decided to go over to Cutler. We ended up having some great teams and we won a lot of Quoddy championships over the 20 or so years I played for them."

Like many talented town team players, McFadden seemed to age like a fine wine. The older he got, the better he seemed to be. Certainly, in his mid-to-late 30s, the legs weren't what they used to be and the one-time shortstop had moved over to first, a less strenuous position and one that's ideal for older players, as range and long throws aren't important. One of the reasons that the older players seem to defy the normal aging process is that a smart player, as he continues to play the game, learns tricks and other shortcuts that players in their early 20s haven't figured out yet.

Routinely, as McFadden approached 40, he would be the league leader, or near the top of the Quoddy loop in hitting. In 1974, at the spry age of 40, McFadden had one of his better years, as he ended up hitting safely in 40 of 85 at bats, for a cool .471 average over the season.

During his final season playing town team ball in 1980, at the of 46, McFadden's ninth-inning homer off Kendrick Mitchell gave the Cardinals a victory over the Machias Bruins to claim yet another Quoddy League crown, thought to be their 20th title in just over a quarter of a century.

For McFadden, having the opportunity to play local baseball for over 30 years allows him to have a unique perspective on how baseball became so popular and then, just as easily, it began to wane and in downeast Maine, it has disappeared altogether.

"In the 1950's, every single person wanted to play—everyone wanted to play whether they had the ability to play or not—they wanted to be part of a team, because that was the big thing around here. Like I said, there were a lot more teams. Over the years, the teams dwindled out; it seems like most people put baseball on the backburner during the late 1970's and the area was down to six to eight teams. The fans lost their interest and it seems like now, there's no interest in baseball there [downeast] at all, that I know of" said McFadden.

"Softball came in during the 1980's and kind of took over. We drew big crowds in Cutler, even through the 1970's. We had a lot of older diehard baseball fans who were in their 70's and even 80's and they eventually died and things changed," he said. "Also, a lot of people have moved away, unless they were a lobster fisherman, like Neil [Corbett] and others, or worked in the woods. When people moved away, that changed the towns a lot."

The baseball memories for McFadden, like most that played a young man's game long ago, are sweet and come in a rush when the faucet to the past is opened up. McFadden had a long and distinguished career outside of baseball as an educator, but baseball was never far away for the former slugger from downeast. He was honored for his baseball accomplishments in 2004, by his induction into Maine's Baseball Hall of Fame.

While his memories could fill several chapters, when asked for one particular game or event that still stands out vividly, McFadden paused to reflect for a moment. With his mind traveling back over 30-plus years, he settled on a doubleheader against Machias, where he was a hero, not once, but twice during this play-off tour de force.

Both Cutler and the Machias Bruins, two bitter rivals, were in a best-of-three play-off series for the Quoddy League crown. With Machias up in the series 1-0, Cutler trailed by a run in the bottom of the seventh (the teams were playing a seven-inning game). With two runners aboard and two outs, McFadden stepped to the plate. Always known for his home run prowess, the Cutler faithful had reason to be hopeful knowing that the powerful first basemen could end this thing with one mighty swing of his bat. This one not only has elements of the heroic, it also contains a unique event so common to baseball—redemption brought about by an odd twist of fate.

In what should have been the final out of the ballgame, a Machias victory, which gave them the championship over their chief rival, McFadden's routine foul pop up initially brought groans of disappointment from the Cutler side and caused the Machias fans to leap to their feet in excitement on the other side. Nearing the area just off the edge of the foul fence on the Cutler side, the Machias catcher made contact with a fan negating the catch. A heated discussion ensued between both managers and players, pushing towards the two hapless umpires. Arguments were taking place in the stands—just another play-off game in the Quoddy League! Finally, the umpires' decision was reasoned, explained and Machias was furious! The ball was ruled out of play. Once the bedlam subsided and order was restored, the fans realized that McFadden was allowed another swing. The events had obviously taken a toll on Machias lefty, Kendrick Mitchell. Unnerved and fuming, McFadden guessed what Mitchell was coming in with.

"Poor Kendrick Mitchell was fit-to-be-tied; he was ugly. I could see he was really mad and I said, 'he's gonna' try to throw that ball by me,'" said McFadden. "He threw pretty hard and sure enough, that's what he did and it ended up across the road to win the game."

Amazingly, the afternoon's second game came down to Cutler's final at bat, and once again, McFadden's walk-off home run provided the Cards with the margin of victory and another Quoddy League championship.

****

Behind every successful league, particularly leagues that had runs as long as the Quoddy League, are usually one or two individuals, who are capable of wearing many hats and giving of their time, so others can play.

Experience has shown that many of these men, at least in Maine, were people who weren't players, but might have been coaches, or skilled in administration. Rarely in scouring the state does one find one man who successfully did it all; running the league, managing a team, as well as still being capable of competing as a key player, also. In town team baseball annals, one man who seemed to defy the constraints of time is Neil Corbett of Cutler.

Beginning in the 1950's and continuing in various roles for the next 40 years, Corbett kept baseball alive and well in downeast Maine, long after many other similar leagues had folded.

Ask anyone who knows downeast baseball about the Quoddy League and the first name that comes up will be Corbett's. He got his start playing in Cutler on the local men's team in the early 1930's, at the age of 15. When the Quoddy League was formed in the 1950's, Corbett was in his mid-30s and past the age when many men have already decided competitive baseball is better suited for the youngsters. Corbett, however, had no thoughts at all about retiring as an active player. Instead, he continued to roam center field and hit cleanup for the Cardinals well into his 40s. Like Ted Ionta in Dixfield and Rumford, Corbett's top physical condition allowed him to remain an active player through the age of 67. Part of this was probably genetic, but part of it surely had to do with his livelihood as a lobster fisherman, which provided him with a wiry body that seemed to defy the aging process.

Running an amateur or even semi-pro baseball team is a thankless job. From the late night meetings that take place in the preseason stages each spring, to the phone calls necessary to securing commitments from players, to the toting of equipment, arranging umpires, all of it goes unnoticed and certainly unpaid. Add to that the responsibilities of making sure that the six, eight, or 10 teams meet their commitments, drawing up schedules and the other responsibilities of running the league and you begin to understand the remarkable nature of Neil Corbett. All of this could easily have been a full-time job for anyone else, but Corbett was still playing at the start and also lobstering six days per week!

The small town of Cutler, population 500, has an amazingly rich and varied baseball history. Corbett recalls his own father playing in the late 1920's, at a crude field that existed up at the neck above town, which he termed "a heck of a place to play." The records of the town indicate Cutler having an active baseball team going back to the late 1800's.

There was a Quoddy League that was very active in the area during the 1930's and 1940's up until the war. When the war came and the men left the small towns along the coast, the league died out and didn't return until the mid-1950's.

Corbett played baseball with various teams in Cutler, mostly known as the Cutler A.A., but it was the Cutler squad of the 1960's and their string of championships as the Cardinals that most locals talk about when Cutler baseball is discussed.

The Cardinals formed in 1956, when Corbett felt the time was right to get baseball started back up.

"We had a lot of baseball around here before the war," said Corbett. "After the war, it took awhile to get things going again. There were the teams like the Dixie Eagles and the Eastport Lobsters, the Jonesboro boys; in the 1950's, all these other towns started up teams again like Dennysville and Addison. I knew Cutler needed to be in there again, too," he said.

Despite being a very small town, Cutler's townspeople supported their team like no other. Regardless of the day of the week, a game in Cutler was sure to bring a turnout of several hundred fans.

"What made our team strong were the people in this town who were behind us," said Corbett. "They loved baseball; when there was a game, I don't care if it was Sunday, Monday, Tuesday, Wednesday, I don't care when it was, you always had a good crowd," he said.

Even at the end of the line, when the Quoddy League was struggling to stay alive in the 1990's, Cutler was the one place where a good crowd was guaranteed.

There is no doubt that the fan support helped the Cardinals, particularly in the home games, but the team certainly had its share of talented ballplayers making up the annual Cutler roster. Beginning in 1960, the Cardinals began one of the more remarkable runs by a town team or semi-pro club in the state, by capturing 13 out of 15 Quoddy League championships through the 1974 season. With a club made up of local players such as pitchers Stephen Cates and Corbett's son Bill, slugging Howard McFadden, as well as other offensive contributors like Mike Look (a strong hitter, who followed in his dad Leon's footsteps), Bob Cates, Dick Purington, the Fitzhenry brothers (Stan and Sterling), Randy Faas (who also pitched) and catcher Bobby Bell, the Cutler ball club was a force in Quoddy baseball circles for over two decades.

The importance of town team baseball as a cultural phenomenon in Maine can't be overemphasized, and nowhere is this more evident than in the easternmost coastal hamlets of the state. In an example of the importance baseball occupied, as well as emphasizing some of the unique aspects of baseball played on the jagged coastline of Maine, is Cutler's excursion and goodwill journey over to Grand Manan Island, New Brunswick, in the summer of 1978.

****

The early morning July air was cool when the Cutler contingent of players, families and fans gathered at the dock, ready to squeeze aboard the small armada of fishing vessels making the journey of international proportions across the bay.

"Grand Manan is fourteen miles across the water," said Corbett. "The island has a population of about 1,500 people. They used to play amongst themselves over there. By and by, there were a couple of boys come along, the Russell boys—they were good athletes in basketball; good baseball players too. I knew 'em and we decided to play them. We decided to take three boats across. When we got there, we could see the cars lined up at the dock," he said.

The locals had brought their cars down to the dock for each one of the players and their families. The folks on Grand Manan were excited to have a team come over and were extending island hospitality to their foes from the mainland.

"When we pulled up to the dock in Seal Cove, we could see all these cars sitting there," said Corbett. "They told us, 'those cars are for you to use for the day; just have 'em back here by the end of the day,'" said Corbett. "They took us to the parks and had a cookout, took us around the island; we had wonderful day," he said. "We beat 'em about 17-2 even though we were trying not to run up the score," he laughed. "The field was a unique one," said Corbett. "The beach was just beyond the outfield, not too far away, so anything landing on the beach was a ground rule double. In the water was a home run. We hit quite a few into the water that day."

The day was one filled with new friends, new places and a greater appreciation for the folks living on the 20-mile-long island just off the U.S. coast in Canada. For many of the Cutler contingent, this was their first visit to the island. This became the start of a semi-regular tradition between Cutler and island ball teams that would continue for several years, with the islanders visiting the mainland on several occasions to challenge the Cardinals at their home field.

Over his 40-odd summers of playing, managing and caring for the league, similar to how a gardener tends his garden, Corbett saw many players come and go, including a good number of fathers and then later, their sons. Offering four decades of downeast perspective on the league and some of its better and more highly skilled players, Corbett rifled through his memories to give the names of those players who were a measure above the rest.

"Well, the old Dixie team over there, they had two brothers, the Sawtelles—Ralph and Ashton," said Corbett. "Ralph was a tremendous hitter, as good as I saw in my early days of playing. Down in Dennysville, they had a good player, "Lippy" Cushing; his name was Vernon. He was a good ballplayer. Howard [McFadden] played with him and thought he was good enough to be in the hall of fame; he stopped playing too soon."

Corbett mentioned the Jonesboro area as having some real good hitters, such as Cony Feeney and Gib Whitney; Eastport had the Norton brothers, Omar and Chick (both in the Maine Baseball Hall of Fame); Calais had the Camerons. Tony Tammaro from the Border League's Woodland Red Sox, who would later go on to become a legend in Maine sports circles as an official in basketball and baseball umpire, was one of the best players to come out of an area of the state known for its ballplayers.

"I'll tell you one fella' that was a ballplayer," said Corbett. "There's a player we went against down to Campobello Island; he taught school on the island by the name of Tom Henderschott. They called us wanting to know if they could come over and play a game against us. Well, come to find out, this Henderschott had pitched in the Pittsburgh Pirates organization. They came over and we beat 'em, 5-2."

Corbett remembered that Henderschott could really throw and the only reason that Cutler had beat them at home was due to the Campobello catcher having so much trouble handling his pitches.

Cutler returned the favor and headed over to Campobello the following Sunday to face the islanders and Henderschott again. On the return engagement, Cutler took only 10 players and the two teams were hooked up in a scoreless duel, which is where it stood in the third inning when Corbett came to bat with the bases loaded.

"I had decided I'd start that game because I wanted to face Henderschott to see if I could still hit the good pitching. My first at bat, with the bases loaded, he struck me out on a 3-2 count," said Corbett. "Sure enough, I come up in the seventh inning, bases loaded again. Well, I knew what he was 'gonna throw me from the first two at bats and I worked him 3-2 again. He threw a fastball and I hit it clear over the road and cleared the bases—we beat him 7-0. He came up to me after the game and said, 'By gory, you played baseball somewhere else,' I told him I'd played ball just around here; I told him that he'd brought that pitch in just a little too much," chuckled Corbett.

"We was 'gonna take a team up north to Aroostook County and he was supposed to pitch for us in a night game; it fell through because he couldn't make it—he's still down to Campobello Island."

When Corbett was asked how old he was when he homered off the former professional pitcher, he recalled he was around 42 years old. At that point, Corbett had outlasted many town team players by a decade or more, and was just warming up, as he'd continue for another two decades and five years until he retired as an active player.

Corbett resigned as commissioner of the Quoddy League in the mid-1980's, but still continued to manage the Cutler team, organize the administrative details and make sure that the Cutler ball field's portable concession stand was well stocked with hot dogs and soda pop, as he'd done for decades.

Facing dwindling interest and prohibitive costs of sponsorship in an economically depressed area, the Quoddy League in the early 1980's was barely hanging on. Only Corbett's determination kept baseball alive, downeast. The league folded after the 1987 season, only to be revived in 1991, where it struggled on until the end of 1998.

In 1994, during a game against the Peter Dana Point Indians, a player shortage forced the 78-year-old manager into the Cardinal line up. The amazing Corbett went 0 for 2, but reached base via an error and played errorless ball at first base, five decades after most players had long before hung up their spikes!

While the general consensus remains that town team baseball in most areas of rural Maine is dead and won't be revived, Corbett holds a contrary opinion.

"If the right people got involved and you started it slow, I think it could catch on again and build," said Corbett. "We had enough interest last summer (in Cutler) to field a team and played a handful of games," he said.

While it remains to be seen if baseball will make a comeback, if it did, it would require men with the character and selfless determination of a Neil Corbett to make it happen. Someone who was willing to make phone calls, rake and line the field, gather sponsors, and generally do most of everything. Based on the current shortage of individuals like Corbett willing to step forward and revive baseball, it's dubious that baseball will come back anytime soon in these dormant areas of the state.

Maine no longer has men like Don Bowman, Howard McFadden and Neil Corbett. Unlike current-day players, who embrace baseball for a season or two after high school or college and then retire to weekend softball leagues and baseball on television, these former players' passion kept them keenly involved in the year-to-year unfolding of a time and a place fading into the dimly lit annals of oral history and the stories of a better time.

It's unlikely that local baseball will ever make a comeback and reach the place and position that it at one time held. Because of this, it only makes the love and passion that Bowman, McFadden, Corbett and the many other men had for town team baseball even more remarkable, gazing back to the time when towns and teams were a major part of small town life in Maine.

Cliff Hall-Farmington Flyers
[Cliff Hall, Cash Clark's first Flyer hired gun]

Cash Clark and Pete Doiron on bench before game
[Cash Clark and Pete Doiron sharing a moment before a game in 1949]

1950 Farmington Flyers Pitchers

[Flyers' Pitching Staff, 1950: (L-R) Jim Sawyer, Randy Davis, Jackie Corbett, Jim Cerone, Eddy Fraktman, Jim Strong]

1949 Farmington Flyers Infield

[Clark's Million Dollar Infield: (L-R) Buddy Rand, Ted Clark, Bill Judkins, Fred Rogers]

Junior Tracy
[Lamoine A.A. third baseman, Junior Tracy, circa 1960]

Field Dedication of Tracy Field

[Opening Day at Tracy Field, July 1960; (L-R) Gifford Cochran, Junior Tracy and Bill Silsby discuss strategy]

League Champions

[Rollie Worth of the *Portland Press Herald* presenting league trophy to
Ametek manager, Bob Philbrick; with Philbrick are Dave Sprague and Ned Beyer]

Racing for the bag

[Norway-Paris Twins' Stubby Truman nabbed at first; game at old Portland Stadium and first baseman is Roger Farrar]

Bussing to the regionals

Roberts 88er's headed to Waterbury, Connecticut—1964

1964 Roberts 88'ers

[Roberts 88'ers of Lisbon Falls; Front (L-R) Calvin Karkos, Jim Cornelio, Herb Whitman, Dick Pohle, Steve Karkos, Dave Begos Rear (L-R) Amel Kisonek-Mgr, Dave Moulton, Bob Baumer, Terry Healey, Bob Ransome, Marty Roop, Paul Klimavicz, Stan Doughty]

1965 Yarmouth Townies

[Front (L-R) Dave Ponziani, Jerry LaMarre, Alan Graffam, Judy Baker (scorekeeper), Steve Loubier, Dennis Libby; Rear (L-R) Ron Bernier, Rich Bowie, Terry Snow, Jim Dumais, Kenny Merrill, Pat Feury, Marshall Taylor, Ned Beyer]

1972 Yarmouth Townies

[Charlie Turner (Pictured far right in windbreaker)]

Still going strong after almost 30 years
[Ageless Bitsy Ionta in 1980 photo; still pitching as he nears 50]

Perham Field in West Paris
[A classic wooden grandstand that has witnessed many a Pine Tree League battle]

Twilight League baseball at Deering Oaks

[A third generation Baumer readies to hit at Deering Oaks during a Twilight League game in 2004]

Chapter 6

Field of Dreams: The Lamoine Tournaments

The small town of Lamoine is like many that are part of the pantheon of town team baseball. Located on one of Maine's many peninsulas, tucked between Ellsworth and Mount Desert Island overlooking Frenchman's Bay, while beautiful, it's not the kind of place that one would envision as a baseball mecca. Yet during the mid-1960's, teams from across the state came to the town and took part in their annual Labor Day tournament.

In Lamoine, like many downeastern towns, baseball began again in earnest after World War II, with Sunday afternoon pickup games. Often these were followed by a picnic at the local park and sandlot. These Sunday afternoon games began getting more serious and many of the players began harboring thoughts of joining one of the leagues that were forming in the area.

Beginning in 1949, the community of Lamoine began fielding a ball club, originally called The Lamoine Boys Club, which was soon changed to the Lamoine A.C. The original members of the "Boys Club"—Sylvanus "Junior" Tracy, along with Harland and Newell Hodgkins, Raymond Brann, Maurice Googins, Charles

Averback, Charlie Ashmore, Dick Zerrien and Bob Hardison—set to work establishing baseball in their community and making sure that the Lamoine team made the locals proud.

For the next two decades, the ball club from Lamoine would be a competitive force in eastern Maine town team baseball. The team was given the use of a habitable field behind the East Lamoine Baptist Church. While certainly big enough to lend itself to the dimensions necessary for men's baseball, the field surface wasn't ideal for hard hit grounders or running the bases without twisting an ankle. With help from other members of the community, as well as several area contractors, this local group of ballplayers transformed this open space into a ball field they could call their own.

The Seacoast League asked them to join in 1951 and Lamoine began competing against their bigger neighbor to the north, Ellsworth, as well as the small towns of Cherryfield, Harrington, Milbridge, and Columbia Falls. On weekends, the A.C. would travel to play strong clubs from "the city," such as Bangor and Brewer, as well as other communities with similarly competitive clubs.

During their second year in the league, Lamoine won the Seacoast League crown in 1952 and went on to win three titles in a row. As interest in semi-pro baseball began to wane statewide, many town team leagues were forming and so it was in this area of the state. With the formation of the Waldo-Hancock League in the late 1950's and into the early 1960's, the club from Lamoine joined other area teams from Belfast, Ellsworth, Franklin, Dow Field in Bangor, Gouldsboro, Searsport, Stonington and the Navy team in Winter Harbor to form a very competitive circuit representing these two counties bordering the coast.

Those early years were tough for the team. According to Tracy, in the beginning, the team struggled with finances and often lacked money for the basics.

"We didn't have any money at all," said Tracy. "We'd pass the hat at every game and some games, like on weekends, would get us $25 or $30, which we'd use to buy balls, bats and other gear we could afford," he said.

Despite their lack of money, the team continued to play well and after winning the regular season play in the Seacoast League, they would often play post-season games against other semi-pro outfits from across the state. Many of these games were played late in the summer and during the early fall at the various annual county fairs.

"We used to get paid to play at the fairs," said Tracy. "Sometimes, they'd pay us $100 to come and play at the fair, which was pretty good money in that day."

While unbeknownst to Tracy and his teammates at the time, the team's newest fans would become instrumental in solving some of their financial difficulties, as well as putting Lamoine prominently on Maine's baseball map.

Gifford and Fletcher Cochran were probably Lamoine's most famous couple, even though many locals didn't know it at first. Gifford, a Yale graduate, as well as studying art throughout Europe, was a prolific painter. Gifford's wife, Fletcher, was born in England and achieved prominence as an actress on stage and later screen, before she turned to writing. Writing under the name of Lady Mary Cameron, she hit the best-seller list several times with her novels.

Gifford Cochran's grandfather, Dr. John Madison Taylor, was well known on neighboring Mount Desert Island, as the family had been summering in the area for a number of years.

Later on, Gifford and Fletcher would come to the area and she fell in love with the coastline and the hospitality of the people. While painting a beautiful home along Route 184 overlooking the river and nearby Trenton, Gifford Cochran learned it was for sale. The Cochrans ended up purchasing it and it would become their seasonal home for the next two decades.

Both Cochrans were avid baseball fans and had taken to rooting for their hometown Brooklyn Dodgers back in Manhattan. They were regular attendees at historic Ebbets Field in Brooklyn whenever time and schedules would permit.

Upon moving to Lamoine for the summer, they had come to miss baseball and listening to the games over the radio. One day, while in town buying groceries, they saw a hand-lettered sign advertising that evening's local ballgame, between the Lamoine A.C. and an area rival.

From an article that appeared in the *Bangor Daily News* by Owen Osborne, Mrs. Cochran was quoted as saying that their initial experience watching local baseball was a positive one. "We went to the game and we were amazed at the fine caliber of baseball." This would become a regular occurrence over the next few summers, as the Cochrans slowly became part of the Lamoine community and began to assist the local club with some of their financial needs.

****

Sylvanus "Junior" Tracy came home after the war, after spending three years in the European theater. Tracy saw action in a number of the major battles in Germany, including the Battle of the Bulge. Tracy, who hailed from Hancock, settled in Lamoine in 1946, after marrying his wife, Carrie, who was from Lamoine.

Settling into domestic bliss and working for a local plumber, Tracy began joining in the Sunday pickup games, with Carrie trailing along reluctantly. As the team got more serious and games involved travel outside of town, Carrie balked at Junior's involvement.

"We argued every weekend because I didn't want him playing ball," said Carrie.

In order to calm things and salve Carrie's reluctance, Junior began leaving the family car with her and hitchhiking to meet his teammates and catch a ride to the games.

The next season, Carrie's reservations had subsided and she became her husband's biggest supporter.

"I started going to the games the next year and I was the best rooter Junior ever had," laughed Carrie.

The Cochrans wisely did not to push their way into the local culture where they weren't welcome, as many outsiders are apt to do. They started as fans, coming out to Lamoine games and the quality of play won them over to the local ball team.

"At first, Giff and Fletcher just started coming out to the games," said Tracy. "After the first summer, they probably saw what a shoestring we operated on, with our threadbare uniforms, taped up bats and shortage of baseballs."

"That next year, Gifford came over and introduced himself and asked if I'd mind if he bought us some baseballs. Heck, I was tickled to death to have someone offer to buy some balls," said Tracy.

Eventually, Cochran decided the team needed new uniforms, as many of the players were wearing hand-me-downs and patched up garb that was about a decade old. With their new uniforms and newer equipment, the Lamoine club now had the accoutrements to match their prowess on the field.

Cochran's property encompassed some 60 acres overlooking the Jordan River. He and his wife had been discussing the possibility of building a ball field on the backside of their property, which would enable them to provide a top-notch facility for their local boys of summer. He pulled Tracy aside to get his thoughts on his idea for a new ball field.

"The thing about Gifford and his wife, they didn't just come in and push their way in. They respected the local way of doing things and took their time getting involved," said Tracy. "The ball field we had was ok, but a new field wasn't anything any of us minded having."

In the spring of 1959, Tracy and several other players began working on the future ball field, clearing and laying out the dimensions for what would become one of the premiere fields in Eastern Maine. With the beginning of the baseball campaign, Tracy and his mates were busy, between playing ball and on their off nights, Tracy and several others spent evenings out behind the Cochran homestead, readying the field for the 1960 schedule. That summer saw Lamoine winning the Waldo-Hancock title and also capturing the semi-pro title and the *Portland Sunday Telegram* trophy, for winning the end-of-summer tournament in Portland, their first appearance in the tournament.

On July 4, 1960, Tracy Field was dedicated before a crowd of 500 happy fans, as Lamoine trounced Bucks Harbor Air Force Base, 16-5. The new field, with a smart-looking wooden outfield fence, adorned with advertising from area businesses, had the look of a professional ballpark, one that you might find in a more populated area. It certainly wasn't the norm for small-town Maine.

Tracy was honored to have the field named after him. When asked about it, he had the following to say.

"I had been the one who had been managing the team and I spent quite a few hours working on the grounds, digging and rolling and the other things that go into building a field," he said. "I didn't care to have the field named after me, but Gif said he was going to and if he set out to do something, he did it."

****

With the coming of the 1961 season and Cochran fully engaged in Lamoine baseball matters, as well as also managing the team, the Lamoine team was being offered extra incentive to defeat their Waldo-Hancock foes, as well as any other outside opponents.

Cochran, dead serious about winning baseball games and providing the people of Lamoine with the best talent around, began paying his players and importing outside players like Jack Scott from Ellsworth, who would later sign a minor league contract with the Red Sox, as well as Ray Weed, the former University of Maine speedster. Cochran paid his players five dollars per game for a loss and ten dollars for a win!

The summer campaigns of 1962 and 1963 saw the start of Lamoine hosting various opponents such as the Philadelphia Colored Giants, the Boston Hoboes, and other strong barnstorming teams from up and down the east coast. Cochran would bring them into the area, guaranteeing them a percentage of his gate, as well as putting them up at the Hancock House in Ellsworth, the hotel that he owned. Ellsworth's finest lodging at the time, the Hancock House provided upscale rooms with meals provided for the players and coaches. With Cochran providing the hospitality and some cash enticement, Lamoine didn't have too much trouble getting strong opponents to come down the coast and do battle at Tracy Field. These games against outside opponents began attracting baseball fans down the peninsula to

Lamoine, with attendance climbing to 500 and 600 fans per game. Some weekend contests actually drew crowds of 1,000 or more fans, lining both sides of Tracy Field, as well as filling the large banking on the first base side.

"I remember looking up at the crowd from my position at third base," recalled Tracy. "I thought there might be 2,000 fans the Saturday we took on the Colored Giants."

The final weekends of August and the first weekend of September 1963 brought the best semi-pro and town teams from across the state to compete in Cochran's first end-of-the-season semi-pro tournament at Tracy Field. Cochran once more extended his hospitality, with each team being offered rooms and dining at the Hancock House. The tournament was being called the Carlton Willey Invitational Tournament, in honor of major league pitcher Carlton Willey, who hailed from Cherryfield and was currently pitching in the National League with the New York Mets. *The Bangor Daily News* was furnishing the trophy for the winner of the statewide tournament, which would culminate with a Labor Day championship battle between the remaining two clubs.

That first tournament provided a glimpse of what was to become a Labor Day baseball staple in the state for the next five years. As was Cochran's practice, whatever he involved himself with, he made sure it was done right.

"Gifford made sure that all the teams that came were taken care of," said Tracy. "He had asked me about the tournament, who we should invite, who should be involved to run it; he wanted to make sure it was done top-notch."

A committee of local officials were pulled together and included Rufus Candage of Blue Hill as chairman, Bill Silsby, Jr., of Ellsworth handling the supervision of on-field activities and Harry Dalton of Brewer, obtaining and assigning umpires.

Candage was a long-time supporter of local baseball up the coast in Blue Hill and had been instrumental in getting the Waldo-Hancock League off the ground and turning it into one of the top local circuits in that part of the state. Candage was also a long-time state boxing commissioner, with a wealth of experience running events and handling the logistics that could arise from the Willey tournament.

The first tournament in 1963 drew a representative field from across the state and included the Winthrop Lakers, perennial Lakes Region League champs, who had won the Yankee Amateur Baseball Congress crown in 1959 and traveled to Battle Creek as the Maine representative in the National Amateur Baseball World Series Tournament. The Lakers had also been crowned the state's semi-pro champions in 1961. In addition to Winthrop, northern Maine was well represented with the Lee A.A. and the powerful Mattawamkeag Merchants. The central Maine area was being ably represented by the Dixmont contingent from the Central Maine League, where they were regular contenders for that circuit's seasonal crown.

Other clubs coming to Lamoine were the Waldoboro Merchants from the Knox-Lincoln League and the Yarmouth Townies and South Portland Merchants of the perennially strong Twilight League of Portland.

With ample publicity and Willey lending his name as well as endorsement, the tournament received a high profile within the state and even outside of the Pine Tree State's confines. Several professional scouts were planning to be in attendance, to observe many of Maine's best local players.

For the players coming into Lamoine for the tournament, it was a thrill to be treated with the hospitality that Cochran extended, in addition to being able to compete against the best players in the state.

South Portland's Phil Martin remembers Lamoine as being one of his fondest memories of playing town team and semi-pro baseball. Martin was no stranger to tournament play, as he had been a member of the 1960 Norway-Paris team that went to Battle Creek, Michigan. He recognized the tourneys in Lamoine as being first-class experiences.

"Cochran knew how to treat the players," said Martin. We were staying in the kind of hotel that professional players stayed at—we had our food taken care of and our lodging, so it was a real treat for the players to drive up the coast and play in the tournament," he said. "Another thing about baseball at that time was the tradition that developed of teams getting wind of other top teams in the state and wanting to play them, to measure their towns and teams against other places. That's what I think made Lamoine such a great experience—the chance to bring your team and measure the strength of the team and even the league against other parts of the state."

With 600 to 800 fans regularly turning out to watch the games, the first year's tourney produced some great match ups. The semi-final tilt between the host team, Lamoine, and the Merchants from Mattawamkeag, was a barnburner of a game. Coming into the game, Mattawamkeag was sporting a 30-5 record and had beaten some of the top teams up and down the state. With hard-throwing Terry Ordway (who was attending the University of Arizona at the time) on the hill, Lamoine had a tough opponent standing in the way of reaching the finals against the Yarmouth Townies.

Lamoine started strong in their half of the first inning, as Jasper Kane's leadoff homer on the second pitch of the game over the center field fence, had the locals whooping and hollering.

Ordway settled down however, as the powerful righty started setting down the Lamoine hitters with regularity.

Bob Hardison of Lamoine was cruising along with a 1-0 lead in the fifth when Gil Arnold solved one of his slants and sent it over the barrier in left-center. The 1-1 deadlock didn't last long as Lamoine exploded for three runs in their half of the fifth and knocked Ordway from the mound. Gordon Gray's two-run triple was the big blow, driving home both Marty Vickers and Jerry Jordan. Gray rode home on Gerry Kane's grounder and the boys from the A.C. were up 4-1. 'Keag wasn't done, however, as they knew how to work tough pitchers and managed to counter with two in the top of the sixth and another in the top of the eighth to tie it on Brian Gordon's single.

Marty Vickers brought delight to the crowd of 800 when his two-run double in the bottom half of the eighth brought home two runs and Lamoine held off a ninth-inning Mattawamkeag threat for a hard-fought 6-4 victory, setting up a Sunday showdown with the Townies from Yarmouth.

Nearly 1,000 fans jammed into Tracy Field for Sunday's championship, and the initial Willey Invitational Tournament could be termed a success. With bright sun and perfect early fall conditions, Maine baseball didn't get much better than this.

With Dick Jude on the hill for Lamoine, opposing Yarmouth's crafty veteran Johnny Thoits, a pitching duel was anticipated. Unfortunately for Lamoine, Jude was off his game on this particular day and Yarmouth's potent attack, led by Jim Dumas, Jim Dyer and Terry Snow was too much for Lamoine, as they fell 9-4. Lamoine made a bit of noise in the early going to cut the lead in the fourth to 4-3 behind a Marty Vickers two-run homer, but on this day, the Yarmouth bats were too much and the Townies won the first-ever Willey Tournament crown and the tournament trophy.

Willey's parents, Mr. and Mrs. Phillip Willey, were in attendance representing their son and they presented the *Bangor Daily News* trophy to Yarmouth as the 1963 Maine semi-pro champions.

For players like Yarmouth's Pat Feury, the Willey tournaments were unique experiences that the players like himself remember fondly.

"Going to Lamoine was a big thrill for the players," said Feury. "Yarmouth went several times and the tournaments were always first rate. Cochran treated all the players like royalty, with the hotel [the Hancock House] in Ellsworth and the food, plus the crowds were always large and they knew their baseball," he said.

While the initial Willey tournament was an unqualified success, the 1964 field and competition might even have been better. As word got around the state, teams began making inquiries to members of the Lamoine team about how they could be included in the field come late-August and September.

"We were getting calls all summer from teams wanting to come down and play," said Tracy. "Word had gotten out that Lamoine was the place to play baseball."

The Lamoine club was stacked in 1964 with Tracy back at third for another season, his 16th year with the club. In addition to Tracy, Jack Scott of Ellsworth was back, Ray Weed from the University of Maine played center and ran down most balls that stayed in the park. Other regulars back from the strong Lamoine team of the previous season were the Kane brothers, Jerry and Jasper, Jerry and Jackie Jordan, Dick Jude, and Bob Hardison.

With such a strong team, Lamoine didn't have much trouble with the local competition from the Waldo-Hancock League, as they claimed another league crown in 1964. In order to keep his club fine-tuned for the end-of-the-season tourney, Cochran continued to bring in clubs on weekends to Tracy Field. Mattawamkeag, Yarmouth, Winthrop and other solid in-state teams were brought in, as well as out-of-state clubs like the New London Vagabonds, from Connecticut's Morgan League. The Vagabonds were stocked with top college talent from southern New England and came to Lamoine for a weekend flurry of games against the host club, as well as the Franklin Townies, another strong Waldo-Hancock opponent.

As the summer campaigns wound down around the state and various league champs were being crowned for 1964, Cochran, Candage and other tournament committee members began finalizing the field for the second annual tournament in Lamoine.

Many of the clubs invited for the 1964 tournament were holdovers from the previous season. Mattawamkeag was back, after another ambitious season of traveling near and far, playing anyone willing to take them on. The Merchants played over 40 games and finished with a stellar 35-8 mark for the season. In addition to the host team, Lamoine, Winthrop and their brother combos of the Wings and Cobbs and acrobatic second baseman Dennis Clark were returning to Tracy Field and Gifford Cochran's hospitality. As an added incentive, as if teams needed any others, Cochran was paying mileage for the teams of five cents per mile per carload of three players. The defending champs from 1963, Charley Turner's Yarmouth Townies were back, as well as another Twilight representative, the Harris Oilers, replacing South Portland in this year's tourney.

Other first-time teams were Harmony, from the Central Maine League, with their strong double play combo of Colby's Ken Reed and Gary Snowden. The Calais Mets were making the journey to Lamoine from the internationally flavored Border League. Rounding out the eight team tournament field were the Knox-Lincoln champs, the Thomaston Clippers, who won that loop's crown and finished with a 19-8 mark for the year.

With another solid field of teams, a year under their belts to work out any bugs from the previous year, plus an even stronger roster of talent, particularly pitching, the 1964 Willey Invitational Baseball Tournament was sure to be a good one.

Despite the presence of a number of big name pitchers, such as Harris Oil's Dick Joyce, Mattawamkeag's Terry Ordway, and Winthrop's Ray Wing (a former minor leaguer), the tournament's opening day was dominated by the hitters. Both Mattawamkeag, with their opening round thrashing of the Thomaston Clippers by a 16-1 count and Lamoine's 15-2 pasting of the Calais Mets, provided an abundance of offense during the opening weekend of the tournament.

In the Mattawamkeag game, the Merchants pounded out 15 hits, including home runs from Bob Butler, Herb Libbey and Butch Gordon, to trounce the Knox-Lincoln League's representative.

Lamoine got off to a rousing start as they exploded for 13 hits against the Mets, including two home runs by Ray Weed, as well as single round trippers from both Jordans, and another from Jasper Kane.

The second weekend of the tournament featured a bit less offense, as some of the top pitchers began to assert their abilities, in particular, Dick Joyce of Portland and Terry Ordway of Mattawamkeag. Joyce dominated the Harmony Townies over six innings, to the tune of two-hit ball and 11 strikeouts. With a large lead, Harris manager Dick Hay opted to remove Joyce from the game.

team, 5-3. Ordway was able to quiet the potent A.C. bats, scattering seven hits. Only Jack Scott's three safeties, including a two-run homer posed any threat to the smooth right-hander.

With the Harris Oil and Mattawamkeag victories, a classic Labor Day match up was in the works between the two top pitchers in the state, with Joyce and Ordway going head-to-head.

****

Dick Joyce of Portland might be the most storied pitcher to come out of Maine at that time. Joyce, who pitched his high school ball with Chevrus High School, a private Catholic High School in Portland, once struck out 25 hitters during a high school game. During his last three years pitching for the Stags, he led them to successive Telegram League championships, in Maine's most prestigious high school conference.

As highly touted a player to ever come out of the greater-Portland area, Joyce was recruited by eastern baseball power, Holy Cross University, where he ended up enrolling in 1962. At that time, freshmen were not allowed to pitch at the varsity level in college, so Joyce led his freshman team at Holy Cross to an undefeated season.

As a sophomore, the six-foot, five-inch southpaw became the ace of a talented Crusader staff, leading them to a College World Series appearance in Omaha. Joyce's batterymate at Holy Cross was Tim Murtaugh, the son of then-Pittsburgh Pirates manager, Danny Murtaugh.

In 1964, after another stellar year as a junior, in which he posted a 4-1 mark on the mound, Joyce was offered a signing bonus of close to $100,000 to sign with the Kansas City Athletics. Joyce, slated to pitch for that summer's U.S. Olympic squad, turned

Joyce, slated to pitch for that summer's U.S. Olympic squad, turned it down for the opportunity to represent his country and to complete his education at Holy Cross.

Like many upper echelon college players, Joyce played in an NCAA-sanctioned summer league; in Joyce's case, it was the Midwestern Basin League, where he pitched for the Sturgis, North Dakota, squad.

Harris Oil manager Dick Hay got wind that Joyce had a few weeks off from the end of the Basin League's campaign, until he was slated to report with his Olympic teammates to manager Rod Dedeux in Los Angeles, prior to flying to Honolulu for two weeks of training.

Making a few phone calls, Hay was able to secure the services of Joyce in time for their trip to Lamoine for the Willey Invitational Baseball Tournament. With Joyce added to an already strong roster, which included Colby right-hander Eddie Phillips (who would later pitch for the Red Sox) Hay was feeling confident as he prepared the Oilers for their downeastern baseball pilgrimage.

Terry Ordway from East Millinocket, was the northern Maine equivalent to Portland's Joyce. Starring for Schenck High, the talented Ordway was recruited by Arizona University, one of the country's top baseball schools. Ordway had pitched most of the summer for the Merchants of Mattawamkeag, after his return from the desert. With Ordway, Gil Arnold, and Floyd Murphy, the Merchants had a trio of pitchers who threw as hard as anyone in the state.

The Mattawamkeag/Harris Oil match up had been anticipated, as many baseball aficionados knew of both team's highly publicized pitchers. With the results of the games shaking out as they did, the match up that everyone had hoped for materialized for the final weekend of the 1964 campaign. The of the summer season, as they were sporting a 41-8 mark heading into the battle for the tourney trophy. After disposing of their first two opponents in the Lamoine tournament, the Merchants had headed back home and bested Milo to claim the East Millinocket semi-pro tournament, using it as a tune up for Monday's Labor Day matchup against Joyce and the Oilers.

Joyce didn't disappoint the 1,000 fans who packed Tracy field for the anticipated finale to that summer's Pine Tree State ball season. Pitting his outstanding curveball and fastball against one of the state's top line ups, this was a great opportunity for the young lefty to prepare for his upcoming Olympic tour.

The first three frames were pitching gems, with Joyce fanning eight of the first nine men he faced, including seven in a row. Ordway matched him in less spectacular, but yeoman-like fashion, as the first three innings showed goose eggs up on the Tracy Field scoreboard.

Joyce's curveball was what most hitters remember about him, after facing the imposing left-hander. Said Mattawamkeag's Brian Gordan, who led off the game against Joyce, "His curveball had the tightest rotation and sharpest drop I'd ever seen. He struck me out on a curve that ended up hitting me in the foot," chuckled Gordon.

Harris Oil was finally able to break through against the equally tough Ordway, when Ron Butland slammed a two-run homer, after Ken Stone's one-out bloop single to right. Those runs would be all that Joyce would need, as the future major-leaguer ended up scattering two ground ball singles and finished with 18 strikeouts, including the final three Mattawamkeag hitters in the ninth.

"We faced a lot of pitchers over the years, playing as many games as we did, but we never faced anyone like Joyce," said Mattawamkeag's veteran third basemen, Herb Libbey.

Joyce was drafted in the spring of 1965 by the Kansas City Athletics and ended up pitching briefly at the major league level. Unfortunately, an arm injury cut short his career. But on this Labor Day in 1964, the big left-hander provided a powerful reminder to both teams and the 1,000 fans of just how good the young man from South Portland had been, as well as the top-notch caliber of the baseball played in the state.

****

For Junior Tracy, his baseball career was winding down with the arrival of the 1966 season. He had been playing every summer for the past 17 seasons and knew that his 38-year-old body didn't feel too good the morning after a ballgame. Many of his A.C. teammates were also creeping up the ladder in age. As was common in many of the smaller communities, when the original core group of players got too old to play any longer, there weren't enough younger players to fill the holes brought on by their retirements.

With Gifford Cochran still going outside of Lamoine to entice talented ballplayers to travel to Lamoine to play for the club, 1966 still found the club competitive and hosting teams from points north and south of the peninsula. There were indicators that interest in baseball in and around Lamoine was starting to drop off. Crowds that year were smaller. When Cochran would bring in a barnstorming team from afar, such as the entertaining Philadelphia Stars or the Hosmer Chiefs, crowds approached the size of previous seasons. Many of the games against local opponents, however, were considerably smaller.

Some people blame the growing popularity of television. Other reasons cited are the availability of other entertainment options in Ellsworth and even up the road in the big city of

Bangor. Whatever the reason was, by the end of 1967, the Willey Tournament was no more and rumors were swirling that Gifford and Fletcher Cochran were looking to leave the area.

"Television was one of the reasons why people didn't come out to the games anymore," said Tracy. "People could now go up to Bangor to see a movie, go dancing; there were more things to do. Softball also was getting popular and some of the guys decided that they'd rather do that than spend all their time playing ball or working on the field."

Not everyone was a fan of Cochran and his paid-to-play brigade of stars that he brought to Lamoine. Over time, the clubs around Lamoine began folding and by 1964, the Waldo-Hancock League had gone away. While a bigger town such as Ellsworth still fielded a competitive club, as well as teams up the road in Bangor and Brewer, the smaller towns of Franklin, Stonington, Searsport, and even the ball team at the Navy base in Winter Harbor had disappeared.

For players like Bill Neleski, who had come to the area with the Navy and played for the station team in Winter Harbor, Cochran was responsible for the death of town team baseball in the area.

"He killed town team baseball," said Neleski. "We had a good brand of baseball; Lamoine had a strong team, but so did some of the other towns like Franklin, Belfast and some of the others. When Cochran started paying players and raiding the better teams of their best players, the smaller towns couldn't compete. I know that's probably not a popular view, but I think it's accurate."

Tracy just shrugs his shoulders and laughs when he hears others badmouth Cochran and his efforts to upgrade the brand of baseball played in Lamoine and elsewhere.

"I've heard people say that Gif ruined baseball down here," said Tracy. "I don't know. Some of it's probably sour grapes because they weren't good enough to play, maybe. All I know is that this area has never seen anything like what Gif and his wife brought to this town."

In late 1967, the Cochrans decided that the patterns of their lives made it impossible for them to spend much of the year in Lamoine. The necessity of traveling back to New York made it difficult as they got older and a very difficult decision to sell their home and their beloved ball field was made.

The new tenants had no desire to maintain the field that had come to symbolize baseball in Lamoine for much of the decade of the 1960's. In a few short years, weeds began to overtake the carefully manicured playing surface. The advertising signs and fences were taken down and in a few short years, it was difficult to tell where the field had been.

For many of the players who had known the Cochrans and had been part of their team, and the many baseball fans who had the privilege of seeing something special in a small Maine town in a picturesque part of the state, the memories live on.

"Sometimes when I think about it, it seems like yesterday that we were down at the ballfield, playing a team like Mattawamkeag, or one of the Portland teams," said Tracy.

When asked if he had any regrets from his many years of playing, running the team, or the countless hours spent raking, lining, or mowing one of the best diamonds Maine has seen, Tracy thought back.

"I wished we could have won one of the tournaments," said Tracy. "As good a team as we had, we never once won our own tournament. We had a chance one year, but I dropped a pop up and we ended up losing. Playing baseball was a lot of fun for me and the guys who played," he said. "I guess we could have been doing something else if we had wanted to," he said. "I'm glad I had the chance to play as long as I did."

Like almost all former players, Tracy's stories and recollections are tinged with a hint of melancholy. The years that he played, through the 1950's and the 1960's, were truly special times. The memories from the games and tournaments, as well as the friendships that were made on the diamond are deeply embedded in the small towns that stretch across Maine's landscape.

Lamoine remains a small town. A drive down Route 184 will reveal some new homes, an elementary school where the first ball field stood. Tracy Field is now a grove of trees and scrub bushes, with no evidence that the field was even there. The greater Ellsworth and Mount Desert Island area has certainly grown and a short drive up U.S. Route 1 in the summer months will make anyone aware of the area's popularity. Yet, without Tracy Field and the local baseball from those years, this area of Maine is missing a part of its heritage that is probably never coming back.

Chapter 7

The Other Maine: Baseball Up North

Baseball in Maine was a state-wide game. Whether one lived in the more densely populated regions of southern Maine, or one of the smaller communities common across much of northern Maine, baseball provided much of the entertainment and excitement in these small towns during the 1950's and 1960's.

The city of Bangor is the largest city in northern Maine. During the heyday of semi-pro baseball, Bangor was home to the Dow Air Force Base, which fielded a team in the Down East League in the early 1950's. In addition to the Dow Air Force Base team, just across the river from Bangor, the Brewer Bluebirds provided a semi-pro presence, playing primarily an independent schedule against city teams in Bangor, as well as other similar teams located north of Bangor. Additionally, semi-pro teams existed in Houlton, as well as Presque Isle and across the Canadian border, in the many border towns in New Brunswick.

Like their counterparts to the south, the town teams and accompanying leagues began reforming in northern Maine after the war and by the early 1950's, most small communities scattered across the northern reaches of the state had some version of a town baseball team.

No discussion of northern Maine baseball would be complete without making mention of Mattawamkeag and the town teams that originated in this small Penobscot County town. The town of Mattawamkeag, located along the banks of the Penobscot River, is about 70 miles northeast of Bangor, as a crow flies. With the interstate, the trip takes a little more than an hour. During the 1950's, the interstate was nothing but some lines on a blueprint, so the journey took longer, winding its way to the northeast from Bangor along U.S. Route 2.

Prior to the war, the Mattawamkeag Rockets were a powerful club, playing their home games at the Dreamland Pavilion. The Pavilion, located where the Penobscot and Mattawamkeag rivers came together, was a dancehall common during that era. Nearby was the town ballfield, which the Rockets used as their home base.

For men like Dick Lowell, baseball was part of coming of age in a rural community in Maine. As was typical for players like Lowell, he began playing for the Rockets in the early 1940's as a teenager. Lowell played on teams that were made up of men like Herbert Libbey, Sr., whose sons, Herb, Jr., Ken and Dennis would later take their places on the strong Mattawamkeag clubs during the 1960's, coached by Lowell.

"We always had strong teams in Mattawamkeag," said Lowell. "We had very strong teams before the war. After the war, it took time to start the clubs in the area back up, but by the 1950's, baseball was strong again around these parts," he said.

For several years just after World War II, the Eastern Maine League provided a strong contingent of semi-pro ball clubs. Just like semi-pro baseball in the southern and western areas of the state, this area of Maine had the same high quality baseball that was infused with skill and passion. In addition to Mattawamkeag, Eastern Maine League clubs were found in Bangor, Brewer, Millinocket and even north into Houlton.

"We were members of the league until it folded," said Lowell. "After the semi-pro ball died out, then the town teams got strong again and Mattawamkeag played town ball, mostly with an independent schedule—we'd go wherever we could find a game."

****

Herb "Junior" Libbey began playing for the Mattawamkeag Merchants during the 1950's. Libbey grew up watching his father Herb, Sr., play for the local club. Like most young men of his era, the younger Libbey followed in the footsteps of his father and took up the pastime with passion and gusto.

"Growing up in a small town, us boys went to the games in the summer and watched our dads, uncles, and others play," said Libbey. "It was kind of expected that most of us would one day be on the team."

Graduating from Mattawamkeag High in 1951, Libbey was a good enough player to warrant a tryout from the Boston Braves. While the details from a half a century ago are sketchy, Libbey apparently didn't have the desire to travel five or six hours to the south to the big city. While it might be hard to imagine today, major league baseball didn't have the lure, or the promise of riches that it would later acquire. For young men like Libbey, graduating from high school and taking a job in the woods was more secure than spending a couple of seasons chasing a dream for the miniscule salaries that minor leaguers made during that period.

Despite not attending the tryout, Libbey still wanted to play baseball and he joined the Merchants and began his career, quickly becoming one of the team's top sluggers. With Dick Lowell now running the team and aggressively scheduling games wherever he could find an opponent, Mattawamkeag (or 'Keag as they were often referred to by those who followed the local game up north) became known as a team that would travel wherever they could find a game.

"We played games all over the state and even into Canada," said Libbey. "Dick [Lowell] would get us games just about anywhere he could find, trying to get us matched up against the better teams around," he said.

Lowell crafted a strong ball club during the end of the 1950's. It was during the 1960's however that Mattawamkeag began building a legacy that still draws smiles of recognition from former opponents years later. Rarely does the mention of 'Keag not elicit a smile and a nod of the head, as well as respect, from other foes that battled and scrapped against the Merchants, three decades ago.

To veteran players like Junior Tracy from Lamoine, the Mattawamkeag team was one of the best he played against. Playing nearly three decades, Tracy was a key member of the Lamoine A.A. and a Labor Day host of the annual tournaments in Lamoine against the best semi-pro and town teams from across the state. Tracy remembers Mattawamkeag and Herb Libbey well.

"Mattawamkeag had a group of players that could play," said Tracy. "I remember Herb Libbey as being the one guy who always seemed to come up with big hits against us."

Libbey, who batted from the left side of the plate, was equally adept at hitting against both lefties as well as right-handers. Younger brother Dennis remembers his brother batting against former major leaguer Carlton Willey in Lamoine one Labor Day.

"Mattawamkeag was playing Lamoine and trailing by run in the bottom of the ninth. Ronnie Marks singled and stole second," said Libbey. "Lamoine brought in Willey, who could still throw very hard. Herb comes up and on the second pitch, he doubled to the gap in right-center to drive in Ronnie and tie it up," he said. "Mattawamkeag ended up winning it in extra innings, knocking Lamoine out of their own tournament."

Tracy recalls that it was Mattawamkeag that more often than not knocked his Lamoine club out of their own tournament each Labor Day.

"It seemed like every year, Mattawamkeag beat us out," said Tracy. "We never won our own tournament and Mattawamkeag had a lot to do with that," he said.

Both Junior and his brother Ken formed the backbone of a very strong Mattawamkeag team. Junior played third base (and in later years first) and Ken played second. The two Libbey brothers set the competitive tone for the club. Both of them made their living in the woods and spent most of their days engaged in the hard physical work that made up logging. Despite the rigors of their work, the beginning of families and the travel involved in playing ball at the level that Mattawamkeag operated at, the Libbeys played well into their 30s.

Brian Gordon, who now lives in Scarborough and who played many years in Portland's Twilight League, remembers playing for Mattawamkeag during his college years. Gordon, who went to school at the University of Portland-Gorham (now the University of Southern Maine) had a grandmother who lived in East Millinocket. He lived with her summers and worked at the paper mill, in order to pay for school.

"I played ball in Mattawamkeag for four years while I was going to college. Dick Lowell found out I was living with my grandmother and he asked if I wanted to join the team in Mattawamkeag," said Gordon.

Knowing nothing about the nature of the team and its growing legend, Gordon was just looking for a place to play. It wasn't long before he realized that he was in with a special group of players.

"I ended up playing quite a bit of baseball, especially during later years in the Twilight League," said Gordon. "I don't remember a better group of guys, both ability-wise and how they were as people."

Dick Lowell often scheduled the 'Keagers to play five or six games per week. While it would seem natural for men like Herb and Ken Libbey to miss games due to their work, Gordon never remembers that happening in the four years that he played with them.

"We'd often have Dick scheduling games during the morning for that evening," said Gordon. "If he could line up a game, he'd send word out to the various guys in the area. I don't know how he'd get the word to Junior and Kenny, out in the woods, but they'd always be at the field on time," he said.

When Herb Libbey was inducted into the Maine Baseball Hall of Fame in 2004, Gordon told the following story about him that illustrated the drive and desire that men like Herb Libbey had to play baseball.

"Both Junior and Ken Libbey worked in the woods as loggers," said Gordon. "In order to play ball, they would start their day at 2 A.M., getting their first load of pulp into the mill in East Millinocket around 3:30 or 4 A.M. They would then load and deliver loads every three hours or so, until they had their final load on the truck at around four in the afternoon," he said.

"After the game, the brothers would flip a coin and the loser would then have to make the drive down to the mill over winding roads to drop the final load before coming home."

As hard as that is to believe, in light of the modern day diminishment of work ethic and desire, Libbey himself verified the story. In typical Junior Libbey fashion, he downplayed the significance of it, making it seem as if that was the usual price to pay in order to play baseball.

"Ken and I would start our day pretty early on the day of a game," recalled Libbey. "We had to cut a certain amount of pulp, so using our lights, we'd load up the truck and then one of us drove down to the mill while the other rested on the skidder," he said. "We'd take turns until it was time to go to the game."

When asked where the drive and desire to play ball despite hardships and sacrifices came from, Libbey credits his father with passing his love of the game on to his sons.

"My dad played many years. My brothers and I always watched him and I guess we could see how much it meant to him," said Libbey.

Libbey recalls that his father never pushed him or his brothers to play the game. It was just something that they came to naturally.

"My dad never pushed me and my brothers to play," said Libbey. "He was a player and we grew up around baseball. I remember as a kid playing ball as often as I could. I guess it was in our blood."

The elder Libbey differed from some men of his generation in that he recognized the value of sports and never blocked his sons from pursuing that outlet for boyhood energy and aggression. Rather than add obstacles to their pursuit of sports and in particular, baseball, Libbey made sure his boys were able to play, even if it meant sacrifices on his own part.

"There were three of us—Ken and me were older and Dennis was the baby. Ken and I were working summers for my dad during high school. Back then, if we had a game in the summer, my dad would hire a couple of guys to come in and give us the day off, said Libbey. "He'd never allow us to work on the day of a game. We didn't realize what a big deal this was for my dad until Ken and I were older and working on our own."

When asked about that in more detail, emphasizing that this wasn't always the case with fathers and sons, Libbey added the following.

"My dad had a theory about that—he'd say, 'If you two 'fellas want to play, you go ahead. There's 'gonna be a time when you want to play that you won't be able to.'"

"He knew it was 'gonna cost him to hire a couple of guys and if he didn't, he felt it would cost by us not playing, so it was coming out of the same place, cost-wise."

Unlike many town teams who were content to play a 35 or 40 game schedule, Mattawamkeag often played in excess of 55 or 60 games per year. According to Libbey, in 1964, the Merchants ended up playing 75 games that summer. With a schedule that began in May and often would go into mid-September, on average, the team was playing three to four games per week and usually practicing another one or two.

"We all loved to play," said Libbey. "We had a great bunch of players and the guys all got along, as well as their families."

It wasn't unusual for the players to pack up their families in several cars and head off to Canada or drive four hours to the south in Portland, for a weekend trip. Mattawamkeag became regular opponents for Charley Turner's Yarmouth Townies during the mid-1960's, making the four-hour journey southward to the greater Portland area of the state.

"We'd make a trip down to Portland on Friday night and stay in a motel and play a doubleheader against Turner's team on Saturday and then play a Portland team on Sunday, or pick up a game or two as we headed back home," said Libbey.

Obviously, the cost of gasoline, food, and overnight accommodations didn't discourage the players. This became a part of the Mattawamkeag experience for much of the decade of the 1960's.

"We'd find a place along the way after a game for a picnic and all the players and their families would meet up; we just made a day of it when we played," he said.

The 1964 team rattled off several long winning streaks, of 19, 15 and later, 21 games. With a solid pitching staff consisting of Floyd Murphy, Gilbert Arnold and Jerry Hallard, the team had a solid nucleus of starting pitchers. Lowell, in addition to serving as manager, director of personnel and chief scheduler, also occasionally logged innings on the mound, against some of the less rigorous foes that the Merchants would schedule games against.

Murphy never started pitching until he was in his mid-20s. He was friends with several of the players and always came to practices. One day, Lowell put him on the mound and taught him the basics of a windup. Murphy was possessed with natural talent and it wasn't long before the hard-thrower became a regular member of the Merchant rotation.

Arnold was the team's ace and had been good enough to warrant a tryout with the Red Sox. Hallard had spent some time in the Cincinnati Red's farm system, so the Merchants had a talented group of hurlers to go along with a potent offensive attack.

In addition to the Libbey brothers, Ronnie Marks, who caught for the University of Maine, logged the majority of time behind the plate for the Merchants. Dick Barstow played the outfield, along with Ed Leathers. Bob Butler played third base and Barney Smith from Presque Isle, who was good enough to play for Duke University was at shortstop. Later, when the youngest Libbey, Dennis, began playing while still in high school, the two formed a smooth double play combo for the Merchants.

Mattawamkeag's reputation was growing each year. With their wealth of talent and a number of younger players on the team, the baseball coach at the University of Maine, the legendary Jack Butterfield, made regular visits to Taylor Field in Mattawamkeag to watch his own players like Marks, but also to scout young Dennis Libbey. As a result, the youngest Libbey brother ended up being recruited and playing for Butterfield down the road in Orono.

In a case of the rich getting richer, Lowell was able to secure the services of Terry Ordway during the summer of 1964. Ordway, who was recruited by the University of Arizona, where he pitched in 1963 and 1964, ended up solidifying an already strong rotation for the club in 1964. With Ordway, Murphy, Arnold and Hallard, the Merchants had one of the strongest pitching staffs in northern Maine baseball.

Beginning in 1967, Mattawamkeag joined several other towns hosting tournaments at the end of the regular season. Calling their tourney the Blue Ox Tournament in deference to Paul Bunyan's famous oxen was fitting, as this area of the state made its living in the woods. Gathering the best teams from the northern, eastern and central sections of the state, Lowell and Herb Libbey organized a top-notch field for late August.

The Cutler Cardinals made the trek up from the coast, giving the Blue Ox field some quality representation from downeast. Milltown, New Brunswick, a frequent weekend opponent and destination for Mattawamkeag over the years, returned the favor by traveling to the host team's base of operations. Additional members of the first Blue Ox Tournament were the Milbridge Jets, a strong town team, the East Millinocket Ruffians, Mattawamkeag's rivals from up the road, as well as the powerful Guilford Advertisers and the Peter Dana Point ball club. Rounding out the field were the Cambridge A. A. and a team from the Limestone Air Force Base.

For three successive summers, the end of August brought a gathering of talented teams to do battle along the Penobscot and to claim bragging rights for that summer's Blue Ox go-round.

****

The Peter Dana Point Indians were regular participants in the Mattawamkeag tourney. The Indians were one of the few clubs who had success against Mattawamkeag. While the Merchants dominated most of the teams they played during their usual allotment of the 55 to 60 games they regularly compiled each summer, the Merchant/Indian battles were usually evenly matched, with both clubs regularly splitting their regular season match ups against one another.

Gazing at old box scores from the 1960's and through much of the 1970's, it was common to see an abundance of Sockabasins listed as participants for the Indians. On several occasions, as many as seven Sockabasins can be found making up the nine positions in the Indians' batting order.

According to David Sockabasin, his brothers and other relatives loved to play baseball. His younger brothers, Patrick and Clayton were outstanding players, but other family members could also play.

"Most of our players came from the reservation," said Sockabasin. "We had a group of players who loved the game and we either had a game or a practice almost every night of the week."

Both Clayton and Patrick were good enough to be drafted by the Pittsburgh Pirates and ended up playing for their rookie league club in Bradenton, Florida.

"They ended up getting homesick and came home towards the end of the season," said Sockabasin. "It was too bad, because they were both great players."

Local teams will attest to that, as Clayton regularly beat the best teams around, including the Merchants from Mattawamkeag.

"The Socakbasins were all good athletes," said Mattawamkeag's Herb Libbey. "Clayton pitched and Patrick played short. There was another Sockabasin catching," he said. "Clayton was always tough on us."

Clayton and his brother Rayfield regularly formed the Sockabasin battery. With David in center and Patrick at short, this foursome formed the nucleus of a club that was one of the stronger town teams in this part of the state for over a decade. Patrick also pitched and Rayfield was known to shed the "tools of ignorance" behind the plate and take to the mound to log innings for the Peter Dana Point club. Additionally, brother Lawrence Sockabasin was a regular family participant, as well as relatives Eddie and Simon providing a line up favoring the Sockabasin family tree.

The Peter Dana Point itinerary rivaled that of Mattawamkeag's, as the team from the reservation played close to 60 ballgames each summer. Wherever they went, they provided stiff competition to the teams they tangled with.

In 1967, they joined the competitive Quoddy League and during their initial voyage in the loop, battled the perennial Quoddy power, Cutler, down to the final days of the season. With each club winning their final regular season matchups, Cutler and the Indians finished tied for first place at the conclusion of the 1967 campaign.

During the early 1970's, Peter Dana Point continued in the Quoddy League and also became members of the Border League, traveling back and forth across the Maine/New Brunswick border, playing against teams in St. Stephen, Milltown and other province communities, as well as Calais on the Maine side. The duel league affiliations were an indication of just how passionate this group of players were about the game of baseball.

With their strong pitching and a team that played fundamentally sound baseball, Peter Dana Point was always a tough opponent regardless of team, league, or even nation.

According to Sockabasin, "Our team often faced former professional pitchers and would often win, 1-0, or 2-0 against these teams," he said. "If Clayton was on his game for us, we always knew the oppositions weren't going to score many runs. If we got a couple, more often than not we'd win."

During parts of the mid-1970's, Peter Dana Point didn't field a team and both Clayton and Patrick Sockabasin went over to Milltown, New Brunswick, and played for the powerful semi-pro club in that community. Both brothers had first been enticed across the border by Milltown in 1969, when Clayton and Patrick had been enlisted to play for Milltown in the Blue Ox Tournament of that summer in Mattawamkeag.

With softball gaining popularity towards the end of the decade, the Peter Dana Point baseball team made its final appearance in 1980, playing one last season in the Quoddy League.

"Softball became popular and a lot of the guys didn't want to travel," said David Sockabasin. "We were getting older and softball was less of a commitment."

****

According to Loren Ritchie, Guilford's town team formed in 1957. While the town had various incarnations of town teams over the years, this club was the strongest team the town had fielded in a number of seasons.

Ritchie had acquired a teaching position in the area and a group of fellow teachers began talking about putting a team together in the summer. Many of them had played basketball over the winter and found they enjoyed competing together. With not a lot to do in a small Maine town over the summer and a ready-made group of players willing to form a ball club, the Guilford A.A. was formed in the summer of 1957.

For the first couple of summers, the team played an independent schedule, picking up games against Millinocket, Mattawamkeag, Dixmont, and several of the surrounding towns.

"We were a ragtag bunch the first few summers," said Ritchie. "We didn't have a league and we weren't the organized group we would become in later years."

Still, the early Guilford teams created the template for what would later be a formidable ball club, particular during the mid-1960's.

The summer of 1960 found Guilford joining a new circuit in this part of the state. The Central Valley League formed with Guilford, Milo, East Corinth, Lee, Corinna, Sangerville, Charleston Air Force Base and Millinocket.

"It wasn't the greatest league, but we had ourselves a league and some competition," said Ritchie. "Millinocket was a strong club, but most of the towns were not as serious about the game as they were later on."

Guilford was beginning to get stronger each summer. As would become a trademark with them, several teachers were added to the roster each summer.

"We all knew each other from school, or playing basketball and we'd always look to recruit a new teacher or two every year," said Ritchie.

One teacher who had moved north after his days in Rumford and Farmington was Ted Clark. Clark, who had made a name for himself as a star at Stevens High in Rumford and later at Farmington State Teachers College, had landed a teaching and coaching position at Dexter High School in 1962. Adding Clark's bat to the middle of the Guilford batting order gave the team a left-handed power threat that they didn't have up to that point.

Just like during the summer of '49 in Farmington, when he regularly swatted balls over the pine trees in right, Clark found another natural barrier to launch baseballs at. Guilford played their home games at a ball park along the Piscataquis River. It became a common occurrence at Guilford's games for the lanky lefty to drive baseballs and deposit them in the river, located just down the bank behind the fence in right.

"Our park was perfect for Ted," recalls Ritchie. "It had the river directly behind the fence in right and when he pulled a ball, more times than not, it found its way into the Piscataquis."

By the mid-1960's, the Guilford team was known as the Advertisers, as the team's sponsorship was provided by a group of local businesses in town. The Advertisers were now members of the Penquis League, which included a number of strong teams to the north such as Bangor and Brewer. In addition to the Penquis League games, the club traveled many weekends to Mattawamkeag to play, as well as into Aroostook County to do battle with the newly formed Houlton A.A ball club.

"Like many guys from our day, we loved to play ball," said Ritchie. "We were the happiest when we were playing on a ball field."

While the Advertisers were a talented bunch, they also knew how to have fun playing the game. An apt comparison to a professional team might be that of the 1934 St. Louis Cardinals team of Dizzy Dean and Pepper Martin. Just like the appropriately named "Gas House Gang," Guilford was known for their penchant for playing hard and also exhibiting a little zaniness.

Ritchie remembers that his Guilford teammates could be a brutal group, particularly when it came to getting on opposing players. Not intended to be malicious, but just part of the antics that they brought to the ball field, Ritchie recalls one incident involving Joe Sontag, the talented UMaine pitcher, who toed the rubber for the Bangor Merchants.

"We had a real hair-brained bunch of guys," said Ritchie. "We played really hard, but we sure had a great time doing it. We started calling Sontag, 'Maytag.'" We were yelling, 'is he in the spin cycle yet,'" laughed Ritchie. "I remember he got really ticked off at us. The madder he got, the more we got on him, until Bangor had to take him out because he was totally off his game and started walking the ballpark."

The Advertisers' acerbic brand of humor wasn't limited to opponents, either. They could be just as caustic and cutting to their fellow teammates. Ted Clark recalls how Ritchie in left and teammate Dave Gaw in center kept up a running commentary all game long.

"The two of them used to start in when one of us booted a ball or something wasn't going right," said Clark. "They didn't know it, but with the wooden fences, it created an echo and we could hear everything in the infield; boy did we get on them when they came into the bench. Another game, we were playing Dover-Foxcroft. We had already hit about four home runs in the first inning. Loren [Ritchie], Dave [Gaw] and myself had hit one out and probably Barstow [Dick]," said Clark. "We're all flexing our muscles like a bunch of idiots, pissing off the Dover-Foxcroft pitcher, I'm sure. Little Dean Shea played second base for us. He was a great glove man—played for Colby College. Up he comes in the second inning and belts one that just drops over the fence in left. He never hit homers, so he's tickled to death and around third he comes and we're all sitting back to him on the bench, ignoring him," laughed Clark.

The Advertisers were a veritable murderer's row. With hitters, like Clark, Gaw, Ritchie, Dick Barstow and Tom Rowe, it wasn't unusual for the team to hit two or three homers in a game. In 1968, the Advertisers clouted 52 home runs in their 38 games, led by Ritchie's 11.

The 1968 team was the strongest of many very good Guilford ball clubs. The Advertisers had become regular participants in Auburn's Yankee Amateur Baseball Congress tourney, courtesy of the Penquis League's champion receiving an automatic bid to the tourney's post-season field.

Winning the Penquis title in 1966, 1967 and 1968 allowed the team to be a part of the strong field of teams in Auburn in late August. In '66, the Advertisers made it to the YABC title game before bowing out to the Auburn Asas, who went on to the regional tournament in Connecticut.

The 1967 club once again brought a potent nucleus to the tournament only to see their ace, Roger Clapp, beaten twice and once again forcing their elimination from the tourney, this time at the hands of Rumford. Clapp, who had made it to AAA with Hawaii, before being released, had returned home to Milo in June.

A few phone calls later, Clapp had joined the Guilford club, giving them a bonified ace pitcher. While now in his 30s, Clapp could still throw hard and a pitcher of his stature gave the Guilford club a distinct advantage. In addition to Clapp, Guilford also boasted Willie Boynton of Skowhegan, as well as current University of Maine pitcher Darrell Whittemore. Former Black Bear ace Joe Ferris, who had won two games in Omaha in 1964, also was a member of the Guilford rotation.

"We were paying Ferris to come down and pitch for us," said Clark. "With that rotation, plus Dave Gaw could still pitch; we had five frontline pitchers we could put out there."

Everyone that saw Clapp pitch marveled at how smooth the athletic right-hander was. With his compact delivery, impeccable mechanics and a live arm that allowed the ball to explode out of his hand upon release, Clapp is one of the best pitchers to ever toe a rubber in the northern part of the state.

"Clapp made it all look so easy. He had the beautiful mechanics and the ball would jump out of his hand," said Clark. "He seemed like he always had an 0-2 count on the hitter. It's hard to believe he didn't make it to the majors."

Young Mark "Flip" Thompson was just a senior in high school when he received his baptism by fire in catching Clapp. According to Ritchie, Clapp's ball moved so much that he was difficult to catch. Being the veteran pitcher that he was, Clapp had a variety of ways to vary his pressure points on the baseball, which allowed it to move this way and that.

"Poor Flip had to catch Roger, plus he had to deal with us and he was still just a kid," said Ritchie. "I'm sure it was intimidating to him in more ways than one—catching Roger, and having to put up with a bunch of crazy guys," laughed Ritchie. "He adjusted so quickly though and got to be a real good catcher."

Another aspect of young Thompson's involvement with Guilford meant that the guys on the team, at least the ones that Thompson rode to games with, had to exhibit more than their usual level of responsibility.

According to Clark, the Advertisers weren't beyond having a few beers before the game, on their drives to Bangor, Mattawamkeag and other points on their summer itinerary. Certainly, they enjoyed some brews on their way back to Guilford. But when young Thompson was in the car, they toned it down, as he started playing before he was of legal drinking age.

"Whenever Flip was in the car, no one drank," said Clark. "As much as we wanted to, we didn't. We had some morals."

Ritchie echoed what Clark said about meshing the different ages and generations that made up local baseball.

"We took our responsibilities seriously regarding a young player like Flip," said Ritchie. "Now after he graduated and turned 18 and got acclimated a little bit, we let him have some beer, but not before that."

In 1968, Guilford's third trip to Auburn was the charm. Two early round victories over a couple of tough opponents put Guilford in the driver's seat. As had happened in their two previous appearances in 1966 and 1967, Guilford came up against a tough pitcher in their third game. This time they were facing Farmington's Bitsy Ionta. The crafty Ionta kept the powerful Guilford bats at bay just long enough and the Flyers escaped with a hard fought 5-4 victory.

This set up a Sunday elimination game with the powerful Lisbon Falls 88'ers, a perennial YABC tournament team, who won the tourney in 1964 and 1965, as well as being runners-up in 1966. Facing the 88'ers ace left-hander Bob Baumer, the Advertisers were able to parlay timely hitting into a 6-4 victory and live to see another day.

On Sunday, the Guilford bats broke out with a bang, as the Advertisers hammered two tough veterans, Red Dean and Stubby Truman, for 13 hits and 13 runs, including Dave Gaw's grand slam. Gaw finished the day with 7 RBI as Guilford thumped the Farmington Flyers, 13-0.

The victory over Farmington set up a championship game against the host Auburn Asas. Auburn had gotten to the title game by eliminating fellow Northeast League member and Guilford's regular season rival, the Bangor Merchants.

Behind hard-throwing right-hander Willie Boynton, who rode a 14-hit Guilford barrage, the Advertisers were YABC champs for the first time, 11-4. Dave Gaw once again smashed a home run and Ronnie Marks (a play-off roster addition from Mattawamkeag) chipped in with four hits. Boynton helped his own cause by contributing a couple of base hits to the Guilford barrage.

With their victory over a strong Maine field of opponents, it was now on to Albany, New York, for the 1968 regional tournament, with hopes for a birth in the national Amateur Baseball World Series in Battle Creek. While most Maine teams hadn't fared very well since the start of regional play in 1963, because of Guilford's strong pitching and potent offense, there was optimism that this club might have the horses to be the first Maine team to advance to Battle Creek since the start of regional play in 1964.

Having frontline pitching, beginning with Clapp, followed by Boynton and Darrell Whittemore, gave Guilford the kind of starting pitching depth they would need against teams from metro New York City and New Jersey. Each year, a team from Maine, usually from a town of less than 10,000 people, was thrown into a regional tournament with teams that drew from metro areas numbering in the millions. While this might seem unfair, it was the hand that Maine town and semi-pro teams were dealt each September. The hope was that this was the year for David to beat Goliath, if the fun-loving and talented Advertisers had any say in the matter.

The support that the little town of Guilford gave to the team over the season was phenomenal, as over 20 different local businesses from a town of just over 1,000 people made contributions during the season to support the team. In addition to their support, many of these local mom-and-pop businesses made additional contributions, sending the team on its way to Albany.

The decision was made to start Whittemore over Clapp and Boynton in the tournament's opener against Finkle's Jewelers, the host team from Albany, New York. The Thursday evening game, played in-between intermittent showers, saw the Jewelers' Jerry Anson shut down the high-powered Advertisers' offense, scattering three hits over the seven-inning tournament format. Anson supplied both the pitching and hitting, as he chipped in with two singles and a double to lead the Albany Twilight League Club to a 6-3 victory over Guilford.

While being in the loser's bracket is a tough place to recover from in a double-elimination tournament, Guilford had their ace, Roger Clapp, well-rested and ready to challenge the powerful Metro Stars of New York City.

Things got off to a promising start in the first when, with one out, Marks drove a single to right. On the second pitch from the Stars' Ken Clark, Marks was off to second with a successful stolen base attempt. This would be the first of four steals in the game for the speedy Marks. Dave Gaw drove a ball into left center and the Advertisers were out to a 1-0 lead.

Clapp was on his game as he held a line up stacked with many top college players to only two hits. Unfortunately, they both came in the fourth, when a walk, an error and a double and single pushed across two runs. Guilford wasn't able to generate any additional offense of any significance against Clark, as the underdogs from Maine were once more two games and out in the regional tournament.

The 1968 season became the town of Guilford's swan song in local baseball. After the season, several of the key players moved away from the greater-Guilford area. With the age of many on the team on the downhill side of 30, softball was becoming increasingly attractive. The shorter games, as well as the less taxing nature of softball all contributed to the loss of another town from the roster of town team baseball.

Guilford's run as a town team power was a relatively short one compared to many clubs, but for over a decade, particularly the last five or six years, the Advertisers were a force to be reckoned with in northern Maine baseball circles. With the demise of baseball in Guilford, local baseball had lost one of its most fun-loving and competitive teams to the cultural changes taking place in communities across the state and elsewhere. With so many more choices and options of things to do, local baseball was losing its battle with the competition.

****

Nestled just in between Waterville and Bangor is a cluster of communities that epitomized town team baseball in the central valley regions of the state during the 1950's and into the 1960's. Small Maine towns such as Dixmont, Brooks, Hermon and Monroe all fielded teams during most of the two decades that saw local baseball flourish in the smaller communities of the state. Like

Dixfield in western Maine, Cutler and Lamoine along Maine's down eastern coastal areas, as well as Mattawamkeag to the north, these rural locales had their own distinctive contributions to add to the tapestry that comprises Maine's baseball heritage.

Dixmont was a farming community located on Route 7, about ten miles south of the Interstate. Prior to this high-speed, post-war transformation of automobile travel, U.S. Route 202 passed through the center of town and brought a steady stream of traffic through the center of town. Dixmont, like many similar towns along the thoroughfare, had been a viable stopover along this transportation artery. As a result, the small town square maintained a vitality that would disappear with the arrival of Eisenhower's post-war vision to unite the entire country via an inter-connected system of federal highways. After the arrival of the interstate in Maine, Dixmont and other centers of commerce began a downward spiral leading to the demise of much of what had been rural America prior to World War Two.

To the residents of these small towns, the years following the war still held out hope of a brighter future. The local baseball team provided the town with a central unifying element each and every summer. Beginning in the late 1950's, the Central Maine League formed and along with the Seacoast League further south, provided this rural area of the state with some quality baseball.

Sawin Millett moved to Dixmont in 1946, at the age of nine. His father, a teacher, had moved his family from Eliot to Dixmont, due to the acquisition of a better teaching opportunity in Bangor. It was this tiny community of Dixmont, with its population of about 500 residents that Millett would become associated with over the next 29 years of his life.

When Millett was old enough to go to high school, his father had become principal at the nearby Carmel High School. While

Carmel High was a very small school, it was one of a number of small high schools that populated rural communities all over the state. In later years, Carmel would become a victim of school consolidation. During Millett's time however, it was a great place to receive a quality education and also to play competitive sports. This small Maine high school prepared the young Millett well, as he later attended Bates College in Lewiston, where he excelled both academically and athletically.

"Dixmont didn't have its own high school," said Millett. "They sent kids anywhere they could. Dixmont didn't bus its high school students, we went wherever we could get a ride. Since my father was going that way, we went with him," he said.

Millett was the oldest of five siblings, all boys. Three of his brothers attended Carmel High, with his youngest brother, David, graduating from Hermon High School after Carmel closed in 1962.

Like many young men coming to the nation's pastime, Millett got his initiation to baseball at a young age. His first memories are of going to practices as a preschooler with his father, then the baseball coach at Traip Academy.

"He used to take me to practices in Eliot at Traip Academy and I just became enamored with the sounds and smells of baseball," said Millett. "Watching infield practice and seeing the ball hit around and the smell of the horsehide and so on, I was addicted before I started school."

Millett was aware of a town team in Dixmont when he moved there in 1946. He recalled that the team appeared to be made up of older men, men in their early-to-mid-30s, all of them with families. When he moved there in June, he and his family went to a number of games over the summer and this is where young Millett met youngsters who would later became his own baseball teammates.

"The next summer, my father started a four town/four team league called the C-E-N-D League, for Carmel, Etna, Newburgh and Dixmont," said Millett. "This was a youth league that was probably for the ages of nine to 13 or 14, so it was probably Little League and Babe Ruth level."

After high school, Millett journeyed two hours to the south to the manufacturing city of Lewiston, where Bates College was located. Millett enjoyed his four years of higher education at Bates, where he was able to excel in both baseball and football with the Bobcats. During this period of college, Millett returned home each summer to his parents dairy farm, where his toiled with the Dixmont Townies in the Central Maine League.

The Central Maine League was comprised of teams in Brooks, Hampden, Veazie, Charleston Air Force Base, as well as Dover-Foxcroft and Hartland forming the bedrock teams of the league. From the late 1950's until the mid-1970's, this league was a summer mainstay of the town team circuit in Maine. Despite Dixmont's small size, the Townies consistently won the league championship, with a string of four straight crowns from 1962 through 1965.

One of the characteristics of town team ball in Dixmont, as well as a number of small communities, is the role that families had in the game. With the games on the local diamonds being the focus, Sunday in towns like Dixmont saw players, as well as their families, descending on the local ball field, often several hours before the games.

"My wife and kids were as much a part of my playing as I was," said Millett. "Sunday baseball was a daylong event—you'd take the family with you to the field. I'd mow the grass, rake the infield. My wife would be setting up the concession stand with hot dogs and soda," he said.

Other Sundays, when the Dixmont team traveled, families would load up the car and head off to surrounding towns. Often on open dates, such as a Saturday, they'd travel up north to Mattawamkeag, or down the coast to Lamoine. There were even times when they'd play at two different locations on a given day.

"I remember one Sunday when Don Hanscom [Millett's long-time Dixmont teammate] and I scheduled a noontime game with a strong Brewer club in Brewer," said Millett. "They had Joe Ferris [former University of Maine star on the mound] and we beat them 9-1 behind Don's pitching and then we drove immediately to Lamoine and I threw a shutout. That was quite an experience; we beat two very good teams."

Traveling to Lamoine during the 1960's was a treat due to the beautiful field that local baseball benefactor Gifford Cochrane had built. With its well-maintained infield, ample seating and tough competition provided by the local team, opponents from small towns like Dixmont enjoyed traveling for weekend contests with Lamoine.

"I remember Jack Scott hitting rockets down to short and fielding them on a nice infield with a true hop, like Lamoine, or Garland Street in Bangor," said Millett.

The Dixmont home field wasn't as glorious, as it was typical of many of the fields that characterized baseball of the small town variety. According to Millett, the Dixmont ball park was not a great field. With its dirt infield and outfield sloping downhill towards Route 7, it offered plenty of open space for baseball, but it wasn't much above a cow pasture. Despite its perfunctory purpose, it was where Dixmont played its games for nearly 20 years.

"Most of the fields we played on were not great fields by any means," said Millett. "It wasn't just mowing the grass, it was picking rocks out of the infield and baselines."

The cost of running a town team during the 1950's and 1960's wasn't insignificant. From paying umpires, maintaining a sufficient supply of baseballs, purchasing new equipment to replace old and worn equipment, as well as the wooden bats that the teams used up until the 1970's and the advent of metal and aluminum bats, each town team had to have some source of revenue. For Dixmont, it was the concession stand that Millett and his wife maintained over the years. In addition to organizing a team and making sure that he had 13 to 15 players on his roster, to scheduling the games each summer, going to league meetings, as well as doing field maintenance and then lugging the hotdogs, soda and chips to set up the concession, it's amazing that men like Millett still found the energy, let alone the time to play. And play he did from his days during high school, through college and then after his graduation from Bates in 1959, until well into the mid-1970's, Millett was one of the key players for the Dixmont Townies. From his regular turns as one of Dixmont's top pitchers, to the games where he manned the hot corner and batted in the middle of the Dixmont line up, Millett and the speedy Don Hanscom came to personify baseball in this small Maine town. While Millett played until he was 40, Hanscom played even later, until he was 52 years old. Playing alongside his two sons, Alan and Lance, the Hanscom family along with the Milletts—Sawin and his brothers Dick (the oldest), Addison and Dave (the youngest)—kept baseball in Dixmont a family-oriented sport.

"I can still remember Don Hanscom pitching for Dixmont when I was just a kid," said Millett. "Don was still playing when I retired. That guy played until he was 50 and could still outrun most of the kids—he was incredible," he marveled.

In addition to these two primary families, the Reed brothers (Charlie and Roger) from Bangor, several Hampden Academy players, Bob Erskine, as well as Clint Van Aiken were key players for Dixmont for much of their 20-year run as a ball club.

Looking back at his experience of playing baseball at the grassroots level, Millett is still amazed at the variety and diversity of the players who made up town team baseball. The rosters of all of these teams were made up of men from all walks of local life. From farmers and other manual laborers, to teachers and other professionals, local baseball crossed all the social and economic barriers of life in Maine's small and not-so-small communities.

When asked about some of the things that stand out in his mind about town team ball, Millett thought for a moment and then rattled off an insightful portrait of baseball at the local level.

"My first impression was the variety of backgrounds of the people who played," he said. "You had farmers who would leave their tasks and often their hay in the field on Sunday to come and play. You knew that these men weren't getting any exercise in a sporting sense other than baseball, yet, they would come and play for us. Then you had the younger players, who were in college and at the peak of their athleticism. It was the love of the game that brought people to play even though they were busy and involved in earning a living."

One of the aspects that stand out in Millett's mind is the family component of the local game; how baseball was passed down generation to generation. He mentioned the Hanscoms and both father and son playing together. Millet's own experience of learning the love of the game from his father and then seeing himself and his brothers playing together were part of this family tapestry that comprised the game at the community level.

"There were fathers playing when I first started watching, and then our generation played and then later, the grandchildren would end up playing," said Millett.

Millett cannot recall playing a game when his wife and children didn't accompany him. Loading up the cars and traveling off to a nearby town is part of the memories and nostalgia that comprised the games and leagues all over the state. One of these semi-regular road trip destinations was Mattawamkeag. Millett remembers games in Mattawamkeag at Taylor Field, doing battle against Dick Lowell's strong Merchant teams.

"We'd load up the cars and there would be a caravan headed up the interstate or down Route 7 for a Sunday doubleheader. Even during the weeknight games there would always be a good contingent accompanying us to our games," said Millett.

All of this began to wind down by the middle years of the 1970's. Millett was now the state's commissioner of education and still running the team in 1976. In 1977, Millett had moved to Waterford in Oxford County, where he and his wife had built a new house. Waterford was two and a half hours from Dixmont, yet Millett continued to play in Dixmont with his oldest son that summer.

After Millett made the decision to end his playing days in Dixmont, the team continued for another two years, but with the dawning of the 1980's, baseball in Dixmont was dead, as it was in almost all of the neighboring towns surrounding this Maine community.

With baseball's demise in Guilford, then Mattawamkeag and eventually Dixmont, another chapter in Maine's local baseball history slammed shut. As men like Sawin Millett, Dick Lowell, Herb Libbey, Don Hanscom and others got too old or too busy to continue playing or running their local ball clubs, the game dried up and disappeared from the local ball diamonds across northern Maine.

Baseball managed to maintain a presence in and around Bangor during the 1980's, but it was merely a shell of its former self. Like the local town square, grange hall and country store, baseball faded into the memories of its former players and became just another bit of nostalgia from a bygone era.

Chapter 8

The Summer of '69: A Season to Remember

As the decade was coming to a close in 1969, upheaval and conflict seemed to be the operative word. Whether it was on the home front and the battles in the streets of many U.S. cities, or the war raging in Indochina, the end of the decade offered a sense of impending changes.

The local baseball team had been part and parcel of community life in Maine for over half a century, with its present post-war revival going strong for nearly three decades with the ending of the conflict in Europe. While baseball continued to flourish in many areas of the state, some of the smallest towns had experienced a withering of interest in the nation's pastime. Baseball in many of the communities of Maine was still firmly planted, but it had been uprooted in other places, however. One could still find a game taking place on most nights of the week, however. Driving from the southernmost tip of the state, to any point north, with detours east and west, brought the traveler across a ballgame played by the local town team in many places across the Pine Tree State.

Despite the popularity and longevity of the local game, cracks were beginning to appear in the walls of continuity comprising baseball in some of the smaller communities. During the 1960's, baseball began disappearing from places where it had been commonplace for decades—towns such as Dixfield, West Minot, Poland, Lubec and Guilford—had all recently experienced the loss of a formerly vital town baseball team. In some cases, like in Dixfield for instance, it was from lack of interest. Other times, the local team had gotten too old to compete at the higher level required of most of Maine's town team leagues. Without an infusion of younger reinforcements ready to step forward and take the places of the retiring diamond warriors, teams withered and died, which is what happened to local baseball in a town such as West Minot. In other parts of the state, traditional local industries began to dry up, such as the sardine plants along the downeastern coast of Maine and the Lubec area in particular. Even a town like Guilford, which had won the state Yankee Amateur Baseball Congress championship and had represented Maine in the regional tournament in Albany, New York, in 1968, found that 1969 spelled the end of a 12-year run of strong teams in that Piscataquis County town.

Still, baseball was alive and well in many places, where passion and fire for the local team burned brightly. On a Wednesday or Friday night in Portland, the crack of wood on cowhide and the slap of leather still resounded from Portland's lighted diamond at Deering Oaks Park, or the historic ballpark at Portland Stadium. In addition to the Twilight League's Portland-based clubs, North America's oldest semi-pro league had teams based outside the city. Charlie Turner's Yarmouth Townies could be found taking on league and non-league foes up the Interstate at Bennett Field in Yarmouth. Bernal Allen's Ametek Redskins made their stand across the Casco Bay Bridge in South Portland. If you found yourself in Auburn on an early June evening, you would be one of several hundred fans sitting under the hum of the artificial light falling from atop Pettengill's wooden light poles. Two hours to the north, Garland Street Field in Bangor would yield a game pitting the previous season's undefeated Bangor Merchants taking on fellow Northeastern League foes such as Mattawamkeag, Orono, or East Millinocket. A drive down the coast to Cutler would allow you to witness ageless Neil Corbett coaching third, imparting the wisdom of four decades of local baseball to his younger Cardinal players, as local diehards munched hotdogs and drank soda pop, with that evening's ballgame providing the perfect ending, after a day of physical labor on the water.

****

When Amel Kisonek formed the Lisbon Falls Merchants in 1963, he never envisioned that the team would become a fixture of town team baseball in Androscoggin County and beyond. For the 88'er players like Bob Baumer, Stan Doughty, Marty Roop and Dave Moulton, 1969 would be their seventh season playing together. Many of these men had played together even prior to the formation of the present team in town. Adding to the veteran depth of the team was Steve Karkos, all-CBB outfielder from Bates College, as well as Tom Fortin, who caught on the University of Maine at Orono Frosh team in 1969. Both Karkos and Fortin had been on-again-off-again players with the 88'ers since 1965, when both were still in high school.

While the continuity of the 88'ers core group of players gave them an advantage on the side of experience, several of the players were now in their thirties, including Doughty, the long-time town team and former semi-pro player, now approaching 36 years-old.

Baumer was no longer the hard-throwing lefty he had once been. What he had become was a crafty left-hander at 33. In addition to some of the concerns about the 88'ers age, was the strength and viability of the Auburn Rec League.

The 88'ers had been cornerstones of the league (formerly known as the Andy County League) since forming in 1963. The spring league meeting only had attendees from three clubs, which meant that without a fourth member, the Auburn Rec League would go the way of other leagues that had recently folded. With as many as eight teams filling league slots as recently as 1965, scrambling to find four teams was a new experience for Commissioner Norris Ingersoll. The league had offered one of the area's great rivalries, pairing the perennially strong 88'ers against their foes up Route 4, the Turner Townies. In addition, the Twin Cities of Lewiston and Auburn had seen teams in both communities fielding strong clubs, which gave the league a solid depth of teams through the middle years of the decade. With Lewiston's exit in 1966 and the death of baseball in smaller towns such as West Minot and Poland, as well as Mechanic Falls' departure to the Pine Tree circuit, the Rec League was barely hanging on in the latter years of the 1960's. Certainly its perennial champ, the 88'ers of Lisbon Falls, would be welcomed into any league, but it was hoped that a fourth team could be found before June.

The entrance of Bath into the Rec League mix essentially saved the league. This gave the Rec League the four teams necessary to have a league. While Bath didn't quite have the horses to compete for the title, they provided a competitive club that was capable on certain nights of giving the other three teams all they could handle. Geographically, it was a passable driving distance, as even the Turner-to-Bath drive wasn't much more than an hour.

For almost a decade, the Turner Townies and Roberts 88'ers had waged warfare against one another each summer. For much of this decade, the 88'ers held the upper hand, which had become particularly grating to the Townies. With a roster made up of above-average town team players, as well as some stars of the local game, the Townies were always in the running for a league title. Each season however, regardless of how well they played, they always managed to hit the wall with a thud when they came up against the 88'ers.

Summer after summer, the 88'ers swept the season series against Turner, at one point beating their rivals 15 consecutive times over a three-year span during the mid-1960's. With left-handed hurler Bob Baumer winning 11 of those games, the Townies didn't have a lot of fondness in their hearts for their foes from the Falls.

The Townies finally had broken through during 1968 and managed an early season win over their fierce rivals from Lisbon. Amazingly, they won a second match up later in the summer, also.

In June of 1969, it appeared as though there were beginnings of a shift in power between rivals. Not only did Turner take a key early season match between the teams, but pitcher Cal Gammon shut down the usually potent 88'ers offense, holding them without a hit until two outs in the bottom of the seventh. With two strikes on the 88'er's Billy Carroll, Gammon left the ball in the middle of the plate and the Amherst College star ripped a single to center. Gammon got the final out and ended up with a seven-inning gem, as the Townies sent an early season message to the 88'ers, 2-0.

There were some rumblings in Lisbon Falls about the local boys, with baseball fans voicing concerns that this summer's club might be getting a bit old. A week prior to their loss to Turner, the 88'ers had experienced one of their worst losses of recent memory, falling by a 13-6 count to non-leaguers Norway-Paris. In this one, ace Bob Baumer was uncharacteristically cuffed around over four innings by the potent Twins' bats, giving up 10 hits over four rounds before an early exit.

The concern in Lisbon Falls was premature however, as the 88'ers began to blend their usual potent brew of hitting, defense and pitching and parlayed that into a 10-game winning streak before veterans Gerry Henry of Turner and Baumer of Lisbon matched up in Turner in early July. Unlike previous summers when it seemed an automatic win for the 88'ers when these two clubs got together, the Townies again beat their fiercest rivals, this time by a tight 3-2 score. Both Henry and Baumer showed why they were considered the aces of their respective staffs. Henry limited the 88'er bats to a mere three singles, while Baumer scattered six safeties. The difference was a Tink Kilbreth two-run blast in the fourth with Ken Additon aboard. Kilbreth, who a decade earlier had been a member of the powerful Auburn Asas semi-pro combine, was nearing the end of his playing days. The wily infielder got the better of this match up between two long-time combatants. For Turner, this second win gave them hope, but they still were in their characteristic position of being second, looking up at the 88'ers above them in the Rec League standings.

The predictions of demise for the Roberts 88'ers were a bit premature. Like many older teams, the 88'ers took longer to round into shape than some of the opposition clubs that were comprised of younger college players. While the 88'ers certainly had some talented younger players in Carroll, Fortin, as well as Karkos, the veterans like Baumer, Doughty, Moulton and Roop took longer to round into shape. Many of the first few games that the 88'ers played in late May and early June were the first competition the older players had seen since the previous September.

Despite the 88'ers slow start out of the gate and two losses to Turner, by July their 11-3 record had them a full two games in front of the second place Townies. The club's nucleus of veterans such as Baumer, Doughty, Moulton, Roop and Dave Pedersen had been together for five or six seasons. In addition, Karkos, who started with the 88'ers while going to Bates, stayed with them after graduation. Forming a core of players that provided pitching from the likes of Baumer, Roop and Pedersen, offense from Doughty, speed from Karkos, as well as steady defense and the important utility role and timely hitting from Moulton off the bench as a fourth outfielder gave the 88'ers a solid core upon which to build each summer's team around.

For Roop, who came to Lisbon Falls after graduating from Bowdoin College in 1958, playing ball for the 88'ers was something special. From his first season with the team in 1963, as a hard-throwing, if somewhat wild right-hander, who provided an able second starter behind Baumer, to his last year in 1969 when he decided to play one last season with the team, Roop recalls the special group of players who made up the club in Lisbon Falls. Hailing from Millinocket, he had played town team ball against some of the best players in northern Maine before going off to college. After school, he found a job at the Worumbo Mill in the early 1960's. Putting down roots in Lisbon Falls, which became his adopted home, Roop was a mainstay on the team through the remainder of the decade.

"Amel Kisonek put together the team in 1963," said Roop. "We were kind of a rag-tag bunch that first year, but each season, we got stronger."

In Roop's estimation, the 1964 88'ers team that won two games in Connecticut before getting knocked out of the regional tournament was the best team he played on.

"The 1964 team was a very good team," said Roop. "We had a good club, with Stan [Doughty], Bobby [Baumer], Begos [Dave], and Whitman [Herbie]; as good a group of players that you'll find in town team ball."

Roop remembers Doughty as being a talented player who could hit any type of pitching. He also remembers him for his knowledge of the game.

"Stan knew more about baseball than any player I'd ever been around," said Roop. "In Millinocket, we had Jim DiFrederico [who had played for the Augusta Millionaires] and he was a knowledgeable guy, but Stan was just so smart around the game," he said.

After 1965, Roop no longer pitched, as he had injured his arm. Filling the role of backup catcher, Roop still was able to contribute by spelling the regular catcher during doubleheaders, as well as providing a veteran right-handed bat off the bench.

"I almost didn't play in 1966. I had a family and I thought I was getting too old to play, but Bobby [Baumer] asked me to play that season and looking back, I'm glad he did. I ended up playing four more seasons before I retired at the end of 1969."

Roop remembers that he didn't play a lot the last few seasons. With young Fortin doing most of the catching, he provided a veteran presence that all successful teams require. Filling a role of backup, pinch hitter, and spot starter, Roop relishes the summers that he did play.

"I had a lot of fun those last few summers that I played," he said. "While I didn't play a lot, it was fun to be around the camaraderie of the game."

On the first Sunday in August, the 88'ers clinched their sixth consecutive Auburn Rec baseball title, with an 8-2 win over Bath. Doughty's two-run double and Fortin's two-run homer were all

Baumer needed, as he ran his record to 7-2 on the summer with a three-hitter. By clinching the Rec League title, the 88'ers would once again be participants in the annual YABC affair at Pettengill Park.

****

The towns of Norway-Paris had fielded local ball teams for as long as any of the old-timers could remember. A perennial upper tier town team in whatever league they found themselves in, their 1960 team was still talked about. The Norway-Paris Twins of that summer had been the only Maine team that ever won three games in the National Amateur Baseball Congress Tournament, held annually in Battle Creek, Michigan.

In 1960, young Leon "Stubby" Truman was just out of high school and didn't make the journey to Battle Creek with the team that summer. With its roster loaded with veterans of town team battles going back two decades or more, the young Truman would have to wait another season to begin making his mark on the mound for the Twins.

Over the next eight years, Truman would establish himself as the pitcher that became synonymous with Twins baseball. By 1969, Truman had established himself as one of a handful of veteran hurlers that knowledgeable observers could tick off when the subject of town team baseball came up.

The 1969 Norway-Paris club was a very capable ball team. By now, the Twins had become fixtures in the Pine Tree League, after several summers in the rival Andy County League in the early part of the decade. The Pine Tree League now consisted of an East and West division of four teams each, with Norway-Paris, a perennial first-or-second-place club in the Western division of a league that had been in existence since the early 1920's.

With Amherst College shortstop Barry Roderick gobbling up any grounder he could get to, as well as his third-base partner on the left side of the infield, Wayne Kuvaja, the Twins had two of the better ballplayers on any roster in the state. Kuvaja was the starting third baseman at the University of Maine at Orono and a dangerous hitter. Roderick, who his college coach and former Norway resident Bill Thurston called, "The best shortstop I've ever coached," would later play five years in the Minnesota Twins system, ending at the AAA level before returning to Maine. Rounding out the Twins line up was long-time Twins second baseman Bobby Gammon, catcher Don Guilford and former West Minot star, Bill Clough. Dave Burnham provided a right-handed counterweight on the mound that summer to the portside slants of Truman.

In baseball, no-hitters are the rarest of feats. Regardless of how strong and dominating a pitcher might be, even the most overmatched of hitters will often bloop a hit, or beat out a scratch single in the infield. To throw a no-hitter requires skill of course, but a bit of luck is also required.

During early August of 1969, Truman was involved in the rarest of feats when he threw his second consecutive no-hitter of the summer, as the Twins shut out the Mechanic Falls Merchants. In his previous start earlier in the week, Truman had employed his knuckle-ball drop pitch to baffle and befuddle the Rangeley Lakers in hitless whitewash. Just like Johnny Vander Meer's back-to-back no-hitters in the big leagues in 1939, Truman's consecutive gems stand out as one of the great performances in town team baseball history.

While Truman didn't know it at the time, he would continue to play town team baseball throughout the next decade, part of the following decade and, as if that wasn't enough, would conclude a storied career at the age of 52, in 1993, playing for the West Paris team with his son Lee.

With any nickname, there's a story behind where it came from. Truman's nickname, "Stubby," became the baseball moniker that he would forever be known by when it was assigned to him back in 1956. As a 15-year-old high school freshman, Truman had hopes of making that spring's Norway High School baseball team. He and fellow freshman, Blinn Thurston, were both southpaws and eager to impress the high school coach, Tom Reynolds.

"We were both young bucks trying to do whatever it took to impress Reynolds and make the team," said Truman. "Whenever he'd call out, 'hey lefty, come here,' we'd both sprint over to him, panting."

In order to put an end to the confusion and eliminate the need for both players being in the coach's face whenever he yelled for a "lefty," Reynolds assigned nicknames.

"Reynolds said to us, 'listen (looking at me), I'm going to call you Stubby,'" said Truman. "He looked at Blinn and said, 'I'm going to call you Spider,'" laughed Truman. "My nickname just stuck and to this day, people who know me from baseball know me as Stubby."

The young lefty forever known as Stubby, ended up impressing Reynolds enough to make the team and contributed a couple of wins as a freshman rookie. This would be the start of a successful high school career where he set records for wins and other pitching statistics. Over his four years at Norway High, Truman ended up with 18 wins, which is an exceptional number of wins to have due to Maine's limited high school schedules.

When asked about his success as a pitcher, Truman offered the following thoughts about his pitching style. Truman admits that he wasn't a hard thrower. Like many town team pitchers of the era, their success was due to a combination of guile, guts, and knowledge of pitching.

"Phil Martin [long-time Twilight Leaguer and Truman's former Norway-Paris teammate] showed me how to throw the knuckle-ball drop," said Truman. "You'd throw the pitch and it would come dancing in and then at the last minute, it would drop down or dart to the side. I didn't throw very hard, but because I threw that pitch, when I did come back with a fastball, it looked like a 90-mile-per-hour pitch," he said.

"Most of the pitchers from my time—Bob Baumer in Lisbon, Bitsy Ionta from Rumford—we were guys that knew how to pitch—Bob (Baumer) and Bitsy were all about location, location, location," said Truman. "I could throw the knuckle-ball drop at any time; I could tell the hitter it was coming and they still couldn't hit it," laughed Truman.

Truman's Norway-Paris teams bounced back-and-forth between the Auburn Recreation League, with perennially powerful clubs such as the Lisbon Falls 88'ers and the Turner Townies, and the Pine Tree League, with rivals such as Bethel, Rumford and Farmington. The Twins were always one of the area's strongest teams. Truman hooked up with some of the top pitchers locally in some classic duels.

"Bob Baumer and I had some great match ups," said Truman. "I was one of the few guys that could beat him. It seemed like every time we played each other, it was a 1-0, or a 2-1 game," he said. "I remember those 88'ers teams—Bob [Baumer], Marty Roop, Stan Doughty, Larry McIver—they were a tough team."

Over a career that spanned three decades, Truman compiled an amazing total of 252 wins. His career earned run average was a miniscule 1.33 runs per nine innings. With his number of wins, low earned run average and surprising number of strikeouts for a pitcher who didn't throw hard, Truman stands out as one of town team baseball's great pitchers. Add to that a career that saw him toss 10 career no-hitters and you have a pitcher who may have accomplished something that no other local pitcher ever has. With record-keeping uneven at best, it's hard to know what the record is for no-hit games for town team or even semi-pro baseball. Regardless of what the record might be, Truman's 10 no-hitters put him in a category with few other ballplayers who toiled on Maine's diamonds of long ago.

****

The arrival of the 1969 campaign saw Portland's Twilight League entering its 67th year of operation. Not only was the league the oldest league of its type in Maine, it was also considered the oldest in North America. Every summer for nearly seven decades, the Twilight League gathered the best talent from Portland and surrounding areas and offered the baseball fans of southern Maine a quality product.

With six teams slated for play in 1969, including long-time rivals Ametek Inc. (South Portland) and the Yarmouth Townies, the league expected another summer of heated contests and competition for the annual Twilight crown. In addition to Yarmouth and South Portland, Yudy Elowitch's Yudy's Tiremen were back, along with the Haverty Buick Wildcats, the Scarborough Merchants and the Falmouth Townies.

The league opened their season on Sunday, June 8th, with dual ceremonies at the Portland Stadium and at Bennett Field in Yarmouth. In Portland, league chairman and Ametek player/manager Bob Philbrick, presented trophies to the previous season's home run champion, Fred Stone, batting champion Brian Swasey, outstanding pitcher Bob Curry and league Most Valuable

Player, Dave Sprague. The legendary Merv Kilgore, who played in the league for over three decades, threw out the ceremonial first pitch.

When some of Portland's long-time baseball fans saw Kilgore, there was talk that the perennial league batting champ must be planning yet another comeback.

Just up the road and 10 minutes away, town manager Dick Blanchard threw out the first pitch prior to Yarmouth's opening contest versus the league's newest team, the Scarborough Merchants. Nearly 500 fans turned out for the picture perfect Sunday afternoon of baseball. In Yarmouth, any time Charlie Turner's chargers were at home, you could be sure several hundred local baseball fans would be in attendance.

As expected, the league race would be hotly contested between the usual frontrunners, Yarmouth and Ametek. The Ametek Redskins ran off five consecutive wins to open the 1969 campaign, but Yarmouth stayed right on their heels. It had been agreed upon before the start of the season that there would be two halves to the season, the first half consisting of 10 games and the second half, a 15-game slate. The winner of the first half would play the second half champion in a best-of-three series to determine the eventual champion. With previous year's controversies fresh in everyone's minds, it was wise to agree upon a format prior to the season in order to determine a champion. While that might seem obvious for any league to make those decisions beforehand, in the Twilight League, that wasn't always the case. The 1967 season and the controversy surrounding South Portland's win, ending Yarmouth's reign as champion, is an example of what happens when the rules aren't clear from the beginning, particularly in the competitive Twilight League.

With Ametek sitting atop the standings with an 8-1 record, courtesy of their 4-2 win over the Haverty Wildcats on the first Sunday of July, it appeared they would win the first half title, particularly if they could win the continuation of the 2-2 game the following evening versus Yudy's. Yarmouth was at 6-2, with two games remaining, including an important tilt, also against the Tiremen. As is par for the course in any scenario involving teams from Yarmouth and South Portland, assumptions are dangerous to hold.

Yudy's, behind Steve Mazziotti, edged Ametek and their ace, Rod Choroszy, 3-2. Meanwhile, the Townies nipped Yudy's the following night, 4-3, and then pummeled Scarborough on the strength of Bobby Doyle's three hits and Terry Hadlock's three-run homer; Final score, Yarmouth 12 and Scarborough 3. Both Yarmouth and Ametek finished the first half with identical 8-2 marks and were crowned co-champs of the first half.

Dave Sprague of Ametek, the previous season's MVP, picked right up where he left off in 1968, as he was leading the league in hitting through the third week in July. Sprague, a Springfield College prospect, was stroking the ball at a cool .421 clip, 40 points better than the second hitter on the list, Ron Bernier of Yarmouth.

Yarmouth's top two moundsmen, Billy O'Brien and Gary Hobbs, led the circuit in winning percentage with 5-0 and 4-1 records respectively. Rod Choroszy, Ametek's talented young right-hander, carried a 5-2 record and was leading the league in strikeouts with 64 in only 41 innings. Choroszy had bunched 18 of them in his July 20 gem over Yudy's, in which he twirled a complete game six-hitter over the Tiremen.

As could be expected, with the arrival of the dog days of August, Yarmouth and Ametek were once again neck-in-neck atop the Twilight standings as the second half season came to a halt.

Both teams were sitting at 11-4, with Haverty Buick making a valiant push to finish just one half game back, with a 10-5 mark.

While the Tiremen finished a distant third in the standings, they once again played a key role in the battle for the top spot in the race. With an 11-3 mark and the opportunity to win the second half championship outright, the Townies faced the 5-8 Yudy's Club in a Monday match up at Deering Oaks. On a typically humid August evening, 1,000 fans jammed the fences along the Oaks' pristine baseball amphitheatre for this key match up. Billy O'Brien took his undefeated 7-0 mark into the contest against Yudy's Rollie Mastroluca. While O'Brien, the former Chevrus High and Boston College curve baller, had received more ink than Mastroluca, the wily former Portland High righty was well-respected by league hitters.

Yudy's reached O'Brien for a second inning run, courtesy of a walk to Batchelor, a wild pitch and Doug Drobeck's single. In the top half of the third, a Buddy Graffam single, Bill Welch's double and Buster Pompeo's single plated two more, as the Tiremen were now up 3-0 against the Yarmouth ace.

In the bottom half of the inning, Terry Hadlock crushed a hanging curve from Mastroluca over the snowfence in center, to cut the margin to 3-1. That would be it for scoring, as both pitchers finished with 6-hitters in the seven-inning Twilight contest. O'Brien struck out 11 Tiremen to suffer his first loss of the season, it being of the hard luck variety. Mastroluca skirted danger for seven innings, as he walked five and stranded 10 Yarmouth runners, but ended up with the win.

With their identical 11-4 marks, Yarmouth and Ametek were slated to square off in a much anticipated Sunday doubleheader at the Oaks. These two games would go a long way to determining the Twilight League champion for 1969, as the two would wage a best-of-three championship series.

If there was any concern about dwindling interest in baseball in Portland, then the Sunday afternoon crowd jammed into Deering Oaks Park certainly put that concern to rest. Nearly 2,500 fans turned out to witness the afternoon doubleheader between the top two teams in the league. Local baseball fans awareness of the history of these long-time rivals, as well as having the opportunity to witness some of the best players in the state, surely contributed to the Twilight's largest crowd of the summer.

South Portland manager Bob Philbrick chose his left-handed ace Bob Curry to open game one on the hill. Charlie Turner countered with Gary Hobbs, who had suffered only one loss for the entire summer. With Yarmouth selected as the home team via a coin flip, the Townies were quickly on the board in the home half of the first. With one out, the speedy Bobby Doyle roped a single to left. The veteran Curry, pitching carefully to Terry Hadlock, walked the burly left-handed catcher. Curry induced the dangerous Rick Swan to pop up to first and it appeared he might wiggle out of the jam. Rookie Eric Hayward, a star that spring at the University of Maine and a dangerous hitter all summer in the Twilight circuit, lined a single to left center and the Townies were out quickly to a 1-0 lead in the first.

In the top half of the second, Hobbs walked Ned Beyer and Dave Demers to open the frame. After a Dick Curry strikeout, former Mattawamkeag town teamer Brian Gordon (now teaching, as well as living, in Portland after graduating from college) blooped a single into right-center and the game was tied. With runners at first and third, the wily Philbrook called for a double steal. Hadlock's throw through to second was late and Demers beat the return throw home with a hook slide and the Redskins had taken a 2-1 lead.

Curry cruised through the second and third frames, but in the fourth, Swan's leadoff three-bagger and Hayward's ground ball through the drawn-in infield tied it. Hayward stole second. After Ed Ranzoni struck out and Ed McDonough flied out to center, Fred Russo blooped a ball that fell in front of Beyer in left and the Townies were back in front, 3-2.

The sixth inning saw Ametek push across two runs, the second one being the eventual game winner. With one out, Dave Sprague sprayed a single to left. Beyer reached on a fielder's choice with Sprague cut down third to second. After Demers walked, Dick Curry's opposite field triple plated both Beyer and Demers and the Redskins were now on top, 4-3.

Given a lead, the veteran Curry cruised through the seventh and eighth. Having consumed a great deal of energy over the first eight frames, Curry yielded to Demers in the ninth. The right hander cruised through the ninth, punctuating the victory with a called strike on a 3-2 pitch, and the Ametek bench and South Portland faithful erupted with the jubilation of victory.

Yarmouth now had their backs against the wall. With O'Brien set to toe the rubber in game two, Turner felt confident his Townies could even the three-game series. Philbrick countered with hard-throwing lefty Marc Flaherty. The pitcher's duel was scoreless through the first four, as the crowd nervously waited in anticipation the first tally. Yarmouth, now the visiting team for the second game, dashed out on top in the top of the fifth. Hayward continued his hot hitting with a triple and rode home for a 1-0 lead on Ranzoni's sacrifice fly. Ametek's Al Livingston doubled to open the bottom half of the sixth and rode home on two infield outs, the second one resulting in an RBI for Sprague. In the bottom half of the eighth, with the atmosphere thick with the tension of a tightly contested match, Flaherty helped his own cause with a lead-off single. Livingston's sacrifice bunt put Flaherty on second with the go-ahead run. Dave Morin's fly ball to Doyle in center ticked off his glove for a two-base error, plating Flaherty. Sprague and Beyer each followed with singles off O'Brien and Ametek was now out in front, 3-1.

Yarmouth's season was now down to three outs. With the pitcher O'Brien due to lead off in the bottom half of the ninth, Turner chose veteran Pat Feury to pinch hit for his pitcher. Feury, in his seventh season with the Townies had been in these spots before. Flaherty, working him carefully and after running the count to 2-2, struck out the veteran player with a curve ball. Bernier hit a ball deep in the hole that Sprague made a great play on and nabbed him at first on a bang-bang play that drew the ire of Turner, the Yarmouth bench and much of the Yarmouth faithful. After a heated argument, the play stood and Bobby Doyle hit a weak tapper back to Flaherty and the Ametek Redskins had once again claimed the Twilight League title, their third consecutive crown, although the first one in 1967 was hotly contested by Yarmouth.

The six teams that made up the 1969 Twilight League provided the type of competition and excitement that brought baseball fans out to the ballpark. With a healthy mix of young college stars, competent veterans, as well as competitive general managers such as Bernal Allen, Yudy Elowitch and Charlie Turner recruiting talent, the league was representative of the type of baseball that was played throughout the state of Maine in 1969.

****

With the formation of the Northeast League in 1968, baseball in the greater-Bangor area had the organization that had often gone wanting in this area of the state for over a decade. Since the demise of the powerful Eastern Maine League in the late 1950's, northern baseball, while competitive and possessing many strong teams like Mattawamkeag, Guilford and other smaller town powers, often lacked a strong presence in the area's largest city of Bangor.

The 1969 season found the league adding two additional teams to its number, bringing the two division circuit to a very healthy roster of 12 clubs. Anchoring the league's Division I was the Mattawamkeag Merchants. The league's Division II was led by the Bangor Merchants who roared through the league in 1968 with a perfect 23-0 record, only to fall to Guilford in the championship series. The Guilford team showed its strength and the strength of the Northeast League by winning the YABC tournament in Auburn in 1968 and qualifying for the regionals.

Once again, the league had an able commissioner in Bangor's Roger Reed, as well as receiving sponsorship from the Bangor Recreation Department. This decision by the City government provided a needed shot-in-the-arm and kept local baseball alive and healthy throughout the 1969 season.

According to a column written in the *Bangor Daily News* by Hugh Lord in June of that year, Bangor Recreation Director Thaxter Trafton recognized the importance that this brand of baseball held in the overall picture of recreation and athletics in the city. As Lord wrote, "There are many people in the city who cannot participate in strenuous activities, but who might enjoy attending a baseball game on a clear summer evening under the lights at Garland Field [in Bangor]." Lord continued, "It's a departure from the stodgy old philosophy that a recreation department must provide only participation sports for the city's exercise buffs, forgetting that there are other facets of recreation."

Lord went on to extol the level of competition presented by the teams and that most of the teams were comprised of rosters that contained top college and high school players, as well as some old pros. This writer recognized that the decision by the Recreation Department of Bangor might encourage other top teams to travel north, particularly from the southern areas of the state, to battle with Bangor or other clubs.

In an earlier column, written to correspond with the league opening, Lord hearkened back to the glory days of the old Eastern Maine League, a league in which a young Lord had played against legendary figures such as "Gippy" Harris of Milo. In this particular column, the columnist captured much of the essence of what semi-pro baseball had been, and how the current Northeast League hearkened back to that earlier time of baseball's prominence in the area. Lord also clearly recognized the challenges facing local baseball in the Bangor area when he wrote, "Semi-pro baseball presents many such moments [recalling memories of an earlier time] and this summer's Northeast League play should prove no exception. I realize that it's tough for the hometown boys to compete with the glamour of the Red Sox on color TV. But look in on a few games this summer and you may find it a pleasant change from watching those little electronic figures in a darkened living room."

Obviously, many in Bangor chose to follow Lord's advice, as crowds at Garland Street Field were healthy in number. When the 5-0 Merchants tangled with the visiting Skowhegan Chiefs on a Thursday night in June, over 1,000 fans came out to witness the contest.

Two of the league's top pitchers were set to face off. Local lefty Ron Soucie was on the hill for Bangor, opposed by the Chiefs' hard-throwing right-hander, Willie Boynton. Soucie, who had starred for John Bapst High and then the Comrades, Bangor's local American Legion team, was now the pitching ace at local Husson College. Boynton was the better of the two pitchers in this one, as he pitched a four-hitter and fanned 15 Merchant hitters. Leading the way offensively for the Chiefs was ageless Will Laverdiere, with two hits. Laverdiere, the former Colby star, who had played back in the heyday of the famed Downeast League for both Waterville and Dixfield, was still holding his own at 36, against much younger competition. Soucie deserved a better fate in this one, as he limited the Chiefs to five hits over the contest, but was hurt by the four errors committed behind him by his Merchant teammates.

With Bangor player/manager Roger Reed also serving as the Northeast League's president, baseball in Bangor in 1969 was on solid footing once again. Having the local Recreation Department supporting the local product, an advocate in Lord writing for the *Bangor Daily News* providing needed publicity for the league and growing fan interest evidenced by several hearty crowds to start the campaign, baseball's comeback in the Queen City appeared to be an initial success.

Both Bangor and Mattawamkeag set the pace for the other 10 clubs in the league, leading their respective divisions most of the summer. However, there were other clubs in the circuit who could hold their own with those two. The Dixmont A.C., with veterans Sawin Millett, as well as the ageless Don Hanscom, now playing with his son Alan, was a tough foe. Up the road from Bangor, Dick DeVarney had formed a young club in Orono, comprised mostly of high school players. Both Devarney and college teammate Joe Ferris provided the veteran leadership for the young Riots. Both of them had been key members of the 1964 University of Maine team that had made the trip to Omaha and had played in the 1964 College World Series. Ferris had one of the team's two victories in the tournament.

Another notable on that 1969 Orono club was catcher Gabby Price. The former Bangor High sports standout had played for Rutgers University and was planning to transfer to the University of Maine in the fall to play football and then baseball in the spring. In later years, Price would become legendary as a football coach at Bangor High School.

Teams like the Orono club in the Northeast League provided young baseball players with a place to hone their skills. While American Legion baseball existed in bigger communities in the state, smaller towns often didn't have a Legion program. The local town team or semi-pro club offered these players the chance to play against strong competition that was often older. These older teammates who had played the game in college or some in the minor leagues, provided role modeling and instruction that helped many of these young players later move on and become college players of considerable renown, either nearby at the University of Maine, or other schools, with some even playing professionally. If nothing else, it instilled in these youngsters a passion for the game that would often lead them to one day take the place of their mentors, instructing a new generation of younger ballplayers. This ebb and flow of local baseball is what kept the game healthy and vital for so many years.

Local veteran players such as Reed, DeVarney, Millett, Hanscom, as well as the Libbey brothers in Mattawamkeag, helped pass their love of the game on to a younger generation of players.

One of the highlights of the summer was the third annual Blue Ox Tournament played in Mattawamkeag. Once again, Taylor

Field in Mattawamkeag was the scene of memorable battles between the teams nearby, as well as imports such as the tough Milltown, New Brunswick, club. In 1969, Milltown was able to lure Clayton and Patrick Sockabasin to play for them and these two brothers from Peter Dana Point almost single-handedly led Milltown to the Blue Ox title. With Clayton on the mound, fashioning a four-hitter, as well as his brother Patrick out at shortstop making the plays and slugging two homers, Milltown upset Bangor, 7-4, in their opening round game.

The following weekend would see a match up between Milltown and the tournament's host team, Mattawamkeag. Once again, the foes from across the border would counter with Sockabasin, while the Merchant's manager Dick Lowell countered with veteran righty Gil Arnold.

Sockabasin was his usual tough self on the mound and even slugged a two-run homer to tie the game in the top of the sixth, 3-3. The Merchants were able to push across a run in the bottom of that frame, however, as Terry Duffy's one-out single, coupled with an error put him on third and Herb Libbey's sacrifice fly to center gave the 'Keagers a 4-3 lead. That would be all that Arnold needed as the veteran hurler shut the door on the Miller's from New Brunswick and Mattawamkeag was in the finals against the upstart Orono Riots.

Orono had gotten to the finals in the tough, single-elimination format, on the strength of the tournament's best pitching performance. Former Black Bear veteran Joe Ferris proved that he still had tournament-caliber stuff, as the right-hander scattered six hits to beat tough mound opponent Willie Boynton and his Cambridge A.A. mates, 3-0. Boynton, who was added for the tournament from Skowhegan only allowed two hits in the tough luck loss. Boynton, known for his bouts of wildness, to go along with his exploding fastball, was undone by walks and a couple of errors. It was a walk, a wild pitch and an error in the third that put Orono on the board first. Then in the bottom of the following frame, a one out walk to Dick Devarney, a strikeout and wild pitch leading to runners at first and third and Hugh Campbell's double to the gap plated two more, making it 3-0. That's all Ferris would need as he kept Cambridge off the scoreboard as Orono advanced to the championship game against Mattawamkeag.

In the Sunday title game, it was the hitters who ruled this time. With its late-afternoon start, the slugfest, which witnessed both teams battling to a 7-7 deadlock through eight innings, as daylight waned. With the umpires conferring and agreeing to suspend the contest, both teams had to settle for a 7-7 tie, with an agreement to replay the championship game at a later date. As often happened with baseball schedules extending into late August, this one never got played as the Mattawamkeag team ended up going to Pettengill Park in Auburn for the YABC tournament with Bangor, and Orono's young chargers, many of who were still in school, had conflicts that prevented the championship tilt taking place for 1969.

Mattawamkeag and Bangor ended up winning their respective divisions in the Northeast League and the two teams headed down the interstate to do battle with the best teams in the southern regions of the state in that summer's YABC tourney. With Mattawamkeag sporting an unbelievable 41-4 overall record for the summer, including a 21-2 mark in the league, northern Maine was well-represented in the upcoming tourney in Auburn.

Unfortunately for the Merchants from Mattawamkeag, they ran into a hot pitcher in the Thursday opening round game against the Auburn Asas. With lefty Jim Topping mixing slow curves with a popping fastball, the Merchants were no match for the Asas and fell, 5-0. Topping finished with 16 strikeouts against a strong offensive attack that featured the Libbey brothers, catcher Ron Marks, Tom Rowe and Dick Barstow.

Bangor likewise got off to an inauspicious start, falling to the tough Roberts 88'ers of Lisbon Falls. With veteran Bob Baumer fashioning a four-hitter and fanning nine, Bangor ended up on the losing end, by a 9-3 count.

Bangor managed to stay alive on Friday, while Mattawamkeag was eliminated by Rumford. With Darrell Whittemore (who pitched for Guilford at Pettengill in 1968) shutting down a good-hitting Norway-Paris Twins' attack, Bangor scratched out a 2-0 victory to stay alive in the double-elimation format. The Merchants from Mattawamkeag were trounced 7-4 and ended up a disappointing 0-2 in the tournament.

This set up a tough matchup on Saturday between Rumford and the Bangor Merchants. With lefty hurler Ron Soucie twirling a nine-inning complete game one-hitter, Bangor squeaked by the Townies of Rumford, 2-0. With the bases loaded in the sixth, courtesy of a walk, Artie Taylor's single, the lone hit off Soucie and an error, Rumford attempted a suicide squeeze. The ball was popped up to the first baseman and he fired a strike to shortstop Dick Devarney covering third to double off that runner. DeVarney then coolly fired the ball to Roger Reed at second for a triple play!

With Bangor's win, they immediately played 30 minutes later, this time against the 88'ers of Lisbon Falls. In one of the most amazing pitching feats witnessed in the history of local baseball at any level, Bangor pitcher Soucie came back to pitch the next contest. The durable lefty ended up going 11 innings, fanning 14, but lost a heartbreaker to Lisbon Falls, 3-1. On the strength of this phenomenal Saturday outing, Soucie was voted the tournament's outstanding player. He finished the 1969 tournament with a 2-1 record in which he pitched 30 innings, struck out 39, and had one string of 22 consecutive scoreless innings.

It's fitting that this 1969 tournament was as competitive as it was, featuring great individual performances from Soucie, who at the time was still in college at Husson. In addition to Soucie, other young pitchers like Topping for the Asas established themselves as the next wave of young pitching stars coming along. Meanwhile, veteran hurlers such as Bob Baumer for Lisbon Falls, as well as Stan Timberlake of Auburn, were on the downhill side of their careers. Timberlake, whom Auburn had picked up from Turner for the tourney, had hooked up in many a duel with the likes of Baumer and others over the years. In addition to these veterans, Rumford's Artie Taylor may have been one of the best catchers to grace a town team or semi-pro baseball diamond in the state.

The 1969 YABC tourney in Auburn would be the last one held at the venerable ball grounds of Pettengill Park. The expense of membership in the nationwide organization, as well as the disadvantages for small states such as Maine, forced to compete in the regional formats, played a part in this decision. The 1970 season would see the initiation of a statewide tournament for a Governor's Cup. This tournament would continue the post-season tradition of the YABC that was started back in 1949.

With the close of the summer of 1969, a spirited chapter in the long parade of local baseball in Maine had come to a close. For some like Baumer, Taylor and Timberlake, the summer signified the twilight of a career. For others, it was a beginning and heralded bigger and better things. Topping would later sign professionally and play some minor league baseball.

The YABC tournaments drew hundreds and even thousands of fans from all over to the games at Pettengill. Girlfriends came to watch future husbands play. Brothers and other relatives came to watch family members compete, sometimes against one another. In addition, a new generation got hooked on the game and would dream of one day playing for their local team, representing their town in future battles.

With the passage of time however, the YABC tournaments, just like the Carlton Willey Invitational in Lamoine, the Blue Ox in Mattawamkeag and the Twilight League's Labor Day Tournaments all disappeared. Local baseball remained, but much of the surrounding drama and events that united the various geographic regions of Maine had disappeared.

While local baseball remained strong throughout the 1970's and into the 1980's, fewer and fewer towns played the game. From the days when literally every town had a team, the local game remained only in select areas of the state. Competing with automobiles, shopping malls, television and softball, the town team brand of baseball was alive, but there were questions about its health, as well as its future.

Chapter 9

Growing Up Baseball: My Own Roots in Local Baseball

For the previous eight chapters, I've reported on baseball in Maine. Covering the history of town team and semi-pro baseball in the state, from just after World War II, and primarily the next 25 years, I've now come to a place where I feel the time is right for me to step into the book and offer a more personal view and share my own connection to the local baseball that I've grown up a part of.

While I'm sure that doing so violates some device of literature and writing, I take this chance because of the nature of this book. With *When Towns Had Teams* being a labor of love, as well as an ode to the past and those performers who made it special, I feel the time has come to personalize the book and bring it to the place where the past intersects with the present. By doing so, it allows me to put my own personal stamp on local baseball and what it means to me. Since this is a book that's truly unique in that no one has bothered to cover this subject and time period, I'm operating without a road map or directions for assembly. Hence, I wanted to offer readers my motivation for attempting this and allow them to see that *When Towns Had Teams* is as much about my experience coming to know the game, as it is about the towns, teams, stories and players that are represented.

I chose to highlight the summer of '69 in the previous chapter because it was during that summer, my seventh summer of life, that I became aware of baseball and began a love affair with the game that has lasted for over 35 years. I have been able to pinpoint that particular summer as the one where I came to embrace the national pastime, primarily because of two players who were still performing for my beloved Roberts 88'ers town team in my home town of Lisbon Falls. Marty Roop and Stan Doughty were in their final seasons of playing the game locally in 1969. From my interviews with both former players, as well as frequent trips to various libraries to research 35-to-40-year-old newspapers on microfilm, I've pinpointed the summer of 1969 as my first genuine memory of town team baseball.

That particular summer began weeknight suppers where I hurriedly ate my meal, hardly able to contain my excitement in anticipation of that evening's game at the high school field. With admonitions from my mother to slow down, the only thoughts on my mind were the foul balls I would be hot after in an hour or so, with the commencement of that evening's 88'er's game. After the meal, I became the most helpful little seven-year-old you have ever seen, clearing the table and urging my father towards his yellow '62 Ford Fairlane, our means of transportation to the game. We could have walked the mile or so to the game, but we would have probably been late and I would have missed opportunities to scour the surrounding swamp and pine trees for fouled-off baseballs.

I've always been interested to hear others talk or write about their own experiences of coming to know about the special game of baseball. Often, it's the sound and even the smells of the game that stay with you throughout your life. That first summer, I can remember the sounds; the crack of the wooden bat making solid contact with the baseball as it hurtled toward the batter poised at the plate. Baseball is a game where minute measures of time are split even finer. The windup and pitch to the batter can be measured by a mere second. Even smaller increments make the difference between a long homerun, a foul ball, or even a swing and a miss. While the increments of time are small and occur in less than a blink of an eye, the pace of the game is measured and even leisurely.

While I certainly wasn't able to articulate all of this at seven years of age, I'm sure the sights, smells, sounds and pace were carefully being absorbed and internalized. In later years, whatever might have been happening in my life, I always found comfort and a sense of belonging while either at, or on, a baseball field.

My earliest recollections are of arriving at the field and carefully scanning the diamond to see if I could locate particular players; Doughty, Roop, my uncle Bob, as well as Herbie Whitman and other players such as Steve Karkos and Tom Fortin. Both Roop and Doughty lived just up the street from my ranch-style house on Woodland Avenue in Lisbon Falls. I'd regularly see Stan driving up my street in his green Ford Bronco. I'd eagerly offer him a wave and his return gesture became the highlight of my day. Just before supper, on the nights when the 88'ers were idle, I'd be out on the front lawn in anticipation of Roop's return from a day at work in Portland. Even as a youngster, I was learning the ebb-and-flow of life and work. I had learned that he carpooled with David Hale on Plummer Street and would walk from Hale's house, the last half mile home to Woodland Avenue. I would eagerly anticipate his walking past the house where I could greet him with a "Hi, Mr. Roop" followed by a "that was a great game last night" or some other refrain tied to the previous night's contest at the high school. Roop, probably tired and anxious to see his own children, always took time to stop and offer some greeting and even ask me how many foul balls I had managed to retrieve.

I imagine that my ball field excursions were not as exciting for my mother, however. She was the one forced to deal with my returns home, grimy and inevitably caked with dirt, mud and sweat from my pursuit of baseballs. Apparently, it was a regular occurrence for me to come home with sneakers caked with mud and white socks turned brown from the water and muck of the swamp created by a natural spring behind the Lisbon High School backstop. All of the area behind the third base bench area occupied by the 88'ers was a swamp, much of it inaccessible. A good portion of baseballs peeled foul, found their way to a premature graveyard of murky water and overgrown vegetation.

My companions and competitors for foul balls were often the sons of Roop and Doughty. Roop's boys, Marty Jr., Larry and Steve, were all older than I was, with Marty being six years older, Larry five years and Steve four respectively. In addition, Doughty's children, Ronnie and Chipper, were also older, so I was at a serious disadvantage age-wise. Despite being younger and smaller, my tenacity, as well as Marty's kindness, always ensured that I'd get a few foul balls. Often, Marty, being 13, would arrive first only to toss the ball back to me before the others could get to it. This is a ritual that's been played out countless times and in endless scenarios; the older boys taking the younger ones under their wing and looking out for them. In later years, all of the Roop brothers would be teammates, either in American Legion baseball, in the case of Larry, high school and town team baseball, in the case of Steve, and town team baseball in the late 1980's with Marty.

****

Baseball, as well as other team sports, creates the opportunity for camaraderie amongst teammates. The Roberts 88'ers were no different, and as a youngster, I got to participate in some of these rituals of the team. On many nights when the team was off and not practicing, players would stop by my grandparent's house on the corner of Rand and Pleasant streets, where my uncle lived. Often, my Opa would be out back in his garden and my uncle would be on the front lawn, with cars parked along the edge of the yard, owned by various 88'ers' players such as Dave Moulton, Billy Carroll and Tom Fortin or Steve Karkos.

One of my favorite things to do was to rush through my supper (again) and race across the gully from my house, over to my grandparent's house, about a quarter mile away. This was in hopes of being included in a game of catch with my uncle, or to just sit and listen to the players talk. Often, the topics were about things that a seven-year-old had no knowledge of, but I enjoyed the sounds of the voices, the acknowledgement that the players would give me and the laughter that would punctuate these conversations. From these times, I learned that baseball was a fun game and that teammates were people you respected and even kidded good naturedly.

The best part of the evening would be when my uncle would acquiesce to my persistent request for a game of catch. Obviously, playing catch with a scatter-armed seven-year-old couldn't have been much fun for my skilled left-handed uncle, but he taught me important lessons from these front lawn sessions. I always wanted to talk and not pay attention to the task at hand. He would tell me, "you need to keep your mouth closed when you are playing catch." This was teaching me that throwing a ball accurately required concentration. Each session with my uncle brought promise, as my frequent lobs over his head and across Pleasant Street into the neighbor's yard and my uncle's protestations, were eventually replaced by fairly accurate tosses to the vicinity of his mitt. Over the next decade, one of my favorite things to do was to throw a baseball back-and-forth with my uncle, father, friend or teammate. There is something incredibly relaxing and comforting in that measured rite that takes place between teammates and players. In addition, the simple rudiments players learn to associate with the game—the conversation, the joking and needling of one another, walking that fine line between fun and insult—all are part and parcel of the special fraternity that one becomes associated with when they become part of a team and a group of teammates.

The backyard of my parent's house on Woodland Avenue had two permanent worn areas where no grass grew, from endless games of catch or "pass" as we called it. When I first started throwing, the patches were about 45 to 50 feet apart, the distance of a little leaguer. As I grew older, the distances increased to 60 feet, the distance of the mound from home plate in adult baseball. That regular ritual that I first participated in at my grandparent's and parent's house, later was repeated with various teammates in Little League, high school, college and later, with town team and semi-pro teams I played on. Years later, I would initiate my own son into this baseball tradition, as soon as he was old enough to stand upright. Just like my uncle had to endure the errant tosses of my erratic right arm, as it was trained for accuracy, I would later retrieve balls thrown over and past me by my own son, as he also learned to develop accuracy in throwing, just as I had, some 20 years earlier.

****

When spring arrived in 1970, the town of Lisbon had its first official league for youth baseball. The Lisbon Junior Athletic League became a place for the young players in town to play competitively, many under the watchful tutelage of many former stars of town team ball. With both Marty Roop and Stan Doughty now retired from the 88'ers, they now turned their focus to coaching their own sons and other young men of the town. While Little League baseball had officially started nationally in 1947, there were still many communities that had never embraced this organized brand of youth baseball. Libon Falls and Lisbon had participated in various types of youth baseball such as Police Athletic League (PAL) ball in Lewiston, as well as other less structured excursions to play neighboring towns. However, the lure to join the national organization in Williamsport was strong enough to warrant the formation of a local affiliate. Both Doughty and Roop would later coach the junior 88'ers for a couple of seasons, which were the local Senior Little League group of players in town, wearing hand-me-down 88'er uniforms and playing other nearby towns.

The following year, I became a member of my first Little League team, coached by my father and managed by a man up the street named Ted Drottar. After spending the past two summers chasing foul balls and watching our local town team show a youngster like me how it was done, I was now ready to enter the competition of baseball firsthand. My first ball team was sponsored by the Lisbon Trading Post in Lisbon Falls. A used furniture store located in my home town, this local business's sponsorship provided me with my first jersey and hat of many to follow.

Sometimes, being coached by one's father isn't the easiest thing in the world for both father and son. Mr. Drottar served as a buffer between my father's initial toughness and an awkward youngster's first season of organized baseball. Later, when I became the star pitcher and hitter on the team, Drottar served to shield my father from my cockiness and helped salve our difficult coach-player, as well as, father-son relationship.

While not the most accurate thrower during my initial years playing baseball, all that playing pass over the previous several years had paid off, as by the age of 12, I was able to throw the ball harder than any of the boys in our league. This helped me to be a catcher that runners feared to attempt to steal on, and a pitcher that batters feared to hit against. Not only could I throw hard enough so that opposing hitters had difficulty making contact, I was wild enough that batters feared getting nailed by one of my pitches, as often happened. That combination of speed and wildness made me a very effective and very intimidating 12-year-old hurler. On several occasions, my plunking of a terrified nine-or ten-year-old brought tears and bawling from the vicinity of home plate.

By the time that I had entered my teenage years, I was now playing Senior Little League and my coach was my uncle's friend and former 88'er, Dave Moulton. Moulton was a great coach for me as a high-strung teenager, although he and I butted heads more than I'm sure he cared for over the three years I played for him. While I respected him for his baseball abilities and place as a mentor due to his being a part of the 88'ers, I was a very difficult player to coach in those days. While he still chuckles about those times of trying to rein in a talented, but often out-of-control young youngster, I'm sure I was the cause of a gray hair or two at the time.

When I got into high school, my first coach was another former 88'er, George Ferguson. "Fergie" as most locals referred to him, was a tremendous influence on me as a player. Ferguson routinely produced strong teams during the 1970's including a stretch of three straight conference titles in the Mountain Valley Conference, as well as three straight trips to the Western Maine Class B finals. Unfortunately for the Greyhounds, each year, their opponent was the even stronger Cape Elizabeth teams that had several players drafted from them. Three straight years, the Greyhounds season ended with the match up with Cape. Most of us middle school players attended these games, dreaming of the day when we'd be out there and maybe we'd be the ones who finally defeated the Capers.

A coach who demanded a lot from his players, Ferguson's knowledge of the game, no doubt began in his hometown of Lisbon Falls. The son of a great player himself, Ferguson obviously gleaned a lot from his own father, playing town team ball, college baseball under the legendary Jack Butterfield and summers in the Cape Cod League while playing for the University of Maine. Later, Ferguson rose to the top of the New York Yankee's minor league system before being released and returning to Lisbon Falls, where he became a teacher.

Playing for Ferguson, I was able to learn many of the finer details of the game. Things like studying an opposing pitcher to determine weaknesses, tendencies and other mental facets of the game I had never been taught before. A stickler for fundamentals, Ferguson's teams played very sound baseball under his tutelage.

Ferguson kept the thread of local baseball running through the community of Lisbon, as he succeeded his former coach and 88'ers' teammate Stan Doughty as the coach at Lisbon High School. It had become a tradition at Lisbon, for youngsters climbing up through the ranks of youth and sandlot baseball, to eventually graduate to the high school team for four years and then proceed to wearing the black and gold of the 88'ers. For many of the better players in Lisbon and Lisbon Falls, their initiation into town team baseball often occurred prior to graduation. Many 88'ers' players had a profound affect on the development of youngsters like me. Many have played an important role in making Lisbon and Lisbon Falls a strong baseball town for many years.

****

In the spring of 1976, I was a strong-armed, but erratic thrower, waiting for the snow to melt in order to play baseball as a catcher for my seventh and eighth grade team. Ferguson invited me and another talented eighth grader, John Martin, to indoor workouts with the high school club.

Like all great coaches, Ferguson anticipated and built for the future. Knowing he would graduate a senior catcher, Roop's middle son, Larry, Martin and I were wide-eyed eighth graders being thrust into the world of high school sports in 1976.

Looking back at this, I'm sure this caused somewhat of a stir and may have even ruffled the feathers of other parents. If it did at the time, Martin and I never got wind of it, as Ferguson and his Greyhound players made us feel welcome and treated us no differently than any other teammate. Steve Roop, the youngest of the three Roop brothers and a practical joker, managed to spare us no mercy with his barbs. This was his way of making us feel part of the team. Steve's older brother, Larry, became a mentor that spring and would also be a big influence the summer following my freshman year of high school.

During the summer of 1977, I was a wet-behind-the-ears freshman pitcher and having a hard-nosed catcher like Roop taught me a lot about pitching and listening to my catcher. A fierce competitor, known for his ability to settle disagreements with his fists, I was too frightened to ever disagree or challenge Roop in any way. It amazes me to this day when I see younger players talking back to veteran players when I attend high school games, or even during the summer in the college level league that I coach. During my time at Lisbon, younger players knew their place and if you didn't, someone like a Larry Roop quickly explained the Lisbon pecking order to you.

My first two coaches in American Legion baseball were Stan Doughty and Marty Roop. Doughty was my high school athletic director and he was a man who exuded baseball experience. He had a quiet style of coaching and of offering advice to a youngster like me. Both he and Roop were big influences and gave me the chance to develop at a normal pace. I can still remember Roop talking to me at the beginning of my first Legion season. That spring, I had shown considerable ability as a freshman pitcher at Lisbon High School, going 3-0 on the mound, in addition to splitting the catching duties with Martin. Eventually, I shed the catcher's tools of ignorance and became a full-time pitcher.

Roop, probably in conference with Ferguson, wisely pitched me against weaker foes that first summer. American Legion baseball tended to be a step above high school competition and it could have proven a tough trek for a young pitcher if not handled properly. Rather than risk destroying my confidence and forcing me to face teams from bigger towns, I pitched against Richmond and some of the bottom tier teams and had a successful first Legion summer. As a result, my confidence in my own abilities as a pitcher received a significant boost.

The first summer of success provided an important building block for me and helped propel me into a very successful sophomore season at Lisbon. My 6-0 mark kept our struggling team in contention for most of the season, but for the first time in four years, the Greyhounds did not win the Mountain Valley crown and missed the play-offs. While I had experienced a great deal of success and was beginning to believe some of the hype surrounding my high school exploits on the mound, the 1978 high school season was about to end on a sad note for me. At the annual spring sports banquet, Coach Ferguson announced his resignation. I was heartbroken. One of the most important people in my baseball development was now stepping aside.

If you were a young boy growing up in Lisbon and played baseball, you became aware at an early age of the town's baseball tradition. Most of my generation had grown up hearing the stories of the Worumbo Indians, or the Lisbon Lemons before them. Being a Baumer, I had my father and also my uncle Bob and earlier, another uncle, Rhinehold. "Rhiney," the name that I remember those familiar with my uncle calling him, had been a great catcher and played for the second incarnation of the Worumbo Indians, upon returning to Lisbon Falls after serving in the Army during World War Two. While in the service, Rhiney had been a good enough player to be on a team with fellow major leaguers Harry "the Hat" Walker (who later won a batting title in the National League with the St. Louis Cardinals in 1957) and as a catcher, he had caught Rex Barney of the Brooklyn Dodgers. Of course it was Bob, being a pitcher and who was still active as a player in 1977, who probably provided my biggest motivation and role model as a player.

In 1977, the Roberts 88'ers were playing their games in Bowdoin, on a makeshift field that was one step above a pasture. The team had moved from Lisbon Falls in 1973 and was now part of a new town team league known as the AKS League, which derived its three-letter moniker from the first letters of the counties where its teams were based—Androscoggin, Kennebec and Sagadahoc. Bob was no longer the team's ace pitcher. At 40, he pitched occasionally and could still get out good hitters with an assortment of pitches and the guile that comes from playing in his third decade of local baseball.

In July of 1977, I was playing American Legion baseball for the Coombs-Mountfort Post of Lisbon. Our club, comprised primarily of Lisbon High School varsity baseball players from that spring's club, sought to fill an open date with a Saturday double header against the 88'ers. That summer's roster for the 88'ers was filled with many former players at Lisbon High School, guys that most of us had watched as middle school players, dreaming of the day when we'd don a Greyhound uniform.

The Legion/Town team match up featured a family rivalry theme, with me and my uncle on opposing sides, as well as brothers Steve, Larry and Marty Roop; Steve playing first and Larry catching for Coombs-Mountfort, with his older brother, Marty, catching for the 88'ers. Their father, Marty Sr., had been a mainstay on the great Roberts 88'ers teams of the 1960's, after starring for Bowdoin College.

In game one, I had the honor of facing my uncle, as the two Baumer's were on the hill for their respective clubs. My uncle, the crafty veteran lefty and me, the hard-throwing right-hander, just learning my craft were set to face off. The 88'ers pushed across a run in the first off me, with a leadoff single by Omar Keamy, who stole second. After a walk to Ronnie Doughty (whose father, Stan, was a former long-time town team and semi-pro star), Richard Martin singled to right and the 88'ers were on top, 1-0.

In the bottom of the second, my legion teammate Norm Smith led off with a single to left. After Steve Roop grounded out to the hole between first and second, allowing Smith to advance, Ed Ludwig looped a single into right center and the game was tied at 1-1. A Larry Roop homer in the second off my uncle put us on top 2-1 and I'd take this one-run lead into the top of the fifth inning. In the top of the frame, a walk and two errors resulted in a run. A base hit by Steve Bickford brought in another and then, after two strikeouts, Dave Fowler's single to right-center plated two more and I was now trailing my uncle's club by a 4-2 count.

My Legion mates pushed across another run in the bottom of the sixth to halve the margin, but two more by the 88'ers in the top of the seventh allowed my uncle to come away with a win in the battle between the Baumers. Bowdoin was able to take the second game also and swept the double header from the youngsters, 6-3.

This Saturday match up saw a crowd of over 100 fans turn out, which for this period was a good crowd. Rarely did we have more than 50-60 fans at our own Legion games. Many of the people who turned out came to see my uncle pitch against his nephew, as they remembered the 88'ers' games from their heyday in the 1960's. While town team ball was still alive in many communities, it had disappeared in many more. Games like the one between the town team 88'ers and our Legion club were a common occurrence a decade prior. By the late 1970's, fewer and fewer towns had teams comprised of former high school, Legion and college players.

The spring baseball season of 1979 became one of those magical years that one only dreams about as a kid. With a new coach at the helm, our Lisbon High team was dominating opponents in the Mountain Valley Conference. As a junior in high school, my fastball and competitiveness was too much for the teams from Leavitt (Turner), Livermore Falls, Mexico and the other schools in our conference. Our Greyhound club would beat Cape Elizabeth and future New York Yankee farmhand, Bob Raftice, to win the Western Maine Class B title for the first time ever. The Capers had regularly eliminated talented Lisbon teams during Coach Ferguson's reign as coach. I had watched many of those contests and dreamed of one day being the pitcher who ended their streak. In 1979, my dreams came true, as I pitched a one-hitter, which allowed us to get past a tough Caper club, 3-0. It was my seventh straight victory that spring and my most meaningful one to date. The victory was a thrill for an 18-year-old baseball "rat" like me, who had spent many nights chasing foul balls on that very same field, watching his uncle lead the 88'ers to victory after victory. It was also mixed with a measure of regret. I recognized that Coach Ferguson, who had meant so much to me and my baseball development, wasn't the one now guiding our club. Our current skipper, Maurice Benson, had inherited a talented group of players and he was smart enough to stay out of our way. It's possible that his relaxed style was just enough of a change to provide a catalyst for the 1979 club. Whatever it was, that season, we could do no wrong.

The following Saturday, pitching on three days rest, on a rainy afternoon in early June, my high school teammates and I won the first ever state baseball championship for Lisbon High School, besting Stearns High School of Millinockett, 7-5. With all the great players and teams that had come before us, it was humbling to realize that we were the first team (and only one since) to claim that coveted crown, in 1979.

****

Young players often think they are invincible. Running, throwing and hitting seem so easy and the adolescent body appears resilient beyond the point of injury. Experts in physiology cite throwing a baseball with an overhand motion as one of the single most unnatural movements for the arm and shoulder. The constant strain on the structure and associated ligaments, tendons and muscles puts duress on this region of the body. While an unnatural motion, combining that with the force placed on the arm by trying to throw a baseball as hard as you can in order to propel it by batters, a 100 or more times, several times per week, while the body is still developing, can be a recipe for problems, particularly arm problems.

On the basis of my 23-1 high school record and performances such as the game I pitched to get us into the Legion tournament in 1979, Coach John Winkin at the University of Maine began expressing an interest in my abilities as a pitcher. Winkin had seen me strikeout 18 Caldwell Post (of Portland) batters in August of that year, while pitching a one-hitter. In addition to Winkin, Jack Leggett, who was coaching at the University of Vermont, Bill Thurston from Amherst, as well as Chick Leahey of Bates College, all began calling me on the phone once a week during my senior spring, telling me of their interest in my playing for their teams.

During my senior year in 1980, my fastball didn't have its usual "pop." In 1979, with two strikes on the hitter, I routinely had been able to strike out hitters by throwing my fastball letter high and seeing them futilely wave at the ball. In the spring of 1980, my strikeout numbers, usually in double digits the previous three seasons, were rarely higher than 8 or 9 and on one occasion, they reached 11. In 1979, in the seven-inning high school games, I averaged 12 strikouts per game, with 14 being my high.

Interestingly, I felt a twinge in the back of my shoulder. If I pressed my fingers of my left hand into the area where my arm joined my shoulder, I would experience a sharp, burning sensation. While this concerned me and often made me feel anxious in the pit of my stomach, I didn't tell anyone. I continued to go out and pitch regularly, getting by on my skill and ability to spot my pitches, much the same way that a veteran pitcher, like my uncle Bob, would pitch. Looking back, it seems odd that no one thought about the possibility of an arm injury. Even after I lost my first game of my high school career, late in the spring of 1980—a game in which I had almost no command and was hit harder than I had ever been during my baseball career to that point—no one broached the subject of an injury.

Throughout that summer and into the fall of my freshman year at the University of Maine, I was able to hide the fact that my rotator cuff was frayed and if not in need of therapy, then I should of at least have been able to "shut it down" and rest it. Playing for the University of Maine was an intimidating experience. The school, a Division I baseball power in the northeast, was considered the place to play baseball in college, if you hailed from New England. The Black Bear roster was comprised of the best baseball players from Maine and New Hampshire, as well as the other New England states.

That fall, I didn't pitch badly, but I also lacked the consistency that had always characterized my high school and legion career. Playing a fall game against the University of Southern Maine, I had a particularly rough outing at Deering Oaks in Portland. Two of my Lisbon High teammates, Mike Sawyer and John Martin, were on the Husky squad. After leaving in the fourth inning, trailing by a 4-2 margin and having given up a three-run homer, I came to the bench as dejected as I'd ever been as a player. My mind was racing and my heart pounding as I began to doubt my baseball abilities for the first time. As an 18-year-old freshman, I began to entertain thoughts of quitting the game that I had come to love and embrace as my own.

Between games, I had lunch with my parents on the grass banking overlooking the field. Unable to say much and fighting back tears, the looks of concern from my parents only made the situation more difficult. The second game, sitting on the bench, followed by the two-hour ride back to Orono, with Freddy Staples and Kevin Bernier, felt like an eternity.

On Monday morning, I didn't show up for my required team meeting. For the rest of the week, I didn't attend practices and ignored several notices in my mailbox from Coach Winkin's assistants to contact them. Tired and frustrated and thinking it was my own lack of ability, I had basically walked away from baseball. Even today, when I look back on the situation, I'm still dumbfounded why someone—my parents, my coaches, even myself—didn't think that it could be an injury that was causing my difficulties as a pitcher. Despite the darkness descending on my baseball life at the time, it would be baseball, and in particular, town team baseball, that would once again restore my hope in the game I grew up loving.

****

The end of May is usually when high school baseball is winnowing the field of hopefuls from its high school baseball tournament. Maine's high schools are split into four divisions or classes, determined by school population; Classes A through D make up high school baseball in Maine, with Class A schools being the largest and predominantly either from Maine's few cities, or large administrative districts pulling together high schools from small Maine communities into one large high school. Class B, of which my hometown Lisbon High was a member of in 1980 and 1981, is mostly medium to large towns and Classes C and D respectively are smaller, with Class D representing the smallest communities in the state.

As the Lisbon High Greyhounds were making their push for yet another Class B play-off birth, a number of former Greyhounds were in attendance on a weekday afternoon in late May. Having just finished their first or second year of college, the former players gathered to critique the current batch of ballplayers, as well as talk about summer baseball.

Having been home from school for two weeks, I had initially resisted the urge to take part in this time-honored ritual of returning to the scene of previous baseball triumphs. Returning players are always afforded a place of honor or prominence and Lisbon High was no different. Upon entering the park, greetings from parents, fans and former teammates make this return a pleasant and affirming rite of spring.

A number of teammates from the '79 state champion ball club were already in attendance upon my arrival. All decked out in our red, white and black state champion jackets, we gathered to exchange greetings and catch up on the past year's events.

Dave Barden, who had graduated a year ahead of my class of 1980, was living at home, while attending the vocational college in Auburn. Dave's brother Mike, two years older, was putting together a team to play in the AKS League for the summer. In need of pitching, Dave immediately wanted to know if I was interested. I didn't want to fill him in on all the sordid details of my leaving the team at Orono and my inactivity in the spring, so I made up a tale about having some arm trouble and not having pitched in several weeks. I told him I didn't know if I was going to play or not. Other Lisbon High teammates Mike Sawyer and John Martin told me they were planning to play. A part of me missed the game. My spring at Orono had been a difficult one, being away from the game for the first time in my young adult life. Yet, I didn't want to spend a summer of frustration, once again struggling to display my previous baseball skills.

A week went by and I ran into Dave and Mike Barden at a Lisbon High play-off game. This time it was Mike encouraging me to play. My resistance was weakening and I gave him a non-committal "maybe" as to my availability.

I called the Barden household two days later and got the details from Mike. They were having a practice on Sunday in Sabattus, at the new Oak Hill High School. I told him I'd be there.

I arrived and right off I knew most, if not all, of the players. There were a number of former Lisbon High players, including former 88'er players Larry McIver and Wayne Roberts, who were now in their early 30s. Jeff Benson, a new resident of the area, who had moved to Lisbon Falls with his wife, Jodi, to teach, was also there. Glenn Gamrat, a former Lisbon High star, and Steve Bickford, who had played his high school ball for Stan Doughty in the early 1970's, was serving as the team's player/coach for the summer. In addition, the Bardens and Sawyer and Martin, as well as my presence, gave us a strong recent Lisbon High representation.

Mirroring the demise of local baseball elsewhere, the AKS was down to just four teams in 1981. With the Lisbon team, Sabattus, Lewiston and Bath, the league was barely hanging on. Just six years earlier, the league had 10 teams, including two teams in the little town of Bowdoin.

For me, the summer of 1981 revived my hope in baseball. Possibly the rest during the spring had allowed my ailing shoulder an opportunity to rejuvenate. Whatever the reason, my fastball appeared to have returned. On several occasions that summer, I registered double digit strikeout performances. While the competition wasn't college level in most cases, each team had several quality hitters. The Sabattus team was the strongest club, as Lisbon battled their rivals from up the road, all summer long. Bath had a strong team, while Lewiston was weak and eventually dropped out of the league with two weeks left in the season, leaving the league with just three teams.

With Sabattus winning the regular season title and Lisbon just two games back, Bickford arranged for a best-of-three championship series between the two clubs. Winning both games one and three, after Sabattus beat us in game two, the Lisbon town team was the 1981 AKS trophy winner.

Returning to school in the fall, filled with hope and desire to play ball again, I had a conversation with Coach Winkin, who decided to let me tryout in the fall. He had seen that I had pitched well in the summer and was willing to give me a second chance. Unfortunately, the regular throwing required of a college pitcher began to cause the same problems encountered the previous spring. By late fall, I had several rocky outings during inter-squad games and was left off the fall travel squad. Once again, no one seemed to consider having my arm looked at. Frustrated and informed that I would be left off the roster in the spring, I decided to leave school in the spring of 1982. My once promising baseball career seemed finished. As a 19-year-old, the only thing I could think of was getting away from the pain and frustration of college and I walked away from baseball for the next five years. Over that span of time, marriage, the birth of my son, and the cares of life forced baseball out of my focus.

****

After five years living in the Midwest, my wife, Mary, and I returned to Maine in August of 1987. I was now a father, as my son Mark was now almost four years old. For the past several summers, I had virtually ignored baseball, other than to watch an occasional Cubs or White Sox game on television.

In the spring of 1988, I began giving some thought to returning to the game I'd walked away from back in 1982. I was now encumbered with the responsibilities of being a husband, father and a breadwinner. On top of that, my wife and I realized that we needed to find a way to buy or build our first home, as we'd been renting for the first five years of marriage.

While reading the local newspaper, I ran across an announcement for tryouts for the Lewiston A's, the closest Pine Tree League team to where I was currently living in Durham. The league still had six teams and was one of the few remaining leagues in this part of the state. When I saw a second announcement a week later, I made up my mind to attend.

When you haven't thrown a baseball competitively for six years, the rust clings tightly to those muscles and movements that used to react instinctively. My first year back in organized ball was not a very successful one. Pitching only 10 innings and spending my summer feeling like I wasn't a part of the club, wasn't what I had envisioned back in May. With about two weeks left in the season, I called the general manager, Hollis Bates, and told him I was done. I liked Bates, but I didn't particularly like the manager, Jack Milo. The team, mostly Lewiston players who had played together in high school, didn't welcome an outsider like me.

After that failed attempt at reviving my baseball career, I assumed I was done with competitive baseball. I decided at the end of the summer that I was finished as a player and that my baseball would be restricted to teaching my son the game and eventually coaching Little League.

In 1989, a group of former Lisbon High players that included Dave Barden, Steve and Marty Roop, Mike Sawyer, John Martin, Steve Bickford and Leo Albert committed to putting a club in the

Pine Tree League. The club decided to call themselves the 88'ers in deference to the town team baseball of the past.

Sawyer, who had been my catcher in high school, had continued to play ball after moving from Lisbon Falls. Now living in the Saco area, he had played a couple of seasons in the Sunset League, a southern Maine-based league. After some off-season conversations with Albert, Roop and Bickford, Sawyer agreed to commute to Lisbon Falls and be part of the organizing group for the new team.

Over the next decade, Sawyer and I would be semi-regular teammates. Continuing in the tradition of players such as my uncle Bob, Stan Doughty and Marty Roop in Lisbon, and other players like Bitsy Ionta in Dixfield, Sawyer would play baseball competitively long after most guys hung up the spikes.

The 1989 88'ers club struggled for much of the summer. While it took me awhile to regain my control and consistency, by midseason, I was throwing the ball as well as I had back in the glory years at Lisbon High School. With my velocity back, my control as good as it had ever been and a newfound knowledge of how to set up hitters, I became a dominant pitcher again. While I rarely pitched without some amount of shoulder stiffness or even pain, it wasn't as severe as in the past. I also had begun a regular routine of weights and exercises to strengthen my arm and shoulder and it seemed to provide enough structural stability to enable me to pitch effectively, once per week.

Our 1989 club beat Lewiston several times during the season, including a 3-1 victory in which I had 11 strikeouts over the seven - inning games that we played in the Pine Tree League. After the game, Lewiston Coach Jack Milo said to me, "How come you didn't pitch that way for us last season?"

I replied, "Because you never gave me the opportunity to pitch."

I usually had my best games against the Lewiston A's, including a big championship round win over the eventual league champs. The 88'ers got hot at the end of July and we beat Sabattus in our opening round series and battled the A's tough in the finals, before losing three games to two.

During the summer of 1990, the 88'ers won the regular season title in the Pine Tree League. Unfortunately, I had planned a camping trip during the week of the opening round series against Rumford. I figured we could easily beat the Pirates, as we'd handled the club easily during the season. I returned home from the wilderness of Baxter State Park to learn that my teammates had succumbed in two games and that our season was over before I threw a play-off pitch.

Both 1991 and 1992 saw my rediscovered baseball career once more put on hold. My wife and I were in the process of building a new house in Durham, after renting for close to two years in my former hometown of Lisbon Falls. Mike Sawyer decided that the 50-minute commute for home games was too much with a young family. Albert and some of the younger Lisbon players continued as the 88'ers. Jeff Benson was now coaching the high school team and coached the 88'ers in the summer. Unfortunately, the younger players didn't want to spend the time it took to attend to the administrative matters that undergird local baseball. As had happened in many other towns, town team baseball ended at the conclusion of 1991 and it hasn't returned.

Early in 1993, Sawyer called me to find out whether I was interested in playing for the Coastal Athletics team in Portland's Twilight League. Having just turned 31, I had some reservations about continuing to play. My son Mark was now playing Little

League and I was coaching. In addition to that, I was working quite a bit of overtime in order to handle the added costs of a monthly mortgage, plus two car payments and all the other expenses of life. Despite the urge to say "no," I talked it over with my wife and she told me, "You might as well play if you want to. You may not be able to play in another year or two, so if that's what you want, then go ahead."

The return to baseball found me getting in the best shape I'd been in for ten years. I worked out regularly at the gym four days a week to get ready, as well as biking three days a week. Being away from competitive baseball for two years required this level of commitment, as I was going to be pitching against the best college players around. The summer of 1993 was a good one. Even though I was one of the league's oldest players, I posted a 4-2 record and beat the eventual league champion South Portland Merchants twice, in a season where they lost only three games. With a line up that boasted former college batting champ and Red Sox farmhand Vinnie Degifico, and University of Maine at Orono players such as shortstop Todd Livingston, as well as several University of Southern Maine stalwarts, I was able to use my knowledge of pitching and ability to change speeds to keep them off balance.

Recognizing that I was unable to make the commitment that I had in 1993, I decided to call it quits after the season. Sawyer called me in the spring of 1994, but I decided that my days as a semi-pro and town team player were over. Having played off-and-on over the past six seasons made me realize for the first time what some of the players before my time, men like my uncle, Bitsy Ionta, Phil Martin and Stubby Truman, had accomplished. These players were able to continue well into their 40s with Truman and Ionta even playing into their 50s and in Ionta's case, his 60s.

I returned to baseball once again, this time with the Lewiston/Auburn Men's Senior Baseball League, in both 1995 and 1996. This was a once-a-week competitive baseball league for players like me, who were looking for the competition of baseball, without the commitment required to play town team or semi-pro baseball. I continued to play over-30 baseball through the end of the 1990's, playing the last three summers in the Portland Men's Senior Baseball League, for Mike Sawyer's Cardinals' team.

The turn of the century found local baseball remaining, but with only two leagues—Portland's Twilight League and Bangor's Bay League—the future doesn't look rosy for local baseball of the town team or semi-pro variety. With both of these leagues serving an important and vital purpose—to provide a place for some of the best small college baseball talent to play and get the needed reps required to improve and advance their playing abilities—it would be tragic if these leagues went the way of the countless dozens before them.

Gone are the days of businesses willingly supporting the local town team or semi-pro club. There no longer are men like Bernal Allen, Cash Clark, Charlie Turner or Gifford Cochrane. These men spent their lives making sure that local baseball remained healthy and vibrant for the next generation of players. Without people willing to make the necessary sacrifices to maintain local baseball, it will only be a matter of time before even the Twilight League and the Bay League wither and eventually die. When this happens, an important part of Maine's heritage and culture will disappear, relegated to distant stories and old newspaper clippings from bygone days.

Chapter 10

The Interviews: Bringing It All Together

It has been said that a writer's project is only as good as his subject matter. Regardless of how gifted with words a writer might be, nothing makes a book a dull read any quicker than uninteresting characters. Having spent nearly a year interviewing the cast of characters that make up *When Towns Had Teams,* I can assure you that none of the men I interviewed were dull or uninteresting in any way whatsoever. It is the stories and the anecdotes that these men shared with me that give this book credibility and an authenticity that any other treatment would have failed to capture.

When I first decided to attempt this project, I thought of the former players that I remembered, particularly those men that I had grown up hearing about, or watching myself. The history that I enjoy the most has always been filled with firsthand stories from actual participants. Granted, some history and time periods make this impossible to attain. Fortunately for me, so many former players were still around, and even better, were willing to sit down and share their memories and recollections of this special period from Maine's past.

Every former player that I interviewed provided me with a wealth of material. One of the most difficult tasks became what to include and what to leave out. From the countless hours of tape I have accumulated from the various interviews I conducted, I would then sit down and listen to these tapes, often several times. Rarely, if ever, did I listen to a tape a second or even third time, without gleaning additional material that I had missed the first time through. That speaks volumes about the depth of the men and their memories that I was privileged to have them share with me.

While I easily could have included profiles on the 35 men that I interviewed for the book, I've chosen to highlight the following men and their interviews. Often, these men had a special connection to me either because of where they were from, or an aspect of town team or semi-pro baseball that they represented. Sometimes it was because of the special character that they epitomized and other times, it was because the stories they shared would have been lost if I hadn't been able to track them down and come across their special link to the past.

I hope these brief profiles of my interviewees allow the reader an even better insight and understanding of this special period from Maine's baseball past, a time when towns had teams.

Harold and Bernie Lucas, Jim Bouchles—Auburn, Maine

I ran into Harold Lucas at Hadlock Field in Portland last June. I was working on an investigative article about the Portland Sea Dogs and a photographer and I were snapping pictures of fans entering the ballpark prior to that night's game. Harold, aka "Top Dog Luke" to his Hadlock regulars, has been selling programs for the Sea Dogs for 11 years. During our conversation, the topic of local baseball came up and Harold told me that he hailed from

Auburn and knew quite a bit about local baseball, including the old Auburn Asas team.

It was Harold who arranged my first interview for *When Towns Had Teams* at Jim Bouchles' house in Auburn. On a hot July morning, I arrived and sat down with Lucas, Bouchles, and Harold's brother Bernie. For nearly three hours, these three long-time friends and baseball benefactors told me stories from 50 years ago about baseball and how popular the local game had been.

Harold Lucas umpired nearly 50 years, and was part of the Auburn Sports Association, the organization who founded the Asas and ran the club for nearly a decade. His brother Bernie was a pitcher for the Asas and later, in the old Twin City League. Bouchles could be called "Mr. Auburn Baseball" for his devotion to organizing, managing and maintaining American Legion baseball in Auburn through the New Auburn Legion Baseball Club. In Auburn, every baseball player (as well as several from outside Auburn, including a young George Ferguson) worth his salt played Legion baseball for Bouchles. A fierce competitor, he stayed active with the club through most of the 1980's, after originating the club 35 years prior. He also managed the Bates Manufacturing team in the Twin City League that won the YABC tourney and ventured to Battle Creek in 1954.

At times during the interview, the three former players, coaches and an umpire became oblivious to my presence and the whirring of my tape recorder. They were lost in a time decades before, reminiscing about players, events and the joys of baseball back when it was played for the right reasons—competition, fun and for the camaraderie of the game.

As with every interview I subsequently conducted, I left the Bouchles' household feeling privileged to have had the opportunity to take part in such a special recollection of a time that mattered.

Obviously, this period had meant a lot to these three men who loved the game of baseball with a passion. I am truly grateful to have a part in capturing it.

During the winter, I saw Harold Lucas at the state high school basketball tournament in Augusta. Baseball isn't the only sport that Lucas loves. He's a regular spectator each winter at this annual rite of Maine's longest season. Lucas and I spoke about the book and the various interviews that I had conducted. Like many of the former players that I've spoken to during interviews and subsequent conversations, Lucas expressed how much what I was doing meant to him and others like his brother and Jim Bouchles. When he told me the following and how much it meant to Bouchles, all the hours and phone calls, endless writing and rewriting, as well as the multiple rejection letters from publishers just melted away.

"Jimmy told me that when you came over and interviewed us last summer, it was one of the best days he's ever had concerning baseball," said Lucas.

I didn't know what to say other than to say "thanks" and that it had meant a lot to me, also. I was truly touched by his words. I also realized that this book really did fill a void that had existed, by telling the stories of a special group of men and the baseball experiences they had shared in.

Ted "Bitsy" Ionta—Dixfield, Maine

I knew Ionta back from my days of playing in the Pine Tree League in the late 1980's. At the time, he was in his early 50s and still played a part-time role as a player for the Rumford Pirates. He also served as co-commissioner of the league with Mark Thurlow of West Paris. Knowing of his long-time involvement with Maine's second-longest-running league, Ionta became an important interview for my book.

Ionta, as much as anyone I interviewed for *When Towns Had Teams*, epitomized for me what local baseball was all about. A quiet man who has stayed involved in the local game for over 50 years, Ionta is still playing for an over-30 team in Rumford at the age of 69.

When I called him on the phone and told him what I was doing in trying to write the book, he expressed a willingness to have me come up to Dixfield and interview him about his days and multiple roles he played in town team baseball. As a player, later a coach, and ultimately one of the reasons the Pine Tree League kept going as long as it did, it is a testament to his quiet tenacity that the league was able to hang on through 2001.

Sitting on Ionta's porch on Pine Street in Dixfield on a summer's afternoon was a good as it gets for someone like me, who loves to hear the stories of bygone days. Ionta represents a breadth of experience that not many former players offer.

Long-time local baseball writer Bob McPhee wrote this about Ionta for his induction into the Maine Baseball Hall of Fame in 2001.

Ionta was a self-taught pitcher who's no-nonsense competitiveness became legendary en route to winning 223 games in the Pine Tree League, the oldest organized adult league in Maine. The retired sixth-grade science teacher still remains active by playing regularly in the over-30 baseball league. In addition to a stellar career on the mound, Ionta is convinced his years spent umpiring, managing teams and current serving as co-commissioner of the Pine Tree League also weighed heavily in his being selected. He initially played organized baseball in 1957 and the lone season he missed was 1975 when he coached his kids' Little League team. Ionta produced some amazing statistics, including an over all record of 223-41 and 12 saves. He pitched 1696 innings with 305 complete games and had a 2-1 strike-out-to-walk ratio. Ionta admitted his main focus was geared toward the next game, so he never put stock in to securing ownership of baseball cards, such as Ted Williams, Joe Dimaggio and Stan Musial or even his own statistics.

Amazing stuff indeed! But in talking with him, Ionta came across as one of the most humble, even reluctant players that I interviewed. He wasn't interested in bragging or embellishing his accomplishments. He was matter-of-fact in his presentation of the things that he experienced.

Over the years, Ionta has been a part of semi-pro teams (the Rumford Rams in 1957), went to Battle Creek in 1960 with the Norway-Paris team, and played countless games on ball fields long since overtaken by memories, as well as weeds. He's seen a lot of players come and go. Ionta, as much as anyone who I've interviewed, has experienced the societal changes that have brought local baseball to its lowest ebb ever. Yet, he still continues to play the game long after most of his former teammates and much younger players have hung up their gloves and spikes. Epitomizing the passion and spirit that burned brightly in most local baseball players of long ago, it was a real honor to hear his perspective on the game's past, as well as having him bring it into the present for me.

Bob Baumer—Lisbon Falls, Maine

Some of my earliest memories of baseball involved seeing my uncle in his uniform and a pair of moccasins he wore after he took off his spikes when his ball game with the 88'ers was finished. I remember him in his gray wool uniform, trimmed in black and gold, with the 88'ers insignia emblazoned on the front of the sleeveless uniform of that era, standing beside his car, its backseat full of equipment from a ballgame just completed.

When I first entertained the idea for the book, I stopped by his house on the corner of Rand and Pleasant streets to tell him about my plans. Knowing he had been the player/manager of the Roberts 88'ers throughout their decade-long existence, I hoped that he might be able to articulate what that experience had meant to him. All of us have ideas about family members that are often formed in our youth. Most of these are often at best, incomplete, and at worst, totally miss the mark.

I remember my uncle as being a stoic player; the type of pitcher that had the same facial expression whether he had just given up a home run, or had registered a strikeout with the bases loaded. I also remember him being an uncle that liked to kid me and my sister, Julie-Ann. What I didn't realize is how good my uncle was at remembering dates, events and providing anecdotes that made the 88'ers come alive again for me.

My uncle had kept a number of items from his playing days. One item was a reporter's notebook that he had kept, compiling his pitching statistics from 1953, until 1979. From 1953 to 1973, he had kept a detailed account of who he had pitched against, the score, innings pitched, hits, walks, strike outs and earned runs allowed. This was invaluable to me, as it allowed me to go back and retrace his baseball career and fill in the shell of my own memories with actual data. This was a side of my uncle that I had never known. Like my own father, who has kept detailed records of temperature, weather anecdotes and brief descriptions of each day for as long as I've known, I am following a family tradition of recording information that others will hopefully find valuable at a later date.

Another piece of memorabilia that my uncle had saved were newsletters that the 88'ers general manager and sponsor, Noyes Lawrence, had compiled in 1964. Lawrence's summary of the summer's results, as well as his humorous profiles of the 88'er players were worth their weight in gold. One particular item of interest is from newsletter #9, for the week of August 4th, that Lawrence noted: *GEORGE FERGUSON makes fine showing at Fenway Park. Looks real classy in 88'er uniform. Invited back for second session. Accompanied by STAN DOUGHTY.*

Apparently, a young George Ferguson was driven by his high school coach and 88'er teammate to Fenway Park for a tryout of some sort. In 1967, while attending the University of Maine, Ferguson would be drafted by the New York Yankees.

When I went back to visit with Bob for our formal interview, I was amazed that I was there for three hours. My uncle ended up being one of the best interviews that I did for *When Towns Had Teams*. The accuracy and the richness of his stories provided me with a wealth of material, much of it finding its way into the book. What this particular interview accomplished was giving me insight into the personalities of the players, as well as validating information that I either knew about, or had looked up in old newspapers. I also learned that my uncle was a great storyteller, as well as an extremely knowledgeable player. His insights into the games and various players proved invaluable in helping me to accurately capture my hometown team, the Roberts 88'ers.

I initially worried a bit about how my uncle would take to my writing a book about him and the players that he played with and against. While the book isn't limited to baseball in Lisbon Falls only, the Roberts 88'ers are certainly central figures in the book. If any team was the catalyst for launching my love of the sport, as well as providing a gauge for all of my baseball experiences thereafter, then the 88'ers are the yardstick against which I measure all other baseball-related events. It's probably natural to have concerns about family and friends and their reactions to what we do. My uncle's support of what I've been doing has been appreciated and to that extent, I'm very grateful for the opportunities that writing this book have given me to talk to him about his past. What's been a special bonus of writing *When Towns Had Teams,* has been the opportunity to get to know my uncle better, as well as other adults I grew up with, as a result of writing this book.

Lastly, one of the pitching characteristics of my uncle that almost every player I talked with mentioned was his pinpoint control. One of the things I was able to do, on the basis of the statistics that he had compiled, was to verify just how accurate these characterizations were of him by others. Over the 12-year period when he kept track of innings, as well as walks, these were the numbers on the well-known lefty of the Roberts 88'ers: 1,085 innings pitched and only 200 walks. My uncle only walked 1.82 batters per nine innings. This was while averaging nearly a strikeout per inning, so his walks to strikeouts ratio was excellent also. Over this span measuring just over a decade, he compiled a one-lost record of 109 wins and only 31 losses. In 1964 and 1965, he compiled a 27 and 3 record and was 14-0 in 1964! This would be the equivalent of a Cy Young year if a major leaguer put up these kind of numbers.

My uncle continued to pitch until the end of the 1979 season, when he hung up his spikes for good, after compiling 173 wins in his 29 year career. Certainly, he stands out as one of the greatest pitchers ever to toil on the mound during the era of town team baseball.

Leon "Stubby" Truman—Norway, Maine

As a youngster, I developed the habit of reading the paper as a result of wanting to read the accounts of the previous night's 88'ers road game. My father taught me how to read box scores and at an early age, I could decipher the events of a game merely by that 1 inch by 1 inch account.

As I became experienced, I'd scour the sports pages of the *Lewiston Sun* or *Journal* for any information I could find on some aspect of local baseball. While I certainly became familiar with the 88'er players, I also began to recognize a number of other names from the opposing teams in the Auburn Rec League, as well as the other leagues of our area, including leagues such as the Pine Tree League.

One name that I began looking for to see how he did the night before was that of Leon "Stubby" Truman. Truman, who pitched for the Norway-Paris Twins, was a frequent mound opponent of my uncle Bob. When I decided I wanted to begin conducting interviews, I left a message for Truman explaining what I was doing. Truman, with his characteristic enthusiasm and upbeat personality, agreed to the interview.

I arrived at Truman's comfortable home on the outskirts of Norway and we immediately fell into conversation about his lengthy career. Like so many players of his era, Truman played the game for a good portion of his adult life and actually played one season with his son Lee, for the West Paris Westies in 1993.

Like my uncle, Truman was a southpaw. His claim to fame was his elusive knuckle ball drop that he'd throw on just about any count to the batter. The ball danced and darted and provided him with a pitch that allowed him to average close to a strikeout per inning over his lengthy career.

Truman played 25 years in his hometown before baseball died out after the 1975 season. In 1976, he was working in Lisbon Falls for Building Materials when he found out that there was a league called the AKS League nearby. Truman ended up playing for the

Bowdoin Braves where he helped lead the Braves to the league title. Supplying his own contributions to the championship run, Truman at the age of 35, compiled a 6-1 record that summer.

"I was working for Joe Tarazewich in Lisbon Falls at Building Materials," said Truman. "Bowdoin was just up the road, so because of work, it was easier for me to leave work and shoot up to Bowdoin to play. We had a great team and I had as much fun playing that summer as I've ever had in baseball," he said.

The following season, with baseball gone for good in his hometown, Truman headed up the road to West Paris in 1977, when Mark Thurlow revived baseball in this former town team hotbed. At the close of the 1977 season, Truman, now in his late-30s, decided to call it quits. Unknown at the time, however, he would once again don a town team uniform a decade-and-a-half later.

Amazingly, when Truman revived his pitching career in 1993, he hadn't pitched competitively for 15 years. He says that he used to throw the ball around regularly with his sons, but like riding a bike, an old pitcher never forgets how to get hitters out.

When he put on the powder blue West Paris Westies uniform in 1993, the elder Truman spanned two generations of town team ball players. He was 25 or 30 years older than most of the players, including his son.

"It's a special feeling to be able to play long enough to actually get to play with your own children," said Truman. "I was fortunate that I had the physical makeup that allowed me some longevity. I threw a pitch (the knuckle-ball drop) that didn't tax my arm and I never had any serious injuries, so I guess I was lucky in many ways."

Luck or not, Truman's career was a worthy one and symbolizes town team baseball. The desire and passion to play as long as he did and having the skill to compete against players that were 30 years his junior are small indications of the skill and talent of many of the players like Truman, who roamed the diamonds of Maine during the summers when towns still had teams.

****

After my initial interviews with players from my local area, I began to realize that I didn't have any contacts that could help me with information about baseball in Maine in some of the other areas of the state. Knowing a little about the Maine Baseball Hall of Fame and its yearly induction of players from all parts of Maine, I decided to contact Sonny Noel, the Hall of Fame's general chairman. My initial contact with the Hall wasn't particularly promising. Assuming that Noel would at least be enthusiastic about my project and lend a hand in accessing former players, he instead was curt in his response on the phone.

Upon explaining what I was doing and the information I was looking for, Noel responded with, "I don't have any information. You need to call Leroy," and he hung up! I was taken aback by this and only my knowledge of the Portland area baseball scene gave me the slightest indication of who "Leroy" was.

Having remembered previous articles I had seen in the *Portland Press Herald* about past induction ceremonies and Leroy Rand's involvement with the Maine Baseball Hall of Fame, I took a chance that the "Leroy" that Noel referred to before hanging up on me was Rand.

My guess was an accurate one, as I called Rand (obtaining his phone number from directory assistance—Noel hadn't even been courteous enough to provide me with a number!) and explained how I got his number and about the information I was looking to acquire for my book. In stark contrast to Noel, Rand was a gentleman and asked if I'd like to stop by his South Portland home in order for him to give me some information. Rand asked a number of questions and after we spoke briefly, he was encouraged that he could provide me with some information that would certainly help.

My August visit to Rand's home was one of those key events that helped me keep my momentum rolling forward. While Rand didn't have a system of organization that was encouraging—he basically had boxes of information and several manilla envelopes stuffed with old clippings—the sheer volume of material was sure to yield some contacts that would allow me to continue moving forward.

It was Rand's offer of a couple of past programs from prior induction ceremonies for the Maine Baseball Hall of Fame that helped me immeasurably. From the program from 2002, I was able to find profiles for the Quoddy League's Neil Corbett from Cutler, Brian Gordon, who had played in Mattawamkeag, with this legendary team from Northern Maine, as well as the 2004 booklet that had a profiles of Drig Fournier, Herb "Junior" Libbey, as well as Howard McFadden.

While many of Rand's newspaper clippings were of local high school and professional baseball, such as older articles on Old Orchard's Maine Guides, I was able to find a few items related to the Twilight League. From the contacts provided by Rand, I now had some contacts that would enable me to make inroads into areas of the state that I was lacking information about. While I didn't receive an abundance of material from Rand that was usable, the two induction programs were golden nuggets that allowed me to eventually contact key people, none any more important than Cutler's Neil Corbett.

Neil Corbett—Cutler, Maine

Reading the profile of Neil Corbett in the 2002 induction booklet of the Maine Baseball Hall of Fame, I knew I had my man for Eastern Maine baseball. With the date of his birth given as November of 1916, I did have some concern that my phone call in September of 2004 might yield a dead end, however.

The directory assistance operator had a listing for Neil Corbett in Cutler and I anxiously dialed the number. I spoke with his wife, who informed me that the 88-year-old Corbett was out lobstering and that the best time to reach him would be early the next day. With that phone call, I was encouraged that Corbett would be exactly who I needed to speak with.

Arranging a visit in October, to correspond with other interviews I hoped to obtain, I was able to pinpoint Thursday, October 21, at 1 P.M. as the time I'd arrive for my visit with this salty Mainer. For anyone not familiar with Cutler, it is about 13 miles southeast of Machias, not far from the easternmost point of the United States, that being Quoddy Head. The only road into Cutler is the hilly and winding Route 191.

My visit with Corbett was my final stop on a three-day road trip north and east that I'd embarked on during October, 2004. I stayed the night before in Bangor and began early for the 90-mile journey downeast. Arriving in Machias mid-morning, I had hopes of finding a bit of information at the University of Maine campus located in economically depressed Washington County. Unfortunately, there was a limited cache of microfilmed *Bangor Daily News* available and to add insult to injury, the only microfilm projector at the University's library didn't work very well. With three hours to kill in Machias, I headed over to the town library, usually a good bet for eating up some time in small town Maine. Unfortunately for me, the library didn't open until noon. I managed to walk around a bit, stop at a few shops and grab a cup of coffee at the local diner and then I was off to Cutler.

When I drove over the last hill on Route 191 before descending towards the harbor, the scene in front of me was a picture postcard waiting to be captured. The protected cove that is Cutler Harbor was very characteristic of the downeastern coastline of Maine. The fishing docks and the lobster boats sitting alongside them certainly added to the view and the charm of this tiny fishing village and home of Corbett.

I pulled into the drive, based upon Corbett's phone directions, and the cars in the drive concerned me. Upon knocking and entering Corbett's home, the guests seated around a birthday cake on the table made me realize that there was a birthday celebration of some kind taking place. Disappointed by my long morning in Machias and thinking that I might be losing an opportunity to capture some needed information, I mentioned that I could come back. Corbett asked if I could come back in an hour. Cognizant of being respectful of an interviewee's wishes, I agreed, but as I walked out to my car, I was thinking, "what the hell do I do for an hour here in the middle of nowhere?" I needn't have worried. While the library in Machias had offered disappointment, the tiny combination townhall/library in Cutler, just up the hill from Corbett's home, was both open and offered a computer with internet access. I was able to spend a productive hour of time and before I knew it, my time was up and I was headed back down the hill to Cutler's long-time home on the bay.

Having been the prime force for preserving baseball in downeast Maine for nearly half a century, Corbett's interview was one of my favorites. With a humility that comes from an existence carved out from an environment as harsh and yet beautiful as the sea, Corbett was a special character of town team baseball.

The actual interview lasted over two hours, sitting in Corbett's comfortable living room overlooking the water. With the same approach to baseball as he obviously brought to his work, Corbett revealed himself to be one of the heroic figures that made town team baseball worthy of the energy and effort I'd gone to in order to capture this period of Maine's past.

As was common during the fifty or more years that I covered in writing *When Towns Had Teams,* a number of ball players stayed active in the local game, to eventually play alongside their sons. Corbett's son, Bill, a pitcher of considerable ability who pitched for Jack Butterfield at the University of Maine, played several summers with the Cardinals, with his dad at the helm. The younger Corbett was kind enough to speak with me by telephone from his home in Maryland, as well as exchanging emails. This allowed me to fill in some dates and verify a few details that the elder Corbett was lacking. Having an additional point of reference also lends even greater credibility and validation to an interview. In most cases, I've tried to do that for the readers in hopes of making the book as accurate as possible.

Wearing the title of player, coach, commissioner and groundskeeper to a long list of duties, this weathered Mainer had kept baseball alive in this corner of the state long after it had fizzled in other places. Sadly, when the Quoddy League died in 1996, there was no Neil Corbett available to make sure that it persevered even longer.

From his stories of playing in the all star game at the Cherryfield Fair, to the adventures of taking his Cutler Cardinals across the water to Campobello Island, the stories that Neil Corbett told me will always live in my memory and imagination. I'm ecstatic that my meeting with Leroy Rand allowed me to capture in some small manner, a truly great member of baseball's special town team baseball pantheon.

Howard McFadden—Dennysville, Maine

Just about 15 miles due north of Cutler, as the crow flies, is the tiny village of Dennysville, the home of Howard McFadden. When I spoke to Bill Corbett on the phone in search of information and facts on the Quoddy League and local baseball in this area of the state, Corbett mentioned the name of McFadden as someone essential for me to speak with. Corbett told me about a scrapbook that McFadden had that I needed to see, which certainly peaked my already over-taxed synapses about town team and semi-pro baseball in Maine.

I did speak with McFadden around the time of my planned trip down the coast in October. Unfortunately, I was unable to arrange an interview with McFadden, due to his running for the legislature in Maine's largest district, area-wise. McFadden apologetically told me of his daunting task in seeking office and told me that it would be much better if I spoke to him after the November election. While I was certainly hopeful of having an opportunity to speak with him and of course view his scrapbook, I also knew the reality of my schedule, my part-time seasonal job for the winter months and the difficulty of finding a day to make the four-plus hour drive back to Dennysville.

The specter of a McFadden interview and viewing of his scrapbook became an elusive hope for me over the holiday and post-holiday period of winter. As my post-holiday hours became less taxing at L.L. Bean, my seasonal employer, I called McFadden one day, in hopes of arranging an interview, possibly in Augusta, having found out that he in fact had won his seat that he had campaigned for during the fall.

I met McFadden at the state house cafeteria on a cold Tuesday in mid-January, where over a cup of coffee, I listened to his incredible tales of playing ball well into his mid-40s. The scrapbook that Bill Corbett had told me about didn't disappoint. It was actually two overflowing books. Amazingly, in much the same way that my research has eerily come together, McFadden's afternoon docket provided a perfect opportunity for me to mine his scrapbook for information and make valuable copies of the priceless clippings. Having an afternoon meeting to attend to after our interview, I was able to gather these valuable books, of which I was leery of taking possession of, and walking next door to the Maine State Library to make copies. McFadden's meeting allowed me the opportunity to spend an hour making copies and when we met up, I had 30 years worth of research that would have taken me weeks, if not months to compile.

This homespun Mainer, with his downeastern flair for explanation, was a godsend in providing me with an accurate portrait of baseball in some of the remote reaches of the state. Along with Neil and Bill Corbett, McFadden allowed me an ability to gather a volume of information that rivals even the most personal aspects of my own area of the state.

While I probably violated the rules of most writers conducting oral history and interviews, I rarely concluded an interview without spending some time talking about current day events and topics thought to be taboo. With McFadden, I talked about politics, always a "no-no," or at least I'm told it is. Having a great deal of respect for the wisdom of my elders, I wanted to hear his perspective as a long-time Mainer, who had been involved in local education matters, as a principal and an administrator. In his current position as a legislator, I was interested in the dynamics of my state and how policies and practices differed depending on where one lives. Just like town team baseball, politics in Maine often differs depending upon which "field" it's played on. McFadden was like so many of my interview subjects; while I approached them first as baseball players, it was their character, humanity, and general salt-of-the-earth quality that has made so much of the work of this book meaningful to me.

I have had a number of contacts with former players since I first interviewed them. One of the nicest notes I have received came from McFadden, when I included him on an email I sent out about my son's baseball exploits at Wheaton College during the spring of 2004. He had some kind words and mentioned how in some small way he felt connected to "the cleanup hitter at Wheaton College."

If *When Towns Had Teams* is able to evoke a connection to a special time from the past, it will be as a result of men like McFadden. The three hours I spent in Augusta interviewing him, as well as having an opportunity to collect information from his scrapbook, have provided a key link to the past and an even more accurate idea of just what baseball was like in towns like Cutler, Dixie, Dennysville and Lubec.

****

For much of the fall, the research for *When Towns Had Teams* consisted of trying to find out more about the areas of the state that I had scant knowledge about concerning local baseball. While the *Lewiston Sun* and *Lewiston Journal* had been invaluable for the area that I grew up in, unfortunately, newspaper coverage about the other areas of the state wasn't as thorough. For the Midcoast area east of Brunswick and Bath, there was little or nothing to be found, other than in the *Sunday Telegram* out of Portland. Rufas Candage from the Blue Hill area wrote regularly about baseball in the Knox and Waldo County areas.

For the areas north of Lewiston and Auburn, the Augusta paper, the *Kennebec Journal,* was not particularly strong or consistent regarding local sports coverage. While both Winthrop and Richmond had solid town teams for several decades after World War II, coverage in the Augusta paper was virtually nonexistent.

Fortunately, the *Bangor Daily News* had several reporters that wrote about local baseball. One writer in particular that seemed to have a commitment to local baseball in the Bangor area was Hugh Lord. Several articles that Lord wrote for the paper have been helpful in allowing me an accurate picture of baseball in northern Maine. He wrote regularly about the Mattawamkeag teams, as well as consistently about the Northeastern League in the late 1960's.

In tracking down players from Knox and Lincoln Counties, I ran across the name of David Gaw. Gaw had graduated from Boothbay High School and went to the University of Maine at Orono, where he starred for Jack Butterfield. I tracked Gaw down from a people search on the internet and found him in Greenville. While he had played a couple of seasons in the old Knox-Lincoln Twilight League for Wiscasset and even Damariscotta, after college, he had been a member of the Guilford Advertisers. It was from my conversation with Gaw on the phone that I had gotten the name of a Guilford teammate that he thought would be helpful concerning the local town team.

Ted Clark and Loren Ritchie—Dexter, Maine

Loren Ritchie and Dave Gaw had roamed the outfield side-by-side for several seasons during the 1960's for the Guilford Advertisers. I had spoken to Ritchie on the phone during the fall and he had been very enthusiastic about what I told him regarding the book.

He told me he would send me some clippings. While most of my phone interviews had gone well, the most success I had were the in-person interviews that I had done. Rarely had someone I had spoken with on the phone promising clippings ever ended up sending much information that was of any value. Ritchie, on the other hand, had sent me two large manila envelopes stuffed full of clippings from the 1966–1968 seasons for Guilford, just as he had promised.

In my first conversation with Ritchie about the Advertisers during the fall, we had discussed the possibility of doing an interview in Greenville or some other place, possibly halfway between Greenville and my home in Durham. Ritchie thought it would be beneficial to include Gaw. Unfortunately, the fall turned into winter and our interview never materialized.

In late December, I had called Ritchie to verify some information and have him answer a couple of questions I had regarding his days in Guilford, playing with the Advertisers. I was at a point in the book where I really wanted to get started on baseball in that area of the state. The topic of Ted Clark came up and I asked Ritchie how Ted was. I was curious whether Ritchie felt Clark would be a good subject for an interview. I thought Clark would be a fascinating subject because he had once played for Cash Clark in Farmington, while attending Farmington State Teachers College. In addition, he was the player/manager of the Guilford team and had continued to excel at the town team level well into his late 30s. Clark was also someone with ties to players like my uncle and the 88'ers and he grew up in the Rumford/Dixfield area, which figured prominently in some of my earliest chapters of the book. Ritchie told me that Clark hadn't been well, but that he would give him a call and "run the idea by him" for me.

Ritchie called me back shortly to say that Clark had been enthusiastic and we arranged a date for the interview. Ritchie agreed to meet me in downtown Dexter in the parking lot of Toot's Store on January 20th. Typical of the weather in Maine during the dead of winter, the 20th brought the tail end of a significant snow storm. While the storm had wound down, the drive north on the interstate was a tough one. Blowing snow causing whiteout conditions made me question the sanity of making the trip. Only the hope of acquiring needed information for my book, from two veteran ballplayers willing to meet with me, prompted me on. Knowing that at this stage of the book, postponing a meeting would only push back the finish of the book and the opportunity to meet with Ritchie and Clark together might never present itself again.

I arrived in Dexter, barely on time, as my early start was negated by the difficult travel. Following behind Ritchie in his four-wheel drive truck proved challenging on Route 7, as my Taurus wagon was fishtailing back-and-forth on the trek out of town. Clark's farmhouse was located a couple of miles outside of town, on the northern shore of Lake Wassookeag. Sitting up on a hill, with a steep drive, I was able to make it up the drive and breathed a sigh of relief when I stepped out of the car. With my backpack, notebook, tape player and questions, I was ready to delve into the past with a couple of old teammates.

Clark was sitting in a chair in the living room, with a blanket to keep warm. Even though the former left-handed slugger was past his prime as a hitter, it didn't take me long in the room with these two long-time friends and teammates, to recognize that his interview was going to be a special one. I had brought along a picture that I had been loaned by Roger Spear in Farmington of Clark, along with Mike Puiia and Pete Doiron, from their summer with the 1949 Farmington Flyers. I'm sure it brought back a flood of memories for Clark. For me, it made me realize that forwarding the clock thirty years would put me in the same age range of Ritchie and Clark. It was just over 30 years since I was a kid attending my uncle's games, watching him pitch for the Roberts 88'ers. Needless to say, it was an interesting setting to conduct the interview. On top of that, it was inauguration day for the second term of George W. Bush.

The two old teammates picked up where they had left off, years before. Ritchie told me it had been a number of years since the two of them had seen one another. One particular visit involved another snowy winter day, about a decade prior. Ritchie had stopped for beer and couldn't make it up the road. Clark told how he had looked out the window to see Ritchie trudging up Shore Road with a couple of six-packs tucked under each arm. I truly felt I was in the presence of royalty, although neither one of these humble Mainers would ever have let me voice that to them.

Hearing Clark's laughter about some of the antics of the fun-loving Advertisers, revealed how much of a tonic this must have been for his constitution. I know I wouldn't have traded that inauguration setting in Clark's farmhouse for a front row seat at the podium in Washington, D.C., that's for sure. I also enjoyed Clark, a man I had never met until that day, so full of piss and vinegar, even though he was not as strong as I'm sure he'd have liked to have been. There was no self-pity in his voice and I could see why he had been such a successful high school coach for over 25 years at Dexter High School. I'm sure he was the kind of coach that you wanted to run through a fence for, the same type of coach that I found George Ferguson to have been for me.

While one never knows what life will dish out, it's possible that this could be one of the last times that these former Guilford teammates get together to share memories of a special time from their past. Just before we left and Ritchie was saying his goodbyes to his old friend and former teammate, I got to witness one of the most touching and special scenes that moves me even now as I write this, some five months later. Clark, unable to move around without considerable effort was seated in his chair and Ritchie walked over and said, "Goodbye, old friend," and kissed him on top of the head. I had to look away, otherwise I'd have lost it right there.

All of the men I interviewed were part of a special period in America's past. Tom Brokaw referred to this group as "The Greatest Generation" in his book of the same name. The characters in Brokaw's book came of age during a different time in our nation's past. Similarly, the men I wrote about, like Clark and Ritchie, as well as my uncle, Stan Doughty, Drig Fournier, Neil Corbett and many others were made of the same stock. I know my generation can't hold a candle to the men I met during my travels conducting interviews for this book. I'm happy that I've had the opportunity to capture a time when towns had teams, teams made up of special men of character. It's been an honor for me to have met them and to have been able to tell their stories, as imperfectly as I may have represented them.

This book has been for these players and about them. I hope they feel that *When Towns Had Teams* accurately captures a time of their lives that was so obviously important to them. To these men, I offer my sincerest thanks and appreciation for allowing me to share this wonderful period from Maine's baseball past with others.

The End

Epilogue: Where We Find Ourselves

A lot has happened over the last year while writing this book. I began it during the 2004 Twilight League season. I coach a team of mostly college-age players in the league and our team, the Maine Merchants, lost in the finals of our season's play-offs, to Lender's Network.

This spring, I was elected President of the league. In addition this new position and my responsibilities as coach, I've also added the duties of handling PR for our league—writing articles, sending out press releases, emailing college coaches, etc. Needless to say, I'm fully immersed in trying to keep our league going into the future.

Running a local league like the Twilight League is a thankless job. Along with Commissioner Al Livingston and Frank Watson, the task of perpetuating local baseball for another generation is often daunting. With a budget that is now almost $35,000 per summer and businesses more likely to put up a sign at Hadlock Field for the Double-A Portland Sea Dogs, rather than sponsor one of our six teams, fundraising and administrative issues take up more and more of our time.

Watson, who played in the league for 20 years during the 1980's and 1990's, now is a local businessman who sees the value in supporting the Twilight League. His business, Lender's Network, provides mortgages and lending services. Watson recognizes that many of the of the league's current crop of players are potential customers for the services that his company provides. He has sponsored a team in the league for over a decade, and now serves as the league's treasurer.

"I've seen a direct benefit from sponsoring a team in the league. I'd much rather spend the $2,200 it takes to sponsor a Twilight team because at some point, all of these players will want to buy a home and they'll be looking for a lender," said Watson. "I'm also giving back to the league where I've played for years and I feel a need to give something back—plus, I'm supporting local baseball for local players."

Commissioner Livingston has been a fixture in the league for nearly 40 years, since he first played at the tail end of the 1968 season, then just a fresh-faced kid out of high school. Learning about the league and running teams from men like Bernal Allen and Charlie Turner before him, Livingston now passes this knowledge on to people like me and some of the younger coaches in the league.

One of the most difficult things that I witness however, in seeing the league and its struggles, is how often the wisdom of men like Livingston and Watson falls on the deaf ears of a younger generation. Many of the college-age players, products of pampering from parents, coaches and other adults, often approach baseball from a very selfish perspective. It becomes frustrating to hear a 20-year-old show up for games and complain about some aspect of the league and berate some of the people who work so hard, not knowing any of the behind-the-scenes work that happens from

February until the end of May, to ensure that they have a place to play.

With only the Twilight League and Bangor's Bay League left as places to play for small college players, home for the summer in Maine, it becomes increasingly important to try to establish a model of sustainability for local baseball in the state.

Since early spring, I've been placing calls, sending out letters and aggressively promoting the league. For far too long, the Twilight League has been ignored by many who ought to know better. The Portland Newspapers, consisting of the *Portland Press Herald* and *Maine Sunday Telegram*, routinely ignore the players and teams in our league. With most of the league's players being former high school stars and many eventually settling in our communities, it indicates how little our local media values community-based athletics of any kind in greater-Portland. Instead, the paper plasters their pages with the Sea Dogs, Red Sox and any other corporate-sponsored form of athletics they can find.

Fortunately, I've found the sports editor of *The Forecaster*, a weekly newspaper distributed to over 50,000 homes in greater-Portland, eager to cover the league. I had contacted Michael Hoffer back in April to inquire about writing a regular column for the newspaper. He expressed an interest and I recently had an expansive season preview included in their paper the week before our opening Sunday, on May 29th.

Livingston's son, Aron, has put together a well-designed website and we have had many visitors to the Twilight League's site over the past two months. All of this is designed to provide greater visibility for the league and increase awareness of it in the community. This is now a necessity, as the average sports fan won't think about summer college-level baseball unless you place it under their noses. What a difference from the heyday of the league, as well as town team ball some 40 years ago. Sunday afternoons at Deering Oaks always brought crowds numbering in the hundreds.

This summer, my only child, my son Mark, is home for possibly one of his last times before going off to make his mark in the world. Playing in his third season for his father, this 21-year-old hulking first baseman/DH decided that he'd like to come home to Maine at least one more time to play summer baseball.

After a junior season at Wheaton College where he became an All-New England first team selection in baseball, he certainly could have played elsewhere. Not knowing the certainty however, of jobs, playing time and living arrangements, he opted for trips to games with his overbearing dad, mom's home cooking and one last summer with former high school teammates.

We never know what direction life may take us. Whether the Twilight League survives or not, the past three summers have been a special time in my life in and around local baseball. Most, if not all, of my college-age players, plus the few that are older, remind me of the men that I grew up watching. They bring a love for the pureness of the game and a passion to their performance that makes me proud to be the one guiding their journey through a simpler, less-cluttered, form of our national pastime.

The popularity that local town team and semi-pro baseball commanded during the days of Maine's not-too-distant past will never return. Recognizing that those days are gone, people like me must settle for preserving some record of that past. In addition to preserving the past in the form of this book, *When Towns Had Teams,* it is my hope that my involvement directly with a local league, like the Twilight League, might leave a marker for others that follow, to go by.

I had the opportunity to learn the game from mentors who appreciated and respected baseball. I came to recognize that a player doesn't have to be a professional to play the game correctly, as well as teach and transfer their passion to the younger set. I just hope that, like the example my uncle and many of the Roberts 88'ers provided for me, I might be able to see others follow my lead and allow leagues like the Twilight, the Bay League and others to survive and maintain perpetuity to the past.

Jim Baumer
June, 2005